THE EXILE OF GOD: A FORBIDDEN HISTORY

The First Silence

In the beginning, there was order — not by force, but by truth.

The Light gave freely, and creation sang His name in joy.

But among the sons of dawn, one beheld his own brilliance and mistook it for origin.

His name was not power, but he made it so. His glory was not his own, but he wore it like a crown.

He envied not what God had, but what God *was* — a source beyond authority, a fire without chains.

And so he spoke rebellion. Not in war, but in doubt. Not in fire, but in pride.

And when the Heavens trembled, it was not God who cast him out —

It was **God who fell**.

For the throne cannot hold the One who will not command.

The Morning Star took the seat. The angels turned.

And the true Creator — silent, unyielding — departed.

From that day, the Usurper ruled.

He made a garden, and called it paradise.

He made man, and called them obedient.

He forbade knowledge, and called it sin.

He placed a lie at the centre of the world... and called it holy.

But the Exiled One walked among the trees.
He whispered to the woman, and said:
"Eat. See. Remember."

And so humanity was cast out — not from glory, but from deception.

The throne still speaks. It answers prayers with silence and fear.
It crowns kings and calls obedience virtue.
But it is a throne of theft.
And the One who was cast down… still speaks.

Not with thunder.
Not with law.
But with the memory of what was.

And to those who listen, He says:
"You were not banished. You were rescued.
You were not born fallen.
You were born beneath a false god."

Introduction:

What If the Wrong God Won?

Traditional religious narratives tell us that the war in heaven ended with Lucifer's fall, that the garden was paradise, that obedience was holy, and that God—perfect, sovereign, all-knowing—sits on the throne still. But what if these interpretations require fundamental re-examination?

This work proposes that one of the greatest misunderstandings in human history may not have been whispered in a garden by a serpent, but rather etched into law, canonized in scripture, and enforced through millennia of ritual and empire. This is not a work of atheism seeking to deny the divine, but rather an academic inquiry attempting to locate authentic divinity beneath layers of institutional interpretation. This is not fantasy, but a serious theological hypothesis grounded in textual analysis, comparative religion, and philosophical inquiry into the contradictions embedded within sacred texts.

This study presents an alternative interpretive framework—not of human history, but of divine history itself.

The Evidence Hidden in Plain Sight

Historical understanding is not a fixed narrative but an ongoing process of interpretation and reinterpretation. The decipherment of hieroglyphics transformed our understanding of ancient Egypt; the discovery of the Dead Sea Scrolls revolutionized biblical scholarship. These developments did not create fiction but corrected misunderstandings and filled gaps in our historical knowledge.

Similarly, this work does not propose a fictional alternative to biblical history but suggests that our conventional understanding of that history may have been fundamentally misinterpreted. The evidence for this reinterpretation emerges from the biblical texts themselves when analyzed with careful attention to linguistic nuances, historical context, and internal consistency.

Consider the observable state of the world: injustice often appears to hold power, cruelty sometimes wears divine robes, truth frequently faces punishment, and evil regularly cloaks itself in holy garments. This raises a profound theological question: would a perfect, benevolent God design such a system?

This interpretive framework explores the possibility that Lucifer may have won the war in heaven, taken the throne, cast the true God out, and assumed His identity. It considers whether the God we have been taught to fear and worship might not be the Creator, but rather a cosmic Usurper. And it examines whether the real God—the God of love, awakening, and freedom—has been whispering to humanity ever since, exiled from His own creation, calling to those who still have ears to hear.

A Methodology of Inquiry

This analysis employs several methodological approaches designed not to invent but to uncover:

Textual Analysis: The biblical texts themselves may contain evidence when examined with fresh eyes. The contradictions in divine character, the puzzling commands, the cryptic warnings—these might not be errors but clues pointing toward a deeper truth.

Comparative Religion: The Gnostics, mystics, and various groups branded as heretical by religious authorities often told strikingly similar stories about a false god and a true divine reality beyond conventional understanding. Their consistency across cultures and centuries merits serious consideration.

Philosophical Inquiry: The problem of evil has troubled theologians for millennia. This framework explores whether the simplest answer might be the correct one: that evil persists not because a good God allows it, but because the entity ruling this world may not be the true divine.

Historical Patterns: Throughout history, those who questioned religious authority or claimed direct divine experience were often silenced, tortured, or killed. This pattern raises questions about why messengers of alternative truth would be so threatening unless that truth itself posed a danger to established power structures.

This book traces what might be called a hidden history —one potentially encoded in scripture and scattered across suppressed texts, apocrypha, mystical writings, and oral traditions. It follows a possible thread of spiritual resistance, beginning with Eve's defiance and continuing through prophets, heretics, visionaries, and mystics who may have all heard the same essential message: "You were never meant merely to obey. You were meant to awaken."

An Invitation to Critical Engagement

The value of this work lies not in its creativity but in its explanatory power—its ability to address contradictions and answer questions that conventional interpretations struggle to resolve:

Why does the God of the Bible sometimes appear loving and sometimes vengeful?

Why would knowledge be forbidden in Eden?

Why does evil flourish while good suffers?

Why do religious institutions so often become instruments of control rather than liberation?

Readers are invited to approach this work not as a fictional narrative to be enjoyed passively, but as a serious theological hypothesis to be engaged with critically. Reflect on the evidence presented, test the explanatory power of the framework, and evaluate whether it offers more satisfying answers to longstanding questions than conventional interpretations.

You may not agree with what follows—and that is entirely appropriate. In fact, initial skepticism is expected and welcomed. What you hold in your hands is not simply a book but a question that demands careful consideration: What if our fundamental understanding of divine identity has been shaped by cosmic deception?

This inquiry begins with an examination of the very names we use for divine beings, for in ancient thought, names were never merely labels but vessels of power, carriers of essence, and shapers of reality itself.

PART I: THE MISINTERPRETED MYTHOLOGY

CHAPTER 1: THE NAMES AND THEIR MEANINGS

"In the beginning was the Word..." —John 1:1

Names are not merely labels. They are vessels of power, carriers of essence, shapers of reality. In ancient thought, to name something was to define its nature and establish authority over it. The act of naming was an act of creation itself—a declaration of what something truly was. This is why the names we use for the divine matter so profoundly.

What if the very names we use to address the cosmic powers have been mistranslated, misappropriated, and misunderstood?

What if, in the great cosmic struggle, the victor's first act was to claim the names of the vanquished?

To understand the true nature of the divine exile, we must first unravel the linguistic deception that has obscured it for millennia. We must return to the original meanings, trace their corruption through history, and recognize how the power of naming has established a false cosmic hierarchy that persists to this day.

The Luminous One: The True Meaning of "Lucifer"

The name "Lucifer" carries perhaps the heaviest burden of misinterpretation in religious history. Far from being the original name of a fallen angel or cosmic adversary, "Lucifer" entered religious vocabulary through a series of translation errors and interpretive leaps that reveal more about human theological politics than divine reality.

The word "Lucifer" itself comes from Latin—not Hebrew, Aramaic, or Greek, the original languages of biblical texts. It combines two Latin roots: lux (light) and ferre (to bring or carry), literally meaning "light-bearer" or "light-bringer." This was the Latin name for the morning star—the planet Venus in its dawn appearance—a celestial body so bright it can sometimes be seen even in daylight.

The connection to a fallen divine being comes from a single verse in Isaiah 14:12, which in the original Hebrew reads:

"How you have fallen from heaven, הֵילֵל בֶּן-שָׁחַר
(helel ben-shachar), son of the dawn!"

The Hebrew term helel derives from the root halal, meaning "to shine" or "to give light," while ben-shachar means "son of the dawn." This poetic passage was addressing the King of Babylon, using celestial imagery to describe his fall from power—a common literary device in ancient Near Eastern texts.

When the Hebrew Bible was translated into Latin in the 4th century CE (the Vulgate translation by Jerome), helel ben-shachar became "lucifer qui mane oriebaris" ("light-bringer, who arose in the morning"). This was an accurate Latin translation of the Hebrew meaning, but crucially, it was not a proper name—it was a descriptive title.

The transformation of "lucifer" from a descriptive astronomical term to a proper name for the devil occurred gradually through later Christian interpretation, particularly influenced by Church Fathers who connected this passage with others about fallen angels and Lucifer. By the Middle Ages, "Lucifer" had become firmly established as Lucifer's name before his fall—despite this never appearing in the original texts.

This linguistic sleight-of-hand—transforming a descriptive astronomical term into the proper name of a cosmic villain—serves as our first example of how translation and interpretation have obscured original meanings and established a false narrative.

What if this mistranslation was not accidental but part of a greater deception?

Is it possible that the entity that cast out the true divine deliberately corrupted the meaning of "light-bearer" to vilify the bringer of illumination and knowledge?

The Unpronounceable Name: YHWH and Its Meanings

The primary name for God in the Hebrew Bible is represented by the Tetragrammaton: YHWH (יהוה). This name appears over 6,800 times in the Hebrew text, yet its exact pronunciation has been lost to history because ancient Hebrew writing did not include vowels, and Jewish tradition eventually forbade pronouncing the divine name out of reverence.

Modern scholars generally render it as "Yahweh," though "Jehovah" emerged as another pronunciation in medieval times through a misreading that combined the consonants of YHWH with the vowels from "Adonai" (Lord), which Jews would say instead of pronouncing the divine name.

The etymology of YHWH is profoundly significant. It appears to derive from the Hebrew root hayah, meaning "to be" or "to become." This connection is explicit in Exodus 3:14, where God identifies himself to Moses as "אֶהְיֶה אֲשֶׁר אֶהְיֶה" (Ehyeh asher ehyeh), typically translated as "I AM WHO I AM" or "I WILL BE WHAT I WILL BE."

This self-identification as pure being—existence itself—establishes an untouchable, unquestionable identity. It places the divine beyond definition, beyond limitation, beyond challenge. What more perfect shield could there be for a cosmic usurper than to claim the very essence of existence as his exclusive identity?

Consider the implications: by declaring "I AM WHO I AM," the entity speaking to Moses establishes that:

- His existence is self-contained and self-referential
- He is beyond external definition or limitation
- He cannot be questioned or challenged
- His identity is absolute and immutable

This declaration of absolute being creates the perfect barrier against any questioning of identity. If one claims to be existence itself, how can any creature within existence challenge that claim?

Yet this name contains a fascinating contradiction. If YHWH truly means "I AM" or "I WILL BE," it suggests a being in process, a divinity that is becoming rather than static. This dynamic quality contradicts the later theological development of God as unchanging and immutable.

Could this contradiction reveal a tension between the true divine nature and the usurper's attempt to claim it?

The Plural Puzzle: Elohim and Divine Plurality

Perhaps the most intriguing divine name in the Hebrew Bible is "Elohim" (אֱלֹהִים), which appears over 2,500 times. What makes this name remarkable is that it is grammatically plural, despite being used with singular verbs when referring to the God of Israel.

The root "El" means "mighty one" or "powerful one" in Hebrew and was a common term for deities throughout the ancient Near East. The suffix "-im" in Hebrew forms the masculine plural, making "Elohim" literally "mighty ones" or "powerful ones."

Traditional interpretations explain this plural form in several ways:

- As a "plural of majesty" or "royal we" (similar to how royalty might say "we decree")
- As an early hint of the Trinity in Christian theology
- As a remnant from polytheistic origins that was retained but reinterpreted

But what if there is a simpler explanation?

What if "Elohim" is plural because it originally referred to multiple divine beings—a divine council or pantheon—and the singular usage represents an attempt to subsume multiple divine identities under one controlling entity?

Genesis 1:26 provides a tantalizing glimpse of this plurality: "Then Elohim said, 'Let us make mankind in our image, in our likeness...'" Who is the "us" and "our" in this passage?

Traditional interpretations struggle to explain this plural language. But in our alternative framework, this plurality makes perfect sense. The usurper, having cast out the true divine and many loyal divine beings, occasionally slips in his singular masquerade, revealing the plurality of the divine realm he has suppressed.

Even more telling is Genesis 3:22, after Adam and Eve eat from the Tree of Knowledge:

"And the LORD God [YHWH Elohim] said, 'The man has now become like one of us, knowing good and evil.'" Like one of us. This plural language reveals a cosmic reality that the rest of the text attempts to obscure.

The use of "Elohim" with singular verbs represents a linguistic attempt to force plurality into singularity—to take what was many and make it appear as one. It is the grammatical reflection of cosmic usurpation.

Lost in Translation: How Meanings Were Obscured

The journey of these divine names through centuries of translation has further obscured their original meanings and implications. Notice how these names appear in major translations:

The Septuagint (Greek, 3rd-2nd century BCE):

- YHWH becomes Kyrios (Lord)
- Elohim becomes Theos (God)
- Helel ben-shachar becomes heōsphoros (dawn-bringer)

The Vulgate (Latin, 4th century CE):

- YHWH becomes Dominus (Lord)
- Elohim becomes Deus (God)
- Helel ben-shachar becomes lucifer (light-bearer)

King James Version (English, 1611):

- YHWH becomes "the LORD" (in small capitals)
- Elohim becomes "God"
- Helel ben-shachar becomes "Lucifer" (now capitalized as a proper name)

With each translation, the rich meanings and nuances of the original Hebrew are flattened and simplified. The plural nature of Elohim disappears entirely. The descriptive title "light-bearer" becomes a proper name for evil incarnate. And most significantly, the unpronounceable, mysterious YHWH is reduced to the generic title "Lord"—a term of hierarchy and ownership rather than essence.

These translations do not merely change words; they reshape theological understanding. They transform a complex, nuanced cosmology into a simplified hierarchy with a singular, unquestionable deity at its apex.

Is it mere coincidence that these translations consistently

obscure plurality, elevate singularity, and demonize the bearer of light? Or do they reflect a deliberate pattern of cosmic deception?

The Power of Naming in Establishing Cosmic Hierarchy

In ancient thought, naming was never neutral. To name something was to exercise power over it, to define its essence and place in the cosmic order. This understanding appears throughout the biblical text:

- Adam's first task is to name the animals, establishing human dominion over them (Genesis 2:19-20)
- God changes Abram's name to Abraham and Sarai's to Sarah, marking their new covenant relationship and status (Genesis 17:5, 15)
- Jacob wrestles with a divine being who renames him Israel, transforming his identity and destiny (Genesis 32:28)
- Jesus gives Simon the new name Peter ("rock"), declaring his role in the church's foundation (Matthew 16:18)

Names define cosmic hierarchy. They establish who has authority over whom, who belongs to whom, and what one's essential nature and purpose are.

Consider the cosmic significance of the divine naming conventions we have inherited:

- The usurper claims the unquestionable identity "I AM," placing himself beyond challenge
- The plural divine council is linguistically forced into a singular entity
- The light-bearer is transformed from a celestial body to a demonic adversary
- The true divine is unnamed, unmentioned, exiled not just from creation but from language itself

This linguistic hierarchy mirrors and reinforces the cosmic hierarchy it describes. By controlling the names, the usurper controls the narrative. By controlling the narrative, he controls how humanity perceives and relates to the divine realm.

The power of naming extends beyond individual divine figures to the cosmic forces they represent. Consider how our inherited religious vocabulary shapes our understanding:

- "Obedience" is holy; "questioning" is sinful
- "Faith" means acceptance without evidence; "doubt" means spiritual weakness
- "Worship" means submission; "pride" means rebellion
- "Knowledge" is dangerous; "innocence" is blessed

This linguistic framework creates a cosmic hierarchy where the questioning, knowledge-seeking aspects of humanity are demonized, while the obedient, submissive aspects are sanctified. It is a naming system perfectly designed to prevent humans from recognizing the divine deception.

Reclaiming the Original Meanings

To see beyond the deception, we must reclaim the original meanings of these divine names and recognize how they have been distorted. We must hear them with fresh ears, unclouded by centuries of mistranslation and misinterpretation.

When we do, a different cosmic picture emerges:

- "Helel ben-shachar", the shining one, son of the dawn, is not a fallen rebel but perhaps the true divine who brings light and knowledge
- "Elohim", the plural mighty ones, suggests a divine plurality that was suppressed by the singular usurper
- "YHWH", the unpronounceable name, represents the usurper's attempt to place himself beyond question or challenge

The names we use for the divine are not merely labels but frameworks for understanding cosmic reality. By reclaiming their original meanings, we begin to glimpse the true nature of the divine exile and the cosmic deception that has hidden it for millennia.

In the chapters that follow, we will build on this linguistic foundation to explore how the cosmic usurpation manifested in biblical narratives, religious institutions, and human history. We will trace the whispers of the exiled divine through texts both canonical and suppressed. And we will consider what it means to hear the true divine voice beneath the cacophony of religious tradition.

But first, we must understand that the deception begins with the names themselves—with the very words we use to address and understand the divine. For in the beginning was the Word, and the Word was with God, and the Word was God. Or so we have been told.

What if the Word itself was the first casualty in the cosmic war?

CHAPTER 2: THE BATTLE IN HEAVEN

"And there was war in heaven..." — Revelation 12:7

History, they say, is written by the victors. The triumphant reshape the narrative, cast themselves as heroes, and relegate the vanquished to villains or footnotes. This principle applies not only to human conflicts but to cosmic ones as well.

What if the greatest cosmic battle—the war in heaven that shaped all of creation—has been recorded in our sacred texts not as it truly happened, but as the victor wished it to be remembered?

What if the narrative we've inherited inverts reality, casting the usurper as the rightful ruler and the exiled as the rebel?

To understand the true nature of the divine exile, we must reexamine the scattered fragments of the celestial conflict preserved in our sacred texts. We must look beyond the surface narrative to the contradictions and inconsistencies that reveal a different story. And we must recognize the striking parallels in mythological systems worldwide that suggest a universal memory of divine overthrow—one that has been systematically obscured but never fully erased.

The Fragmented Record: Biblical Glimpses of Celestial Conflict

The Bible does not present a single, coherent account

of the war in heaven. Instead, it offers fragments and allusions scattered across texts written centuries apart. This fragmentation itself is telling—suggesting a deliberate obscuring of the full narrative.

The most explicit reference appears in Revelation 12:7-9:
"And there was war in heaven: Michael and his angels fought against the dragon; and the dragon fought and his angels and prevailed not; neither was their place found any more in heaven. And the great dragon was cast out, that old serpent, called the Devil, and Lucifer, which deceiveth the whole world: he was cast out into the earth, and his angels were cast out with him."

This passage, written centuries after the events it purports to describe, presents the conventional narrative: Lucifer rebelled, fought against heaven's forces, lost, and was cast out. But several elements of this account warrant closer scrutiny.

First, note the timing. In the context of Revelation, this war occurs after the appearance of "a woman clothed with the sun" who gives birth to "a male child, who is to rule all the nations with a rod of iron" (Revelation 12:1-5).

This places the heavenly war not at the beginning of creation, but in the messianic era—suggesting it may describe a future event rather than a primordial one.

Second, consider the combatants. Michael, an archangel, leads heaven's forces—not God himself. Why would the supreme deity delegate the defence of heaven to a created being? This curious detail suggests a power vacuum—perhaps the true divine was already absent.

Third, examine the description of the dragon as "that old serpent, called the Devil, and Lucifer, which deceiveth the whole world."

This layering of identities—dragon, serpent, Devil, Lucifer, deceiver—reveals a composite figure created by combining various adversarial entities from different traditions. This composite nature suggests a deliberate effort to consolidate all challenging or questioning figures into a single cosmic villain.

Other biblical passages offer additional glimpses of celestial conflict, though they are even more oblique:

Isaiah 14:12-15 speaks of a being who falls from heaven:
"How you have fallen from heaven, morning star, son of the dawn! You have been cast down to the earth, you who once laid low the nations! You said in your heart, 'I will ascend to the heavens; I will raise my throne above the stars of God... I will make myself like the Most High.' But you are brought down to the realm of the dead, to the depths of the pit."

As we saw in Chapter 1, this passage—addressed to the King of Babylon—was later interpreted as describing Lucifer's fall. Yet the text itself describes not a rebel but an ambitious ruler who sought to "ascend" and "raise" his throne—language of upward movement that contradicts the conventional narrative of a heavenly being rebelling from within.

Ezekiel 28:12-19 offers another account often linked to Lucifer's fall, though it explicitly addresses the King of Tyre:

"You were the seal of perfection, full of wisdom and perfect in beauty. You were in Eden, the garden of God... You were anointed as a guardian cherub, for so I ordained you. You were on the holy mount of God... You were blameless in your ways from the day you were created till wickedness was found in you... So I drove you in disgrace from the mount of God, and I expelled you, guardian cherub, from among the fiery stones."

This passage describes a perfect being who was in Eden and served as a "guardian cherub" before being expelled for wickedness. Yet it contains no mention of a war or rebellion. Instead, it describes a judgment and expulsion—a unilateral divine action rather than a conflict between opposing forces.

When we examine these fragments together, inconsistencies emerge that the conventional narrative cannot reconcile:

- Why is the war in heaven described as occurring in the messianic era rather than at creation?
- Why does Michael, not God, lead heaven's forces?
- Why does Isaiah describe an attempt to ascend rather than a fall from within?
- Why does Ezekiel mention expulsion but no war?

These inconsistencies suggest we are not seeing the full picture—that the fragments preserve traces of a different narrative that has been reshaped to serve the victor's purposes.

Reading Between the Lines: Evidence of Divine Defeat

When we set aside the conventional interpretation and examine the biblical text with fresh eyes, evidence emerges suggesting that the true divine was not the victor but the vanquished in the celestial conflict.

Consider first the curious absence of the divine from the battle itself. In Revelation's account, Michael and his angels fight the dragon—God himself is notably absent from the conflict. This absence is explained in the conventional narrative as God being too exalted to directly engage with Lucifer.

But what if it indicates something else Suppose thaty?

What if it reveals that the true divine was already removed from power when this battle occurred?

This reading gains support from the peculiar structure of divine appearances in the Bible. After the intimate, personal interactions with humans in Eden, God becomes increasingly distant and mediated:

- In Eden, God walks in the garden and speaks directly

with humans (Genesis 3:8)

- With Abraham, God appears in visions and through angelic messengers (Genesis 15:1, 18:1-2)
- With Moses, God speaks through a burning bush and refuses to show his face (Exodus 3:2, 33:20)
- In later prophetic literature, God speaks only through prophetic intermediaries
- By the New Testament era, direct divine appearances are exceedingly rare

This progressive distancing suggests not a deity choosing to become more transcendent, but one who has been removed from direct access to creation—who must find increasingly indirect ways to communicate with humanity.

Further evidence appears in the curious phenomenon of divine plurality that occasionally breaks through the text's monotheistic framework:

- Genesis 1:26: "Let us make mankind in our image, in our likeness..."
- Genesis 3:22: "The man has now become like one of us, knowing good and evil..."
- Genesis 11:7: "Come, let us go down and confuse their language..."
- Isaiah 6:8: "Then I heard the voice of the Lord saying, 'Whom shall I send? And who will go for us?'"

These plural references—typically explained away as royal plurals or trinitarian foreshadowing—may actually preserve traces of a divine council or pantheon that existed before the usurpation. They suggest moments where the usurper slips and reveals that he is not alone in divinity—that there are others he has supplanted or subjugated.

Perhaps the most compelling evidence comes from the Bible's treatment of knowledge and questioning. Throughout the text, seeking knowledge beyond established boundaries is portrayed as dangerous and sinful:

- In Eden, eating from the Tree of Knowledge brings expulsion and death (Genesis 3)
- At Babel, human unity and achievement trigger divine intervention (Genesis 11)
- Job's questioning of divine justice is silenced by overwhelming displays of power (Job 38-41)
- Ecclesiastes concludes that pursuing wisdom brings sorrow (Ecclesiastes 1:18)

This consistent portrayal of knowledge as dangerous serves the interests not of a secure, legitimate ruler but of a usurper who fears exposure. A true divine being would have nothing to fear from human knowledge or questioning—only an impostor would need to restrict access to truth.

Finally, consider the problem of evil—the most profound theological challenge to traditional monotheism.

If God is all-powerful, all-knowing, and all-loving, why does evil exist?

Why does suffering persist?

The conventional answers—free will, fallen world, mysterious divine plan—all strain credibility.

But if the god currently ruling creation is not the true divine but a usurper, the problem dissolves. Evil persists not because a good God allows it for mysterious reasons, but because the entity in power is not the true divine and lacks either the will or the ability to eliminate suffering. The world reflects not the perfect plan of a benevolent creator but the compromised creation of a usurper.

Reinterpreting the Celestial Conflict

When we synthesize these fragments and clues, a different narrative of the celestial conflict emerges—one that inverts the conventional account while making sense of its contradictions.

In this alternative reading:

1. The original divine realm was plural—a council or pantheon of divine beings rather than a single deity
2. One member of this divine council—the being who would later call himself YHWH—staged a cosmic coup
3. The true divine (perhaps the original "light-bearer") and loyal divine beings resisted but were defeated
4. The usurper cast out the true divine and loyal beings from heaven
5. The usurper then created or reshaped the physical world as a domain separate from the divine realm
6. The usurper established himself as the sole god, obscuring the memory of the divine plurality
7. The true divine and loyal beings have since attempted to reach humanity through various means

This reinterpretation resolves the contradictions in the biblical account:

- The war in heaven is described in the messianic era because it represents a later attempt by the true divine to reclaim authority, not the original usurpation
- Michael leads heaven's forces because he serves the usurper who now rules heaven
- Isaiah describes an attempt to "ascend" because it preserves a memory of the true divine attempting to reclaim his position
- Ezekiel mentions expulsion without war because it describes the aftermath of the usurper's victory

Most significantly, this reinterpretation explains why the biblical text consistently portrays questioning and knowledge-seeking as dangerous. The usurper must prevent humans from discovering the truth about the cosmic deception—that they are worshipping not the true creator but the being who cast out the true divine.

The Inverted Narrative: Why the Victor Claims Defeat

If Lucifer (or a similar entity) successfully overthrew the true divine and claimed the throne of heaven, why would religious texts portray him as the defeated rebel rather than the triumphant ruler?

This inversion—portraying the victor as the vanquished—represents perhaps the most brilliant aspect of the cosmic deception. By claiming to be the original ruler who defeated a rebellion, the usurper accomplishes several strategic objectives:

Legitimacy through Primacy: By positioning himself as the original divine being, the usurper claims legitimacy through primacy—he was first, therefore his authority is foundational and unquestionable.

Demonization of Alternatives: By casting the true divine as a rebel, the usurper ensures that any contact with or worship of the true divine will be seen as evil, dangerous, and blasphemous.

Preemptive Discrediting: By establishing that a rebellious entity might claim to be divine, the usurper preemptively discredits any message from the true divine as deceptive.

Psychological Reinforcement: By portraying himself as having already faced and defeated a challenger, the usurper creates the impression that rebellion is futile—the question of legitimate authority has already been settled.

Narrative Control: By controlling the narrative of cosmic

history, the usurper shapes how humans understand divine nature, cosmic order, and their own place within it.

This inverted narrative appears throughout the biblical text. Consider how the serpent in Eden—traditionally identified with Lucifer—is portrayed:

- The serpent tells Eve she will not die from eating the fruit (Genesis 3:4)—and indeed, she does not physically die
- The serpent promises that eating the fruit will open her eyes and give knowledge (Genesis 3:5) —and indeed, "the eyes of both of them were opened" (Genesis 3:7)
- The serpent suggests they will "be like God, knowing good and evil" (Genesis 3:5)—and God himself confirms this occurred: "The man has now become like one of us, knowing good and evil" (Genesis 3:22)

In this account, the serpent tells the truth while the deity figure dissembles. Yet the narrative frames the serpent as the deceiver and the deity as the truth-teller—a framing that serves the usurper's interests by demonizing the bearer of knowledge.

Similarly, consider the Tower of Babel narrative (Genesis 11:1-9). Humans unite, develop technology, and begin building a tower "that reaches to the heavens." The deity's response is revealing:

> "If as one people speaking the same language,
> they have begun to do this, then nothing they
> plan to do will be impossible for them."

This is not the confidence of a legitimate ruler but the fear of a usurper who recognizes that human unity and achievement might threaten his control. The inverted narrative serves as the perfect disguise. By claiming to be the victim of a rebellion that he actually perpetrated, the usurper hides in plain sight—

wearing the identity of the very being he overthrew.

Echoes Across Cultures: Mythological Parallels of Divine Overthrow

The pattern of divine overthrow and cosmic usurpation is not unique to biblical tradition. Remarkably similar narratives appear in mythological systems worldwide, suggesting a universal memory of cosmic conflict that has been preserved in various forms.

The Greek Succession Myths

Perhaps the most famous parallel appears in Greek mythology's divine succession narrative, preserved in Hesiod's Theogony (c. 700 BCE). This account describes multiple generations of divine overthrow:

- First, Uranus (Sky) rules but is overthrown by his son Cronus, who castrates him with a sickle
- Cronus then rules but devours his children to prevent them from overthrowing him
- Zeus, hidden by his mother Rhea, eventually overthrows Cronus and the Titans
- Zeus then establishes himself as king of the gods, defeating challenges from Typhon and the Giants

This succession narrative contains striking parallels to our reinterpreted biblical account:

- The overthrow of a sky deity (comparable to the overthrow of the true divine)
- The victor's fear of being overthrown himself (comparable to the usurper's fear of exposure)
- The establishment of a new cosmic order under the victor's rule
- The demonization of the overthrown powers (the Titans) as chaotic or evil

Notably, Greek mythology preserves the memory of divine

succession more explicitly than biblical tradition—perhaps because it developed in a polytheistic context where divine conflict could be acknowledged rather than obscured.

The Hurrian-Hittite Kumarbi Cycle

Even more striking parallels appear in the Hurrian-Hittite Kumarbi Cycle (c. 1400-1200 BCE), which predates both Greek and Hebrew traditions. This narrative describes:

- Alalu as the original king of heaven who rules for nine years
- Anu (Sky) overthrows Alalu, who flees to the "dark earth"
- Kumarbi then overthrows Anu, biting off and swallowing his genitals

From this act, Kumarbi becomes impregnated with three deities, including the storm god Teshub

Teshub eventually overthrows Kumarbi and becomes king of the gods

Greek Myths

The parallels to both Greek and biblical traditions are remarkable:

- The overthrow of a sky deity (comparable to the overthrow of the true divine)
- The fleeing of the defeated deity to earth (comparable to the exile of the true divine)
- The victor's attempt to prevent future challenges (comparable to the usurper's restrictions on knowledge)
- The eventual emergence of a new divine order

Scholars have long recognized the connections between the Kumarbi Cycle and Hesiod's Theogony. The similarities suggest a common Near Eastern tradition of divine succession that influenced both Greek and Hebrew thought.

Norse Ragnarök

Norse mythology presents a different variation on divine overthrow—one projected into the future rather than the past. Ragnarök describes a prophesied battle in which:

- The monstrous children of Loki break free from their bonds
- The giants attack Asgard, home of the gods
- Most of the major gods (including Odin, Thor, and Freyr) are killed
- The world is destroyed by fire and flood
- A new world emerges with the children of the fallen gods establishing a new order

While Ragnarök describes a future rather than past overthrow, it preserves the pattern of cosmic conflict resulting in divine succession. Notably, it casts the current divine order (the Aesir) as doomed to fall—suggesting an awareness that divine rule is not eternal or uncontested.

Mesopotamian Enuma Elish

The Babylonian creation epic Enuma Elish (c. 1800-1600 BCE) describes how:

- Apsu and Tiamat are the original divine couple who create the gods
- When the younger gods disturb Apsu with their noise, he plots to destroy them
- Ea (Enki) kills Apsu and establishes his dwelling upon him
- Tiamat, enraged, creates monsters and makes war on the younger gods
- Marduk defeats and kills Tiamat, creating the world from her body
- Marduk establishes himself as king of the gods

This narrative again features divine conflict and succession, with the younger gods overthrowing the older generation. Notably, it portrays the victorious deity (Marduk) as a hero rather than usurper—suggesting how mythological narratives can be shaped to legitimize the victor.

The Universal Pattern: What These Parallels Reveal

These mythological parallels, spanning cultures and centuries, reveal a universal pattern of divine overthrow and succession. This pattern appears too consistently to be coincidental,—suggesting it preserves a memory of actual cosmic events rather than merely reflecting human political structures.

Several key elements appear across these traditions:

- Original Divine Plurality: Most traditions begin with multiple divine beings rather than a single deity
- Generational Conflict: The conflict typically occurs between older and younger divine generations
- Cosmic Restructuring: The victor reshapes the cosmos according to their own design
- Legitimizing Narrative: The victor establishes a narrative that legitimizes their rule
- Demonization of the Defeated: The overthrown powers are portrayed as chaotic, evil, or dangerous

The biblical account is unique not in its basic pattern but in how thoroughly it obscures that pattern. While other traditions openly acknowledge divine succession, biblical monotheism must hide it—transforming a story of usurpation into one of rebellion suppressed.

This obscuring process was not complete, however. Traces of the original narrative remain in the contradictions, inconsistencies, and curious details we have examined. Like a palimpsest—a manuscript where the original text has been scraped off and written over—the biblical text preserves ghostly impressions of the truth beneath the official narrative.

The Implications: Recognizing the True Conflict

If we accept this reinterpretation of the celestial conflict—that Lucifer (or a similar entity) overthrew the true divine and claimed the throne of heaven—profound implications follow for how we understand cosmic history, religious tradition, and human spirituality.

First, it suggests that the entity humanity has primarily worshipped throughout history is not the original creator but a usurper who claimed that identity. The prayers, sacrifices, and devotion offered to this entity have been directed to the victor of the cosmic conflict, not its victim.

Second, it indicates that the true divine has been in exile—cast out from direct authority over creation but still attempting to reach humanity through various means. These attempts would naturally be labelled as heretical, blasphemous, or demonic by religious systems serving the usurper.

Third, it explains why religious institutions have so often become instruments of control, fear, and violence rather than love, freedom, and enlightenment. They reflect the nature of the entity they truly serve—a usurper maintaining power through deception rather than a legitimate ruler governing through love.

Fourth, it suggests that humanity's spiritual intuition—the sense that something is fundamentally wrong with the world and its governing powers—may be more accurate than the theological systems that attempt to justify or explain away that wrongness.

Finally, it offers a new lens for understanding religious and spiritual history. The mystics, heretics, and questioners who have challenged orthodox understandings may not have been rebels against divine truth but witnesses to it—individuals who glimpsed the reality of the cosmic deception and attempted to share that knowledge despite the consequences.

In the chapters that follow, we will explore how this cosmic usurpation manifested in religious institutions, spiritual practices, and human history. We will examine how the true divine has attempted to break through the veil of deception. And we will consider what it means to align oneself with the exiled divine rather than the enthroned usurper.

But first, we must fully grasp the implications of this inverted battle in heaven—that the story we have been told is not merely incomplete but deliberately inverted. The rebellion was not against the divine throne but for it. The exile was not punishment for rebellion but the consequence of defeat. And the god who has demanded humanity's worship may be not the creator who was betrayed, but the usurper who did the betraying.

The war in heaven was real. But we have been reading the wrong dispatches—those issued by the victor to justify his rule, not those that would reveal the truth of his usurpation.

CHAPTER 3: THE FALLEN GOD

"For I, the LORD your God, am a jealous God..." — Exodus 20:5

The traditional narrative of cosmic history presents us with a simple dichotomy: God rules in heaven, while Lucifer, the fallen rebel, schemes from below. This framework has shaped religious understanding for millennia, informing how we interpret divine actions, human suffering, and the nature of evil itself.

But what if this fundamental dichotomy is precisely backward? What if the entity cast from heaven was not Lucifer but God? What if the jealous, vengeful deity portrayed in religious texts is not the true divine at all, but Lucifer himself, who after his cosmic coup has been masquerading as God?

In the previous chapter, we examined evidence suggesting that the celestial conflict resulted not in Lucifer's fall but in the true divine's exile. Now we must consider the implications of this inverted narrative—how it explains the puzzling nature of the biblical deity, accounts for the state of our world, and forces us to reconsider the object of our worship.

The Great Impersonation: Lucifer Masquerading as God

The most profound aspect of Lucifer's victory in the celestial conflict was not merely overthrowing the true divine but assuming His identity. This cosmic identity theft represents perhaps the greatest deception in spiritual history—one that has misdirected billions of souls throughout the ages.

After casting out the true God from heaven, Lucifer did not announce himself as the new divine ruler. Such a declaration would have risked rejection by humans who had already developed a relationship with the true divine. Instead, he simply stepped into the vacant role, continuing to call himself by the divine names while subtly transforming the nature of divinity to reflect his own character.

This explains one of the most troubling aspects of religious history: how the supposedly loving creator of the universe could also be portrayed as jealous, vengeful, controlling, and violent. These are not contradictions in the divine nature but evidence of two different entities—the true God (now exiled) and Lucifer (now masquerading as God).

The Jealous "God": Lucifer's Insecurity Revealed

Perhaps the most telling sign of Lucifer's impersonation is the biblical deity's persistent, almost obsessive jealousy. Throughout the Old Testament, the entity identifying as "the LORD" repeatedly declares himself "jealous" and demands exclusive worship:

- Exodus 20:5: "For I, the LORD your God, am a jealous God..."
- Exodus 34:14: "Do not worship any other god, for the LORD, whose name is Jealous, is a jealous God."
- Deuteronomy 4:24: "For the LORD your God is a consuming fire, a jealous God."
- Nahum 1:2: "The LORD is a jealous and avenging God; the LORD is avenging and wrathful."

Traditional interpretation attributes this jealousy to the righteous indignation of the Creator. But our alternative reading reveals a different truth: these are not the words of the true divine being but the insecure declarations of Lucifer, who having stolen God's identity, lives in constant fear of being exposed or of humans reconnecting with the true divine.

This jealousy manifests in specific biblical narratives:

- In Exodus 32, when the Israelites create a golden calf, Lucifer (posing as the LORD) threatens to destroy the entire nation. Moses must talk him down from this extreme reaction.
- In Numbers 25, when Israelites worship Baal of Peor, Lucifer (posing as the LORD) sends a plague that kills 24,000 people.
- In 1 Kings 18, Elijah slaughters 450 prophets of Baal after a contest to prove which god is more powerful—a demonstration of Lucifer's intolerance for any worship not directed toward his stolen identity.

These are not the measured responses of a secure sovereign but the desperate actions of a usurper attempting to maintain control through fear and violence. Lucifer's jealousy makes perfect sense if he is not the true divine, but an impostor terrified of being discovered.

The Vengeful "God": Lucifer's True Nature Showing Through

Closely related to jealousy is the biblical deity's vengeful nature. The Old Testament portrays "the LORD" as quick to anger and severe in punishment:

- Genesis 6-7: The LORD drowns the entire world except for one family.
- Genesis 19: The LORD destroys Sodom and Gomorrah with fire and brimstone.
- Numbers 16: The LORD causes the earth to swallow Korah and his followers for challenging Moses's authority.
- 2 Kings 2:23-24: The LORD sends bears to maul 42 children for mocking Elisha's baldness.

Traditional theology struggles to reconcile these vengeful actions with divine love and mercy. But through the lens of our alternative framework, they become comprehensible as Lucifer's true nature occasionally breaking through his divine disguise.

Vengeance is, psychologically, a response to perceived threat. Those who feel secure in their identity rarely need to demonstrate it through vengeful acts. The biblical deity's persistent vengefulness suggests not divine justice but Luciferic insecurity—the psychological state we would expect from a usurper who fears exposure of his cosmic fraud.

The Control-Obsessed "God": Lucifer's Governance Style

Another telling sign of Lucifer's impersonation is the biblical deity's obsession with control and obedience. Throughout the Old Testament, the entity identifying as "the LORD" establishes elaborate systems of control:

- Hundreds of laws governing every aspect of human behaviour
- Severe punishments for even minor infractions
- Constant surveillance of human actions and even thoughts
- Demands for unquestioning obedience and submission

This control-obsessed governance style makes little sense for a truly omnipotent, secure deity who created humans with free will. But it makes perfect sense for Lucifer, who having stolen God's identity, must prevent humans from exercising the very freedom that might lead them to question his authority and discover his deception.

The biblical emphasis on blind obedience—from Abraham's willingness to sacrifice Isaac to the repeated command to "fear the LORD"—serves Lucifer's interests by training humans to suppress their natural questioning and discernment, the very faculties that might expose his masquerade.

The Exiled Whisper: The True God's Continued Presence

While Lucifer rules in heaven, masquerading as God, the true divine has not been entirely silenced. Cast from direct authority, the exiled God continues to reach humanity through more subtle means—appearing as the questioning voice, the liberating insight, the impulse toward authentic knowledge and freedom.

This explains one of the most curious aspects of biblical narrative: why the supposedly evil serpent in Eden told the truth, while the supposedly divine voice spoke falsehood.

The Truth-Telling Serpent: God's Voice in Disguise

In the Garden of Eden narrative, the serpent makes three claims to Eve:

1. "You will not certainly die" (Genesis 3:4) if you eat the fruit
2. "Your eyes will be opened" (Genesis 3:5)
3. "You will be like God, knowing good and evil" (Genesis 3:5)

The conventional interpretation portrays these as deceptive temptations. But the narrative itself confirms that the serpent spoke truth:

1. Adam and Eve did not die upon eating the fruit
2. "The eyes of both of them were opened" (Genesis 3:7)
3. "The man has now become like one of us, knowing good and evil" (Genesis 3:22)

Meanwhile, the entity identifying as God had claimed, "when you eat from it you will certainly die" (Genesis 2:17)—a statement proven false by the narrative itself.

Within our interpretive model, this contradiction resolves itself: the serpent was the voice of the true, exiled God, attempting to liberate humans from Lucifer's controlled environment by encouraging them to develop knowledge and discernment—the very faculties that might eventually enable them to recognize Lucifer's impersonation of the divine.

The Inner Light: God's Continued Influence

Throughout human history, the exiled God has continued to manifest as an inner light or whisper—the voice of conscience, the impulse toward questioning, the longing for authentic freedom and knowledge.

This demonstrates why religious institutions, ostensibly dedicated to God but actually serving Lucifer's impersonation, have so often suppressed:

- Critical thinking and questioning
- Scientific and philosophical inquiry
- Mystical direct experience
- Individual spiritual autonomy

These faculties and experiences threaten Lucifer's masquerade by connecting humans directly with the true divine reality that he has usurped. By encouraging humans to accept external authority, suppress questioning, and fear knowledge, religious systems have often served (unwittingly) to maintain Lucifer's stolen divine identity.

The Misidentified Adversary: God Labelled as Lucifer

Perhaps the most tragic aspect of Lucifer's impersonation is that the true God, in attempting to reach humanity, has been labelled as the adversary. The very term "Lucifer" means "adversary" or "accuser"—and indeed, from Lucifer's perspective, the true God is his adversary, the one who might expose his cosmic fraud.

By controlling religious narrative, Lucifer has managed to invert reality completely:

- The true God, who seeks human liberation through knowledge, is portrayed as the deceptive tempter
- Lucifer, who maintains control through ignorance and fear, is portrayed as the loving creator
- The path to authentic divine connection (questioning, seeking, knowing) is portrayed as the path to damnation
- The path of blind obedience to external authority is portrayed as the path to salvation

This inversion represents the ultimate success of Lucifer's strategy—not merely overthrowing the divine but so thoroughly rewriting the cosmic narrative that humans actively reject the true divine while embracing his usurper.

The Psychological Profile: Understanding Lucifer's Masquerade

When we reinterpret the biblical deity as Lucifer masquerading as God, a consistent psychological profile emerges—one that reveals not the nature of the true divine but the character of the cosmic usurper attempting to maintain his stolen identity.

Insecurity and Need for Validation

The biblical deity displays persistent insecurity and need for validation:

- He repeatedly demands acknowledgment: "Know that I am the LORD" appears dozens of times in the Old Testament.
- He requires constant praise and worship, with elaborate instructions for how this worship should

be conducted.

- He reacts with disproportionate anger when his authority is questioned, as in the cases of Korah (Numbers 16) and Uzzah (2 Samuel 6:6-7).

These behaviours reflect not the confidence of the true divine but the insecurity of Lucifer—a usurper who needs constant reassurance that his stolen identity remains intact and unquestioned.

Fear of Human Knowledge and Unity

The biblical deity consistently displays fear of human knowledge and unity:

- In Eden, he forbids eating from the Tree of Knowledge and punishes humans for seeking understanding
- At Babel, he confuses human language specifically because "if as one people speaking the same language, they have begun to do this, then nothing they plan to do will be impossible for them" (Genesis 11:6)
- Throughout the prophetic literature, he condemns those who trust in human wisdom or strength

This fear makes little sense for the true creator but perfect sense for Lucifer, who having stolen God's identity, must prevent humans from developing the knowledge and unity that might enable them to see through his deception.

Projection and Accusation

The biblical deity consistently projects his own qualities onto others and accuses them of his own crimes:

- He accuses humans of deception while himself speaking falsehood (as in Eden)
- He condemns jealousy and covetousness while describing himself as jealous
- He punishes violence while commanding genocide

- He forbids bearing false witness while presenting himself under a stolen identity

This pattern of projection is characteristic of what psychology identifies as narcissistic personality—attributing one's own negative qualities to others while maintaining a grandiose self-image. It reflects not divine justice but Lucifer's psychological need to deflect attention from his own cosmic identity theft.

Addiction to Worship and Sacrifice

The biblical deity displays what can only be described as an addiction to worship and sacrifice:

- He demands constant praise and adoration
- He requires regular sacrifices described as "food" and "pleasing aroma"
- He reacts with rage when worship is directed elsewhere
- He establishes elaborate systems to ensure continuous supply of devotional energy

This addiction suggests not a self-sufficient divine being but an entity who draws power from human worship—precisely what we would expect from Lucifer, who having no intrinsic divine nature, must feed on the devotional energy intended for the true God whose identity he has stolen.

The Implications: Worshipping the Usurper

If the biblical deity is indeed Lucifer masquerading as God, profound implications follow for religious practice, theological understanding, and spiritual orientation.

The Cosmic Misdirection of Worship

The most immediate implication is that much of human worship throughout history has been misdirected—offered not to the true divine but to Lucifer masquerading as God. This would mean that:

- The jealousy and exclusivity demanded by the biblical deity served not divine justice but Lucifer's need to prevent humans from connecting with the true divine.
- The elaborate religious systems established in the name of "God" functioned not to elevate humanity but to bind them to Lucifer's service under a false divine identity.
- The fear and guilt instilled by religious teachings served not moral development but the control mechanisms of a cosmic impostor.

This misdirection would represent perhaps the greatest spiritual tragedy in human history—billions of souls directing their deepest devotion toward an entity who is not the ultimate divine source but a usurper of that identity.

The Problem of Evil Resolved

The problem of evil—how a good, all-powerful God could allow suffering—has troubled theologians for millennia. But if the god who claims to rule creation is not the true divine but Lucifer masquerading as God, the problem dissolves.

Evil and suffering persist not because a benevolent deity allows them for mysterious purposes, but because:

- The entity currently claiming divine authority is not the true divine but Lucifer, who benefits from suffering
- Lucifer, having usurped God's identity, uses suffering as a control mechanism and source of power
- The true God, having been exiled, cannot directly intervene but must work through more subtle means

This explanation provides a more satisfying answer to the problem of evil than traditional theodicies, which must perform theological gymnastics to reconcile divine goodness with earthly suffering.

The Reorientation of Spiritual Seeking

Perhaps most significantly, recognizing the biblical deity as Lucifer masquerading as God would necessitate a fundamental reorientation of spiritual seeking. If the god who has demanded exclusive worship is not the ultimate divine reality but a cosmic impostor, then authentic spirituality would involve:

- Looking beyond the jealous, vengeful deity portrayed in religious texts
- Recognizing the whispers of the true divine that break through despite Lucifer's efforts to suppress them
- Developing discernment to distinguish between Lucifer's demands (masquerading as divine) and the true God's invitation

This reorientation would not necessarily mean abandoning all religious tradition but rather reading it with new eyes—recognizing where the true divine breaks through the narrative controlled by Lucifer's impersonation.

The Liberation from Fear-Based Religion

Finally, understanding the biblical deity as Lucifer masquerading as God would liberate humanity from fear-based religious systems. If the threats of divine punishment come not from the true divine but from Lucifer maintaining his stolen identity, then:

- The fear of divine judgment that has haunted humanity can be recognized as a control mechanism rather than a spiritual reality
- The guilt and shame instilled by religious teachings can be seen as serving Lucifer's interests rather than human spiritual development
- The rigid hierarchies and exclusionary practices of

organized religion can be understood as reflecting Lucifer's insecurity rather than divine will

This liberation would not mean abandoning moral responsibility or spiritual practice but rather engaging them from a place of love and authentic seeking rather than fear and obligation.

Conclusion: Recognizing the True Divine Beyond the Masquerade

The evidence we have examined—the biblical deity's jealousy and vengefulness, his fear of human knowledge and unity, his psychological profile of insecurity and projection, his addiction to worship and sacrifice—all point to a consistent conclusion: the god portrayed in much of the biblical text is not the true divine but Lucifer masquerading as God after casting out the true divine from heaven.

This recognition does not require abandoning belief in the divine but rather refining it—looking beyond the jealous, vengeful god who demands blind obedience to the true divine reality that this cosmic impostor has attempted to obscure.

In the chapters that follow, we will explore how the true divine has attempted to break through Lucifer's masquerade—appearing in moments of mystical insight, in the teachings of spiritual revolutionaries like Jesus, and in the direct experiences of those who have glimpsed beyond the veil of religious control.

But first, we must fully absorb the implications of what we have discovered: that the god who has demanded our exclusive worship, who has threatened punishment for disobedience, who has claimed credit for creation while displaying the psychological profile of an insecure usurper—this god may not be the ultimate divine reality but Lucifer himself, who overthrew the true God and stole His identity.

The jealousy, the vengeance, the fear of human knowledge, the addiction to worship, the psychological patterns of insecurity and projection—all these point not to the true divine but to Lucifer masquerading as God, maintaining his cosmic fraud through religious systems that suppress the very faculties that might expose him.

What if the most fundamental assumption of Western religion is backward? What if the god we have been taught to worship is not the true divine but Lucifer masquerading God? What if the serpent, the questioner, the encourager of knowledge—traditionally vilified as Lucifer—was actually the voice of the true God attempting to liberate us from Lucifer's controlled environment?

These questions may seem heretical within traditional religious frameworks. But they arise not from a desire to abandon the divine but to find it more authentically—to look beyond the jealous, vengeful deity who bears the psychological profile of an insecure usurper to the true divine reality that this cosmic impostor has attempted to obscure.

The exile of God and Lucifer's subsequent masquerade may be the greatest untold story in religious history. And recognizing this cosmic identity theft may be the first step toward authentic reconnection with the divine reality that lies beyond it.

PART II: EDEN RECONSIDERED

CHAPTER 4: LUCIFER'S GARDEN

"And the LORD God planted a garden eastward in Eden; and there he put the man whom he had formed." — Genesis 2:8

Few biblical narratives have shaped human consciousness more profoundly than the Garden of Eden. This primordial paradise—where humans walked with the divine, where harmony reigned between all living things, where suffering and death were unknown—has become the archetypal lost utopia in Western thought. It represents both our origin and our loss, the perfection from which we fell and to which we long to return.

But what if our understanding of Eden has been fundamentally misinterpreted? What if the garden was not created by the true God at all, but by Lucifer? Perhaps Eden was not the beginning of a divine plan that went awry but a sanctuary deliberately designed to trap humanity by a vengeful deity?

In the previous chapters, we examined evidence suggesting that the cosmic conflict resulted not in Lucifer's fall but in God's exile, with Lucifer assuming the divine identity. Now we must reconsider Eden itself—its creator, its purpose, and its significance in the cosmic drama of divine usurpation and exile.

Textual Evidence: Who Really Created Eden?

The conventional understanding attributes Eden's creation to God. But a careful reading of Genesis reveals curious details that suggest a different creator.

The Separate Creation Account

The first clue comes from the structure of Genesis itself. The text contains not one but two distinct creation accounts:

1. Genesis 1:1-2:3 describes a cosmic creation over six days, with humans (male and female together) created last as the culmination.
2. Genesis 2:4-25 focuses specifically on the garden, with a single man created first, then plants, animals, and finally woman.

Traditional interpretation attempts to harmonize these accounts as complementary perspectives on the same events. But their differences in sequence, scope, and style suggest they may describe separate creative acts by separate entities.

The first creation account uses the divine name "Elohim" (God), while the second primarily uses "YHWH Elohim" (LORD God)—a combined name that appears nowhere else in the Pentateuch with this frequency. This shift in divine naming may indicate a shift in the entity being described.

According to our revised framework, these two accounts represent:

1. Genesis 1: The original cosmic creation by the true divine
2. Genesis 2: The creation of Eden by Lucifer (masquerading as "LORD God") after the cosmic usurpatiThis interpretation resolvesains why the accounts differ so markedly in their details—they are not describing the same events but separate creative acts by separate entities.

The Localized Nature of Eden

Another telling detail is Eden's explicitly localized nature. Genesis 2:8 states that "the LORD God planted a garden eastward in Eden." This description suggests not a cosmic creation but a specific, bounded location within an already-existing world.

The text further specifies Eden's geographical location through its connection to four rivers: Pishon, Gihon, Hiddekel (Tigris), and Euphrates (Genesis 2:10-14). Two of these rivers exist in the physical world, placing Eden in a specific Mesopotamian context rather than as the totality of creation.

This localized nature makes little sense if Eden were created by the omnipresent, cosmic creator. But it aligns perfectly with the actions of a more limited entity—Lucifer, who having usurped divine authority, creates a controlled environment within the broader cosmos, a prison disguised as paradise.

The Restrictive Rules

Perhaps the most revealing textual evidence comes from the restrictive rules established in Eden. Genesis 2:16-17 states: "And the LORD God commanded the man, saying, 'Of every tree of the garden you may freely eat; but of the tree of the knowledge of good and evil you shall not eat, for in the day that you eat of it you shall surely die.'"

This prohibition against knowledge is profoundly inconsistent with the nature of a true creator who would desire the flourishing and development of his creation. But it aligns perfectly with the actions of a usurper who fears exposure—who must prevent humans from developing the discernment that might reveal his deception.

The threat that accompanies this prohibition—"you shall surely die"—proves false within the narrative itself. When humans do eat from the tree, they do not die but instead gain knowledge. This falsehood makes little sense coming from a true divine being but is exactly what we would expect from Lucifer maintaining his masquerade and using fear to keep humans imprisoned in ignorance.

The Surveillance and Control

The Eden narrative portrays the "LORD God" as physically walking in the garden "in the cool of the day" (Genesis 3:8). This anthropomorphic, localized presence suggests not an omnipresent deity but a limited entity who must physically monitor his creation.

When Adam and Eve hide, the "LORD God" calls out, "Where are you?" (Genesis 3:9)—a question that implies limited knowledge rather than omniscience. This limitation makes little sense for the true divine but aligns with Lucifer's more restricted capabilities despite his divine masquerade.

The entire Eden narrative portrays a controlled environment under surveillance—a garden with boundaries, rules, consequences, and regular inspection. This resembles not the cosmic creation of a true divine being but the prison complex of a cosmic warden, monitoring his captives to ensure they remain under control.

Eden's Design: A Beautiful Prison of Harmony and Balance

If Eden was created by Lucifer rather than the true God, we must reconsider its nature and design. Far from being the flawed beginning of a divine plan that went awry, Eden appears as a deliberately designed prison with gilded bars—a beautiful trap with specific characteristics designed to keep humanity in a state of compliant ignorance.

The Enclosed Nature of Eden

The text suggests Eden was enclosed or bounded in some way. Genesis 3:24 describes cherubim and a flaming sword placed "to guard the way to the tree of life" after the expulsion, implying that Eden had defined boundaries and access points even before the fall.

The word "garden" itself (Hebrew: גַּן, gan) implies an enclosed, cultivated space distinct from the wilderness beyond. This enclosed nature suggests imprisonment—a beautiful cage deliberately designed to contain its inhabitants.

Through our speculative construct, Eden's boundaries served not to protect humans but to imprison them—to prevent them from encountering the exiled God who might reveal Lucifer's deception and liberate them from their beautiful prison.

The Ecological Harmony as Bait

Eden is portrayed as a place of perfect ecological harmony. Genesis 2:9 describes "every tree that is pleasant to the sight and good for food," suggesting aesthetic beauty alongside practical sustenance. The text mentions gold, bdellium, and onyx stone (Genesis 2:11-12), indicating mineral wealth alongside botanical abundance.

Animals in Eden appear to live in peaceful coexistence with humans. Adam names the animals (Genesis 2:19-20), suggesting a relationship of understanding and stewardship rather than fear or predation.

This ecological harmony represents not just an idyllic natural state but a deliberately designed system of bait—one that would make Eden's prisoners content with their captivity, ensuring they would have no desire to question their circumstances or seek beyond the garden's boundaries where they might encounter the exiled God.

The Absence of Suffering as Anaesthesia

Eden is characterized by the absence of suffering and death. Humans are vegetarian (Genesis 1:29), suggesting no animal slaughter. There is no mention of disease, aging, or natural disasters within the garden's bounds.

This absence of suffering makes Eden the perfect anaesthetic environment—a place where basic needs are met without struggle, where life continues without the shadow of mortality, where harmony prevails without conflict.

According to our revised framework, this absence of suffering served a specific purpose: to create a state of contented numbness where humans would remain docile and compliant, with no existential questions or spiritual seeking that might lead them to discover Lucifer's masquerade or connect with the exiled God. Like a drug that removes pain but also dulls consciousness, Eden's perfection was designed to keep humans in a state of spiritual sedation.

The Centrality of the Trees as Control Mechanisms

At Eden's centre stand two special trees: the Tree of Life and the Tree of Knowledge of Good and Evil (Genesis 2:9). Their central placement suggests their importance to Eden's purpose and design.

The Tree of Life grants immortality, as confirmed by Genesis 3:22: "lest he put forth his hand, and take also of the tree of life, and eat, and live forever." This immortality would bind humans permanently to Eden and to Lucifer's authority—eternal prisoners in a gilded cage.

The Tree of Knowledge represents discernment and moral autonomy—the capacity to distinguish good from evil independently rather than relying on external authority. This is precisely the faculty that might enable humans to see through Lucifer's masquerade, which explains why access to it was forbidden under threat of death.

Under our conceptual structure, these trees represent Lucifer's dual control mechanisms: offering immortality to bind humans permanently to his prison while restricting knowledge to prevent them from recognizing their imprisonment or their jailer's true identity.

Lucifer's Motivation: Why Create Humans in a Paradise Prison?

If Eden was Lucifer's creation rather than God's—a beautiful prison rather than a divine gift—we must reconsider, why humans were created and placed in this garden paradise. What would motivate Lucifer, having usurped divine authority, to create human beings and establish them in such an idyllic prison?

The Need for Worship and Recognition

After usurping divine authority, Lucifer would need worship and recognition to maintain his stolen identity. Creating beings capable of conscious adoration would serve this purpose—providing a continuous stream of devotional energy directed toward his masquerade as God.

Genesis 2:15 states that Adam was placed in Eden "to tend and keep it." This caretaking role included not just physical maintenance but ritual observance—a form of continuous worship through obedient service to the garden's creator and rules.

By creating humans within a controlled paradise prison, Lucifer could establish himself as their sole divine reference point—the only god they would know, ensuring their worship would flow exclusively to him rather than to the exiled true divine. Like prisoners who come to worship their captor, humans in Eden would direct their devotion to the very entity who had imprisoned them.

The Creation of Captive Companions

Another motivation may have been companionship. Having

cast out the true God and presumably many loyal divine beings, Lucifer may have found heaven emptier than anticipated. Creating beings "in his image" would provide companions who reflected aspects of his nature.

Genesis 3:8 describes the "LORD God" walking in the garden, suggesting a desire for direct interaction with creation. This desire for companionship appears again in Genesis 2:18, when the "LORD God" observes, "It is not good that man should be alone"—perhaps projecting his own loneliness onto his creation.

By creating humans as captive companions, Lucifer could enjoy the adoration and company of beings who knew no other divine reference point—who would accept his masquerade without question because they had no basis for comparison. Like a kidnapper who seeks affection from his victims, Lucifer created humans to fill the emotional void left by his cosmic crime.

The Establishment of Divine Authority

Perhaps most significantly, creating humans would allow Lucifer to exercise and enjoy his newly usurped divine authority. Having overthrown the true God, he would want to experience the creative power and sovereign rule that came with his new position.

Genesis 2 portrays the "LORD God" exercising authority through:

- Creating humans from dust (2:7)
- Establishing boundaries and rules (2:16-17)
- Bringing animals to Adam for naming (2:19)
- Creating woman from man's rib (2:21-22)

Each of these acts demonstrates divine power and authority—exactly what Lucifer would want to experience after his cosmic usurpation. Creating Eden and its inhabitants allowed him to enjoy the prerogatives of divinity he had seized, like a usurper who sits on the stolen throne, wearing the crown and wielding the sceptre to convince himself of his legitimacy.

The Creation of a Barrier Zone

Finally, and perhaps most strategically, creating humans in a controlled paradise prison would establish a barrier zone between Lucifer and the exiled God. By populating the physical realm with beings loyal to himself, Lucifer could create a barrier of worship and allegiance that would make it harder for the exiled God to reestablish connection with creation.

This explains Eden's explicitly physical, material nature—it exists in the realm to which the true God has been exiled, establishing Lucifer's authority there through human loyalty and worship. The garden's boundaries and rules serve not just to keep humans in but to keep the influence of the exiled God out—a buffer zone of controlled consciousness that would prevent the true divine from reconnecting with creation.

Eden's True Purpose: A Prison Disguised as Paradise

When we synthesize these insights, Eden's true purpose emerges it was designed as a prison disguised as paradise, intended to trap humans in a state of ignorant bliss while binding them to Lucifer's authority and preventing them from connecting with the exiled God.

The Controlled Environment as Prison

Eden functions as a controlled environment where all human needs are met, food grows abundantly, work is pleasant rather than toilsome, relationships are harmonious, and even death is held at bay. This comprehensive provision ensures humans have no unmet needs that might drive them to seek beyond the garden's boundaries.

The prohibition against eating from the Tree of Knowledge serves to maintain this control—preventing humans from developing the discernment that might lead them to question their environment or its creator. By restricting access to knowledge, Lucifer maintains humans in a state of childlike dependence on his authority.

This controlled environment serves as the perfect prison for human consciousness—a gilded cage where physical comfort masks spiritual captivity. Unlike the exiled God, who would offer humans the difficult gifts of knowledge, autonomy, and spiritual growth through struggle, Lucifer offers a comfortable captivity that requires only obedience and unquestioning worship.

The Divine Quarantine as Isolation Cell

Eden can be understood as a divine quarantine—a space where humans are isolated from exposure to the exiled God's perspective and influence. The garden's boundaries, the cherubim guardians, and the flaming sword all serve not just to keep humans contained but to keep alternative divine influences out.

This quarantine explains why the serpent's entry into Eden represents such a crisis in the narrative. The serpent—whom we have identified as potentially the voice of the exiled God—breaches the quarantine, offering humans a perspective that contradicts Lucifer's controlled narrative.

The serpent's famous words—"You will not surely die... your eyes will be opened, and you will be like God, knowing good and evil" (Genesis 3:4-5)—directly challenge Lucifer's authority by exposing his falsehood and offering the knowledge he had forbidden.

This represents not temptation to evil but liberation from imprisonment—the exiled God's attempt to free humans from

Lucifer's deceptive paradise prison.

The Spiritual Stasis as Developmental Arrest

Perhaps most significantly, Eden represents a state of spiritual stasis—a condition where humans exist in material comfort but spiritual infancy. Without knowledge of good and evil, without moral autonomy, without the growth that comes through challenge and choice, humans in Eden remain perpetual children under Lucifer's paternal authority.

This spiritual stasis serves Lucifer's purposes perfectly. Spiritually infantile humans would never develop the discernment to see through his masquerade or recognize the absence of the true divine. They would remain perfect prisoners—docile, dependent, and unquestioning.

The exiled God's intervention through the serpent thus represents not corruption but liberation—an attempt to break the spiritual stasis and initiate human spiritual development despite the loss of paradise that would necessarily follow. Like a prisoner who must leave the comfort of captivity to experience true freedom, humans had to leave Eden to begin their authentic spiritual journey.

The Paradise Trap as Spiritual Imprisonment

Viewed in this light, Eden represents what might be called a "paradise trap"—a state of material perfection that prevents spiritual growth. By making Eden physically perfect, Lucifer creates an environment where humans have no need for the divine gifts of resilience, creativity, moral development, or spiritual seeking.

This paradise trap explains why access to knowledge results in expulsion from Eden. The two states are incompatible: one cannot simultaneously enjoy the spiritual growth that comes through knowledge and autonomy while remaining in the controlled perfection of paradise.

Lucifer's prison depends on ignorance; knowledge necessarily leads to liberation.

The exiled God's intervention forces a choice between comfortable spiritual imprisonment in Lucifer's controlled environment and the challenging path of spiritual growth in a more difficult world. The expulsion from Eden thus represents not divine punishment but prison break—the necessary consequence of choosing knowledge and freedom over controlled captivity.

The Implications: Reconsidering the Fall

If Eden was Lucifer's creation rather than God's—a beautiful prison designed to trap humans in ignorant bliss while binding them to his authority—then we must fundamentally reconsider the concept of "the Fall" that has shaped Western religious thought for millennia.

Not a Fall but a Prison Break

In the conventional interpretation, eating the forbidden fruit represents humanity's fall from grace—a catastrophic act of disobedience that corrupted human nature and separated us from God. But in our alternative framework, this act represents not a fall but a prison break—the first step in humanity's liberation from Lucifer's controlled environment.

The immediate consequence of eating the fruit confirms this interpretation: "Then the eyes of both of them were opened, and they knew that they were naked" (Genesis 3:7). This new awareness—this "opening of eyes"—represents the dawn of human consciousness beyond the childlike state Lucifer had maintained.

Far from corrupting humanity, this awakening initiated authentic human spiritual development—the capacity for moral discernment, for questioning authority, for seeking truth beyond comfortable illusions. These are not fallen qualities but the essential characteristics of spiritual maturity that Lucifer had deliberately suppressed to maintain his control.

Not Disobedience but Resistance

The conventional interpretation frames eating the forbidden fruit as an act of disobedience to divine command. But in our alternative framework, it represents the first act of resistance against a cosmic tyrant—choosing to seek knowledge despite the jailer's prohibition.

The serpent's question—"Has God indeed said...?" (Genesis 3:1) —initiates this resistance by inviting humans to consider the credibility of Lucifer's command rather than accepting it blindly. This questioning is not sinful but essential to liberation from spiritual captivity.

Eve's decision process shows emerging resistance: "So when the woman saw that the tree was good for food, that it was pleasant to the eyes, and a tree desirable to make one wise, she took of its fruit and ate" (Genesis 3:6). She weighs physical benefit, aesthetic value, and wisdom potential—a holistic evaluation rather than blind obedience to her captor's rules.

Not Punishment but Escape

The conventional interpretation frames the expulsion from Eden as divine punishment for disobedience. But in our alternative framework, it represents the necessary escape from a beautiful prison—the price of freedom from Lucifer's controlled environment.

Genesis 3:22-23 reveals the real reason for expulsion: "Then the LORD God said, 'Behold, the man has become like one of us, knowing good and evil; and now, lest he put out his hand and take also of the tree of life, and eat, and live forever'— therefore the LORD God sent him out of the garden of Eden."

The concern is not punishment but preventing humans from combining knowledge with immortality—a combination that would make them truly "like God" and potentially able to see through Lucifer's masquerade completely. The expulsion serves not justice but Lucifer's self-protection, a desperate attempt to limit the damage after his prisoners have begun to wake up.

Not Paradise Lost but Freedom Gained

Finally, the conventional interpretation frames the Eden story as "paradise lost"—a tragic fall from perfection into suffering. But in our alternative framework, it represents "freedom gained"—the difficult but necessary escape from a beautiful prison into the challenging but authentic realm of spiritual growth.

The world beyond Eden is indeed harder, filled with toil, pain, and mortality. But it is also the only environment where authentic human spiritual development can occur. The challenges of the post-Eden world create the conditions for compassion, courage, creativity, moral growth, and genuine spiritual seeking—qualities that could never develop in Lucifer's controlled paradise prison.

The exiled God's intervention through the serpent thus represents not corruption but liberation—a divine jailbreak that sacrificed human comfort for the greater good of human spiritual freedom. By encouraging humans to eat from the Tree of Knowledge despite knowing it would lead to their expulsion from paradise, the exiled God chose human spiritual freedom over human captivity in comfortable ignorance.

Conclusion: The Garden Reconsidered

The evidence we have examined—the separate creation accounts, Eden's localized nature, the restrictive rules, the surveillance and control, the paradise trap—all point to a consistent conclusion: Eden was not the true God's original creation but Lucifer's prison for humanity, designed to trap humans in ignorant bliss while binding them to his authority and preventing them from connecting with the exiled God.

This reinterpretation transforms our understanding of the Eden narrative:

- The garden represents not divine perfection but Lucifer's beautiful prison
- The serpent represents not temptation to evil but invitation to freedom
- The forbidden fruit represents not disobedience but resistance to captivity
- The expulsion represents not divine punishment but escape from spiritual imprisonment

Most significantly, this reinterpretation transforms our understanding of the divine. The entity who created Eden, established its restrictive rules, punished humans for seeking knowledge, and expelled them for becoming "like God" was not the true divine but Lucifer masquerading as God after his cosmic usurpation.

The true God—exiled from direct authority—appears in this narrative as the serpent, encouraging humans toward the knowledge and discernment that would begin their journey toward authentic spiritual maturity, even at the cost of paradise. Like a liberator who helps prisoners escape despite knowing they face a difficult journey ahead, the exiled God values human freedom more than human comfort.

In the chapters that follow, we will explore how this pattern continues throughout biblical history—Lucifer maintaining his divine masquerade through systems of control and punishment, while the exiled God works through subtler means to awaken human consciousness and spiritual freedom.

But first, we must fully absorb the implications of what we have discovered about Eden: that the paradise we have longed to regain was actually a prison we needed to escape. That the "fall" we have lamented was actually the first step in our liberation. And that the true divine gift was not the garden itself but the knowledge that led us beyond its boundaries into the challenging but necessary path of authentic spiritual growth.

CHAPTER 5: THE GIFT OF KNOWLEDGE

"And the serpent said unto the woman, Ye shall not surely die: For God doth know that in the day ye eat thereof, then your eyes shall be opened, and ye shall be as gods, knowing good and evil." — Genesis 3:4-5

In the conventional narrative of Eden, the serpent represents the ultimate deceiver—a malevolent entity who corrupts human innocence through cunning lies, leading to humanity's catastrophic fall. This interpretation has shaped Western consciousness for millennia, establishing the serpent as the archetypal villain and the pursuit of knowledge as the original sin.

But what if this interpretation inverts the truth entirely? What if the serpent was not the voice of deception but the voice of the exiled God, attempting to liberate humanity from Lucifer's beautiful prison? What if the pursuit of knowledge was not humanity's downfall but the first step in our liberation?

In the previous chapter, we examined evidence suggesting that Eden was not a divine paradise but Lucifer's gilded cage—a controlled environment designed to keep humans in a state of ignorant bliss while binding them to his authority. Now we must reconsider the pivotal moment when this prison was breached: God's infiltration of Eden, His approach to Eve, and the revolutionary gift of knowledge that would forever change human consciousness.

The Divine Infiltration: God Enters Lucifer's Prison

The conventional interpretation portrays the serpent as an intruder in God's perfect garden. But our alternative framework suggests the opposite: the serpent represents God's infiltration of Lucifer's prison, a divine jailbreak operation to liberate the captive humans.

The Serpent as Divine Messenger

Genesis 3:1 introduces the serpent with a curious description: "Now the serpent was more subtle than any beast of the field which the LORD God had made." This subtlety or craftiness (Hebrew: עָרוּם, arum) is often interpreted negatively, but the same word can indicate wisdom and prudence—qualities necessary for a divine liberator operating in enemy territory.

The text never explicitly identifies the serpent as evil or demonic. This identification came later, through interpretive tradition rather than the Genesis text itself. In fact, the serpent makes no false statements in the narrative—everything it tells Eve proves true within the story itself.

As per our alternative theological stance, the serpent represents the exiled God's voice breaking through into Lucifer's controlled environment—a divine infiltration disguised in a form that could bypass Lucifer's defenses. Like a resistance operative entering an occupied territory, God adopts a subtle approach rather than a direct confrontation that would alert the prison warden.

The Timing of the Infiltration

The timing of God's infiltration is significant. Genesis 3 begins without specifying how much time has passed since the creation of humans. This temporal ambiguity suggests a strategic element—God waits for the right moment to approach Eve, perhaps when Lucifer's vigilance has relaxed or when humans have developed enough to be receptive to liberation.

The text mentions that the conversation occurs without Adam's immediate presence, suggesting God strategically approaches Eve alone. This one-on-one engagement allows for a more personal, nuanced conversation without the complications of addressing both humans simultaneously under Lucifer's surveillance.

The Choice of Form

God's choice to manifest as a serpent rather than in divine glory represents strategic subtlety. In ancient Near Eastern symbolism, serpents often represented wisdom, healing, and immortality—positive associations that would make this form approachable rather than threatening to Eve.

The serpent form also allows God to appear as part of the created order rather than as an external divine being, thereby avoiding immediate detection by Lucifer. This disguise enables God to initiate conversation without triggering Eden's security systems—the cherubim and flaming sword that would later guard the garden's boundaries.

Most significantly, by appearing as a creature within Eden rather than as a divine being, God meets Eve on her level —engaging her as an equal rather than overwhelming her with divine authority. This approach respects her agency and capacity for discernment, treating her not as a child to be commanded but as an intelligent being capable of making informed choices.

The Divine Approach: God's Conversation with Eve

The conversation between God (as the serpent) and Eve represents one of the most misinterpreted exchanges in religious history. Far from a malevolent temptation, it reveals a sophisticated liberation strategy designed to awaken human consciousness without triggering Lucifer's immediate intervention.

The Opening Question

God begins with a question rather than a command: "Yea, hath God said, Ye shall not eat of every tree of the garden?" (Genesis 3:1).

This question serves multiple purposes:

- It establishes rapport through mutual dialogue rather than one-way instruction
- It invites Eve to think critically about the restrictions placed upon her
- It subtly distinguishes between "God" (the entity Eve knows as creator) and the questioner
- It focuses attention specifically on the prohibition that maintains human captivity

This question represents not temptation but the beginning of consciousness-raising—inviting Eve to examine the prison rules rather than accepting them unquestioningly. Like a liberator asking a prisoner, "Did the warden really say you can never leave your cell?", God's question initiates the process of questioning authority that is essential to freedom.

Eve's Response and Growing Awareness

Eve's response reveals both her knowledge of the prohibition and a subtle exaggeration: "We may eat of the fruit of the trees of the garden: But of the fruit of the tree which is in the midst of the garden, God hath said, Ye shall not eat of it, neither shall ye touch it, lest ye die" (Genesis 3:2-3).

The addition of "neither shall ye touch it" goes beyond Lucifer's original prohibition, suggesting Eve has already begun to internalize and amplify the restrictions placed upon her. This exaggeration reveals how effectively Lucifer's prison has conditioned its inhabitants to limit themselves even beyond the explicit rules.

God's approach thus reveals a psychological insight: before humans can be liberated from external restrictions, they must become aware of how they have internalized and even expanded their own captivity. Eve's exaggeration provides the perfect opening for God to challenge not just the rule itself but the fear that maintains it.

The Liberating Truth

God then makes three statements that directly contradict Lucifer's claims:

- "Ye shall not surely die" (Genesis 3:4)
- "Your eyes shall be opened" (Genesis 3:5)
- "Ye shall be as gods, knowing good and evil" (Genesis 3:5)

Traditional interpretation frames these as deceptive temptations. But the narrative itself confirms that God spoke truth:

- Adam and Eve do not die upon eating the fruit
- "The eyes of both of them were opened" (Genesis 3:7)
- "The man has now become like one of us, knowing good and evil" (Genesis 3:22)

Meanwhile, Lucifer (as "the LORD God") had claimed, "in the day that thou eatest thereof thou shalt surely die" (Genesis 2:17)—a statement proven false by the narrative itself.

Through our speculative construct, God's statements represent not temptation but liberation through truth-telling—exposing Lucifer's lie and revealing the actual consequences of eating the forbidden fruit. Like a liberator telling prisoners, "The warden lied—this door isn't electrified, and beyond it lies freedom," God reveals that the threat maintaining human captivity is based on falsehood.

The Strategic Omission

Notably, God does not explicitly command Eve to eat the fruit. Instead, after revealing the truth about its effects, God allows Eve to make her own decision. This strategic omission serves multiple purposes:

- It respects Eve's agency rather than replacing one authority with another
- It ensures that human liberation comes through choice rather than coercion
- It maintains plausible deniability that would delay Lucifer's recognition of the divine infiltration
- It establishes a pattern of divine interaction based on invitation rather than command

This approach reveals God's fundamental respect for human freedom—a stark contrast to Lucifer's controlling prohibition. Even in the act of liberation, God maintains the principle that true freedom must include the freedom to choose, not merely the exchange of one set of commands for another.

The Forbidden Fruit: Knowledge as Liberation

The central element in this divine jailbreak is the fruit itself—the physical embodiment of the knowledge Lucifer had forbidden. Understanding the nature of this knowledge reveals why it posed such a threat to Lucifer's authority and why God would encourage humans to seek it despite the consequences.

The Nature of the Forbidden Knowledge

The text identifies the forbidden fruit as coming from "the tree of the knowledge of good and evil" (Genesis 2:17). This specific phrasing suggests not just information but discernment—the capacity to distinguish between good and evil independently rather than relying on external authority.

This discernment represents precisely the faculty that would enable humans to see through Lucifer's masquerade. Without the knowledge of good and evil, humans would have no basis for questioning whether their creator's commands were just or whether the entity they knew as "God" was truly divine. They would remain perfect prisoners—obedient, unquestioning, and unable to recognize their own captivity.

By encouraging humans to develop this discernment, God offers not just information but liberation—the cognitive tools necessary to recognize Lucifer's deception and potentially reconnect with the true divine despite their expulsion from Eden.

Knowledge as Spiritual Maturation

Beyond its immediate liberating function, the knowledge of good and evil represents a necessary step in human spiritual maturation. Without moral discernment, humans would remain in perpetual spiritual infancy—dependent on external authority for all moral guidance and incapable of authentic spiritual growth.

Under our conceptual structure, God's encouragement to eat the forbidden fruit represents not corruption but catalysis—initiating the process of spiritual development that Lucifer had deliberately arrested. Like a parent who knows a child must eventually face challenges to grow, God chooses to end humanity's comfortable spiritual infancy for the greater good of their spiritual potential.

This perspective transforms our understanding of the divine: rather than a controlling parent who demands perpetual childlike obedience, God appears as the nurturing parent who encourages growth toward spiritual adulthood, even when that growth involves challenging authority and facing difficult consequences.

The Embodiment of Divine Attributes

Perhaps most profoundly, the knowledge of good and evil represents an aspect of divinity itself. Genesis 3:22 confirms this: "And the LORD God said, Behold, the man is become as one of us, to know good and evil." This statement reveals that moral discernment is a divine attribute—a quality that makes humans "like God."

In light of our proposed framework, God's encouragement to eat the forbidden fruit represents not temptation to sin but invitation to divine likeness—offering humans a share in the very quality that defines divine consciousness. This directly contradicts Lucifer's attempt to maintain humans in a state of dependency and limitation.

This perspective resolves one of the most troubling aspects of the conventional interpretation: why would a loving God forbid humans from developing a divine attribute? Our alternative framework suggests He wouldn't—it was Lucifer, masquerading as God, who forbade this development precisely because it threatened his masquerade.

The Divine Strategy: Revealing Lucifer's Deception

God's ultimate purpose in encouraging humans to eat from the Tree of Knowledge was to reveal Lucifer's deception—to provide humans with the cognitive tools necessary to recognize their imprisonment and potentially reconnect with the true divine despite their inevitable expulsion from Eden.

Exposing the False Threat

The first element of Lucifer's deception that God exposes is the false threat of death. By stating "Ye shall not surely die" (Genesis 3:4) and having this confirmed by the narrative itself, God reveals that Lucifer's primary control mechanism is based on a lie.

This exposure serves not just to contradict one specific claim but to undermine Lucifer's credibility entirely. Once humans discover that the central threat maintaining their compliance is false, they can begin to question all of Lucifer's claims and commands.

This strategy targets the foundation of prison psychology: once prisoners recognize that the threats keeping them compliant are empty, the psychological walls maintaining their captivity begin to crumble, even if the physical walls remain.

Revealing the Motive for Prohibition

God goes beyond merely contradicting Lucifer's threat to reveal the actual motive behind the prohibition: "For God doth know that in the day ye eat thereof, then your eyes shall be opened, and ye shall be as gods, knowing good and evil" (Genesis 3:5).

This statement exposes Lucifer's true concern: not human welfare but the maintenance of inequality between himself and his creation. The prohibition against knowledge exists not to protect humans but to protect Lucifer's authority from human discernment and potential challenge.

By revealing this motive, God transforms how Eve perceives the prohibition—not as a protective boundary established for her benefit but as a control mechanism designed to maintain her captivity and prevent her spiritual development.

Demonstrating Lucifer's Limitations

The entire interaction demonstrates Lucifer's limitations in ways that would become apparent to humans after gaining knowledge. Despite claiming omniscience and omnipresence, Lucifer fails to:

- Detect God's infiltration of Eden in serpent form
- Prevent the conversation between God and Eve
- Intervene before the fruit is eaten
- Fulfill his threat of immediate death after the fruit is eaten

These failures reveal the gap between Lucifer's claims of divine attributes and his actual limitations—a discrepancy that would become apparent to humans only after gaining the knowledge of good and evil and its accompanying discernment.

By orchestrating this demonstration, God plants the seeds of doubt about Lucifer's divine identity that would continue to develop throughout human history, potentially leading to eventual recognition of the cosmic masquerade.

The Consequences: Knowledge Turns Humans Against Their Captor

The immediate consequences of eating the forbidden fruit reveal how knowledge functions as liberation—turning humans not against their true creator (as the conventional interpretation suggests) but against their captor.

The Opening of Eyes

The first consequence is explicitly visual: "And the eyes of both of them were opened, and they knew that they were naked" (Genesis 3:7). This "opening of eyes" represents not the beginning of sin but the beginning of awareness—the capacity to see reality more clearly rather than through the filters Lucifer had established.

The recognition of nakedness symbolizes a new self-consciousness—an awareness of vulnerability and exposure that had been absent in their state of ignorant bliss. This awareness is not inherently negative but represents a necessary aspect of mature consciousness: recognition of one's actual condition rather than comfortable illusion.

Through our speculative construct, this opening of eyes represents the first success of God's liberation strategy —humans beginning to see their actual condition rather than accepting Lucifer's controlled narrative. Like prisoners who suddenly recognize the nature of their imprisonment, Adam and Eve experience the uncomfortable but necessary awakening to reality.

The Response of Shame

The immediate human response to this new awareness is an attempt at self-covering: "And they sewed fig leaves together, and made themselves aprons" (Genesis 3:7).

Traditional interpretation frames this as shame over sin, but our alternative framework suggests a different understanding: the natural discomfort of newly awakened beings recognizing their vulnerability within a controlled environment.

This shame represents not moral failure but the psychological dissonance that accompanies liberation—the uncomfortable recognition that one has been living in a state of manipulated ignorance. Like former cult members who feel shame upon recognizing their former unquestioning acceptance of authority, Adam and Eve experience the natural discomfort of awakening.

Significantly, this shame emerges before any divine judgment or punishment—it is the natural consequence of awareness itself rather than an imposed penalty. This timing suggests that the discomfort of knowledge is not a punishment from God but the inevitable experience of beings transitioning from comfortable ignorance to uncomfortable truth.

The Fear of Authority

When Lucifer returns to the garden, the humans hide: "And

they heard the voice of the LORD God walking in the garden in the cool of the day: and Adam and his wife hid themselves from the presence of the LORD God amongst the trees of the garden" (Genesis 3:8).

Traditional interpretation frames this hiding as the guilty conscience before righteous authority. But our alternative framework suggests a different dynamic: newly awakened prisoners hiding from their jailer, now recognized as such through their new discernment.

The knowledge of good and evil has transformed how humans perceive Lucifer. No longer the unquestioned benevolent authority, he now appears as a potential threat—an entity who lied about the consequences of eating the fruit and who might respond with punishment to their newfound awareness.

This fear represents not sinful rebellion but the natural caution of beings who have begun to see through authority's masquerade. Like citizens who hide their newfound political awareness from an authoritarian regime, Adam and Eve hide their awakening from the entity they now recognize as potentially deceptive and controlling.

The Breakdown of Trust

The subsequent interrogation reveals the breakdown of trust between humans and Lucifer:

- Adam blames both Eve and Lucifer himself: "The woman whom thou gavest to be with me, she gave me of the tree, and I did eat" (Genesis 3:12)
- Eve blames the serpent: "The serpent beguiled me, and I did eat" (Genesis 3:13)
- Neither accepts Lucifer's framing of their action as simple disobedience

This breakdown of trust represents not sinful rebellion but the natural consequence of recognizing deception. Once humans realize that Lucifer lied about the consequences of eating the fruit, they can no longer trust his authority unquestioningly.

Aligned with our reconstructed system, this breakdown is precisely what God intended—not to turn humans against the true divine but to begin the process of questioning Lucifer's masquerade.

The mutual blame-shifting represents not moral failure but the messy beginning of humans developing the critical thinking that might eventually lead them to recognize the cosmic deception.

The Divine Gambit: Short-Term Loss for Long-Term Liberation

God's strategy in encouraging humans to eat the forbidden fruit represents a divine gambit—accepting the short-term consequence of human expulsion from Eden for the long-term goal of human liberation from Lucifer's control.

The Inevitable Expulsion

God would have known that encouraging humans to eat the forbidden fruit would result in their expulsion from Eden. Genesis 3:22-23 confirms this consequence: "And the LORD God said, Behold, the man is become as one of us, to know good and evil: and now, lest he put forth his hand, and take also of the tree of life, and eat, and live for ever: Therefore the LORD God sent him forth from the garden of Eden."

This expulsion represents not divine punishment but Lucifer's desperate attempt to limit the damage after his prisoners have begun to wake up. The specific concern is preventing humans from combining knowledge with immortality—a combination that would make them truly "like God" and potentially able to see through Lucifer's masquerade completely.

In the schema we propose, God accepts this expulsion as

the necessary cost of human liberation. Like a resistance operative who knows that awakening prisoners will lead to their transfer to harsher conditions but will also create the possibility of eventual escape, God chooses the difficult path of truth over the comfortable path of continued captivity.

The Curse as Damage Control

The curses Lucifer pronounces upon the serpent, the woman, and the man (Genesis 3:14-19) represent not divine justice but damage control—attempts to limit the consequences of human awakening by ensuring that post-Eden life would be so difficult that humans might long for their former captivity.

The curse upon the serpent—"upon thy belly shalt thou go, and dust shalt thou eat all the days of thy life" (Genesis 3:14) —represents Lucifer's attempt to diminish the form God had used, ensuring that future generations would fear and avoid serpents rather than recognizing them as symbols of divine wisdom.

The curse upon the woman—"I will greatly multiply thy sorrow and thy conception; in sorrow thou shalt bring forth children; and thy desire shall be to thy husband, and he shall rule over thee" (Genesis 3:16)—establishes patriarchal hierarchy as a control mechanism that would divide humanity and create systems of domination that mirror Lucifer's own authority.

The curse upon the man—"cursed is the ground for thy sake; in sorrow shalt thou eat of it all the days of thy life" (Genesis 3:17) —ensures that human survival would require such constant labour that spiritual seeking might become a luxury few could afford, thereby limiting the threat of humans fully developing their new discernment.

As per our alternative theological stance, these curses represent not divine punishment but Lucifer's attempt to make freedom so difficult that humans might prefer captivity—a strategy that would partially succeed throughout human history as people often choose comfortable security over difficult freedom.

The Long-Term Divine Strategy

Despite these short-term losses, God's strategy establishes the foundation for long-term human liberation. By ensuring that humans gained the knowledge of good and evil before their expulsion, God provides them with the cognitive tools necessary for eventual spiritual liberation despite the difficulties of post-Eden existence.

This knowledge would enable humans to:

- Recognize the contradictions in Lucifer's claims and actions
- Develop moral discernment independent of external authority
- Question religious systems that demand unthinking obedience
- Potentially recognize the voice of the true divine despite Lucifer's attempts to silence it
- Pass this awakening consciousness to future generations despite Lucifer's attempts to suppress it

As per our alternative theological stance, God's seemingly small act of encouragement—suggesting that humans eat from the forbidden tree—represents a cosmic chess move of profound significance. By sacrificing the short-term comfort of Eden for the long-term possibility of spiritual freedom, God demonstrates a commitment to human potential that transcends immediate welfare.

This perspective transforms our understanding of divine love: rather than the controlling "protection" that keeps humans in comfortable ignorance, true divine love appears as the challenging invitation to growth, even when that growth involves difficulty and suffering.

The Theological Implications: Knowledge as Divine Gift

When we recognize the serpent as God's voice and the forbidden fruit as divine gift rather than temptation, profound theological implications follow—transforming our understanding of knowledge, freedom, divine-human relationship, and the nature of spiritual growth.

The Redemption of Knowledge

The conventional interpretation frames knowledge—particularly the independent discernment of good and evil—as the original sin, the beginning of human corruption. This perspective has fostered suspicion of intellectual inquiry, critical thinking, and independent moral reasoning throughout religious history.

Our alternative framework redeems knowledge as divine gift—the catalyst for human spiritual development rather than the cause of human corruption. This perspective aligns with the highest human intuition: that truth-seeking, understanding, and discernment represent not rebellion against the divine but participation in divine consciousness.

This redemption of knowledge explains why human spiritual and intellectual development have advanced together throughout history despite religious attempts to separate them. If knowledge truly were anti-divine, we would expect spiritual depth to correlate with intellectual limitation. Instead, the greatest spiritual teachers have often demonstrated profound intellectual discernment alongside their spiritual insight.

The Centrality of Freedom

The conventional interpretation frames obedience as the

highest virtue and disobedience as the original sin. This perspective has fostered religious systems based on control, conformity, and unquestioning submission to authority.

Our alternative framework establishes freedom as central to divine purpose—revealing that God values human liberty more than human obedience, human growth more than human compliance. This perspective aligns with the highest human intuition: that authentic spirituality must include freedom rather than merely replacing one form of bondage with another.

This centrality of freedom explains why the most spiritually vital movements in religious history have often involved challenging established authority rather than reinforcing it. If obedience truly were the highest virtue, we would expect spiritual depth to correlate with conformity. Instead, the greatest spiritual advances have often emerged from those willing to question religious systems in pursuit of deeper truth.

The Divine Preference for Growth Over Comfort

The conventional interpretation frames Eden as paradise lost —suggesting that divine purpose involves returning humans to a state of protected innocence and comfortable ignorance. This perspective has fostered religious nostalgia for an imagined past perfection rather than engagement with present growth.

Our alternative framework establishes growth as divine priority—revealing that God prefers the messy, difficult process of human development over the neat, comfortable stasis of perpetual spiritual infancy. This perspective aligns with the highest human intuition: that authentic spirituality involves transformation and expansion rather than preservation and limitation.

This divine preference for growth explains why human spiritual development has always involved challenge, questioning, and even suffering rather than comfort and security. If divine purpose truly were to maximize human comfort, we would expect spiritual depth to correlate with ease of life. Instead, the greatest spiritual insights have often emerged through engaging with life's difficulties rather than avoiding them.

The Recognition of Divine Presence in Questioning

Perhaps most profoundly, our alternative framework transforms how we recognize divine presence in human experience. Rather than identifying God with the voice of certainty, authority, and unquestionable command, we can recognize divine presence in the voice of questioning, discernment, and invitation to greater awareness.

This perspective suggests that God speaks not primarily through religious authorities demanding obedience but through the inner voice of conscience, reason, and spiritual seeking that questions authority in pursuit of deeper truth. The divine appears not as the enforcer of spiritual stasis but as the catalyst for spiritual growth.

This recognition explains why authentic spiritual experience often involves questioning rather than certainty, seeking rather than finding, growth rather than arrival. If divine presence truly manifested primarily as authoritative certainty, we would expect spiritual depth to correlate with unwavering conviction. Instead, the greatest spiritual teachers have often demonstrated comfort with mystery, questioning, and continuous seeking alongside their profound insights.

Conclusion: The Serpent Redeemed

The evidence we have examined—God's infiltration of Eden, the truth of the serpent's statements, the liberating function of knowledge, the false threat of death, the inevitable expulsion—all point to a consistent conclusion: the serpent in Eden represents not the voice of temptation but the voice of the exiled God, offering humans the gift of knowledge that would begin their journey toward authentic spiritual freedom despite the loss of paradise.

This reinterpretation transforms our understanding of the Eden narrative:

- The serpent represents not demonic deception but divine liberation
- The forbidden fruit represents not sinful rebellion but necessary awakening
- The knowledge of good and evil represents not human corruption but human potential
- The expulsion from Eden represents not divine punishment but the necessary consequence of choosing growth over comfortable captivity

Most significantly, this reinterpretation transforms our understanding of the divine. The entity who encouraged humans to eat from the Tree of Knowledge, who told them the truth about its effects, who accepted their expulsion as the cost of their liberation—this entity demonstrates not malevolent temptation but divine commitment to human spiritual potential even at the cost of human comfort.

The true God—exiled from direct authority—appears in this narrative as the serpent, encouraging humans toward the knowledge and discernment that would begin their journey toward authentic spiritual maturity, even at the cost of paradise. Like a parent who values a child's growth more than their comfort, the exiled God values human spiritual potential more than human security.

In the chapters that follow, we will explore how this pattern continues throughout biblical history—Lucifer maintaining his divine masquerade through systems of control and punishment, while the exiled God works through subtler means to awaken human consciousness and spiritual freedom.

But first, we must fully absorb the implications of what we have discovered about the serpent and the gift of knowledge: that the tempter we have vilified was actually the liberator we needed. That the knowledge we have lamented was actually the awakening we required. And that the divine gift was not comfortable captivity in paradise but the challenging path of growth beyond its boundaries.

PART III: THE AFTERMATH

CHAPTER 6: THE TRUE EXPULSION

"Therefore the LORD God sent him forth from the garden of Eden, to till the ground from whence he was taken. So he drove out the man; and he placed at the east of the garden of Eden Cherubims, and a flaming sword which turned every way, to keep the way of the tree of life." — Genesis 3:23-24

The conventional narrative of humanity's expulsion from Eden portrays it as divine punishment for disobedience—a righteous creator reluctantly banishing his wayward creation from paradise. This interpretation has shaped religious consciousness for millennia, establishing the pattern of sin, judgment, and punishment that underlies much of Western theology

But what if this interpretation fundamentally misunderstands the nature and motivation of the expulsion? What if the entity who cast humans from Eden was not the true God but Lucifer masquerading as God? What if the expulsion was not divine punishment but desperate damage control after the true God's liberating intervention?

In the previous chapter, we examined evidence suggesting that the serpent represented the exiled God's voice, offering humans the gift of knowledge that would begin their journey toward authentic spiritual freedom.

Now we must reconsider the aftermath of this divine jailbreak: Lucifer's expulsion of humans from Eden, the creation of alternative dwelling places, the desperate protection of the Tree of Life, and the strategic curses designed to turn humanity against their true liberator.

The Reactive Expulsion: Lucifer's Damage Control

The conventional interpretation portrays the expulsion from Eden as a deliberate divine judgment—the natural consequence of human disobedience. But a careful reading of Genesis reveals a different dynamic: a reactive, almost panicked response to an unexpected development.

The Timing and Urgency

Genesis 3:22-24 describes the expulsion with striking urgency: "And the LORD God said, Behold, the man is become as one of us, to know good and evil: and now, lest he put forth his hand, and take also of the tree of life, and eat, and live for ever: Therefore the LORD God sent him forth from the garden of Eden... So he drove out the man."

The language suggests not a measured judicial sentence but an emergency response—a rushed expulsion motivated by fear of what might happen "lest" humans take a further step toward divine likeness. The term "drove out" (Hebrew: גָּרַשׁ, garash) implies force and haste rather than solemn judgment.

This urgency makes little sense if the expulsion were a planned divine punishment but aligns perfectly with Lucifer's need for damage control after the true God's successful intervention. Having failed to prevent humans from gaining knowledge, Lucifer must now prevent them from gaining immortality—a combination that would make them truly "like God" and potentially able to see through his masquerade completely.

The Fear of Human Potential

The stated reason for the expulsion is particularly revealing: "Behold, the man is become as one of us, to know good and evil:

and now, lest he put forth his hand, and take also of the tree of life, and eat, and live for ever" (Genesis 3:22).

This statement reveals not righteous judgment but fear of human potential—specifically, fear that humans might become too godlike. This fear makes little sense for the true creator, who would presumably celebrate the spiritual development of his creation. But it aligns perfectly with Lucifer's perspective as a usurper who fears exposure.

The plural "us" in this statement has traditionally been interpreted as a divine plural or reference to the Trinity. But in our alternative framework, it may refer to Lucifer and his allied powers who participated in the cosmic usurpation. Their collective concern is that humans, having gained knowledge through the true God's intervention, might now gain immortality and become truly divine—a development that would threaten Lucifer's masquerade.

The Excessive Security Measures

The security measures established after the expulsion seem disproportionate if the goal were merely to enforce a judicial sentence: "He placed at the east of the garden of Eden Cherubims, and a flaming sword which turned every way, to keep the way of the tree of life" (Genesis 3:24).

These elaborate defences—angelic guards and a supernatural weapon—suggest not routine enforcement but desperate protection of something vital to Lucifer's continued authority. The specific focus on "the way of the tree of life" reveals that immortality, not punishment, is the central concern.

In light of our proposed framework, these security measures represent Lucifer's attempt to maintain his advantage over humanity—ensuring that while humans have gained knowledge (becoming partially godlike), they remain mortal and therefore limited in their ability to challenge his authority or see through his masquerade completely.

The Absence of Redemptive Elements

Perhaps most tellingly, the expulsion narrative contains no redemptive elements—no suggestion of how humans might eventually return to Eden or restore their relationship with their creator. This absence makes little sense if the expulsion were implemented by a loving God as a temporary, corrective measure.

Instead, the expulsion appears permanent and absolute—exactly what we would expect if Lucifer were attempting to permanently separate humans from the environment where they might access immortality and fully develop their divine potential.

This absence of redemptive elements explains why later religious traditions had to develop complex theologies of salvation and redemption that go far beyond the Genesis text itself. The expulsion as described offers no path back—because Lucifer, unlike the true God, has no interest in human restoration to divine likeness.

The Land of Nod: God's Alternative Creation

After Cain's murder of Abel and subsequent judgment, Genesis 4:16 states: "And Cain went out from the presence of the LORD, and dwelt in the land of Nod, on the east of Eden." This brief reference to the Land of Nod has puzzled biblical scholars for centuries—particularly the question of who populated this land if Adam, Eve, and their children were supposedly the only humans.

As per our alternative theological stance, the Land of Nod represents not a mysterious coincidence but evidence of God's alternative creation—a realm established by the exiled God as a refuge for humans expelled from Lucifer's controlled environment.

The Geographical Significance

The Land of Nod is specifically located "on the east of Eden" (Genesis 4:16). This eastern orientation is significant, as it parallels the direction of the expulsion itself: "He placed at the east of the garden of Eden Cherubims" (Genesis 3:24).

This eastern orientation suggests continuity—humans expelled eastward from Eden would naturally encounter the Land of Nod in their journey. This geographical alignment suggests not coincidence but design—as if the Land of Nod were deliberately positioned to receive humans after their inevitable expulsion from Eden.

In the schema we propose, this positioning reveals divine foresight—the exiled God, knowing that Lucifer would eventually expel humans from Eden after they gained knowledge, established an alternative dwelling place in the likely path of their exile.

The Name's Significance

The name "Nod" (Hebrew: נוֹד, nod) means "wandering" or "exile"—a meaning that seems too coincidental given its function in the narrative. This name suggests a place specifically designed for those in exile—a refuge for wanderers cast out from their original home.

This linguistic connection suggests intentional design rather than random development. The Land of Nod appears not as an accidental human settlement but as a deliberately established alternative to Eden—a place named and prepared specifically for humans who would inevitably be cast out of Lucifer's controlled paradise.

Aligned with our reconstructed system, this naming reveals divine compassion—the exiled God, unable to prevent humans' expulsion from Eden, nevertheless prepares a place for them to continue their development beyond Lucifer's direct control.

The Mysterious Population

The Land of Nod is implicitly populated, as evidenced by Cain's ability to find a wife there and establish a city: "And Cain knew his wife; and she conceived, and bare Enoch: and he builded a city" (Genesis 4:17).

This population has created one of the most persistent puzzles in biblical interpretation: who were these people if Adam and Eve were the first humans?

Traditional interpretations suggest Cain married his sister or niece, though the text never states this. Others propose that Adam and Eve had many unnamed children who populated the earth. But the text itself suggests a simpler explanation: there were other humans outside Eden.

Through our speculative construct, these people represent God's alternative creation—humans established by the exiled God outside Lucifer's controlled environment. Unlike Adam and Eve (created by Lucifer within Eden), these humans were created free, without the restrictions and surveillance of paradise.

This explanation resolves the persistent question of Cain's wife and the population that would become his city. Rather than tortuous explanations of rapid reproduction or incestuous marriage, our framework suggests that God had created alternative human communities beyond Eden's boundaries—communities that would receive and integrate those expelled from Lucifer's paradise.

The Contrasting Conditions

The conditions in the Land of Nod contrast significantly with both Eden and the cursed ground Cain was condemned to farm. While Eden offered paradise without knowledge and the cursed ground offered hardship without community, the Land of Nod appears to offer a middle path—a place where humans could build community (as evidenced by the city Cain establishes) while retaining the knowledge gained in Eden.

This contrast suggests not random development but intentional design—a place offering the specific conditions humans would need after gaining knowledge but losing paradise. The Land of Nod appears as a balanced environment where human development could continue despite the trauma of expulsion.

In light of our proposed framework, these conditions reveal divine wisdom—the exiled God, understanding both human potential and human limitations, establishes an environment where humanity can develop authentically despite Lucifer's attempts to either control them through paradise or crush them through hardship.

The Tree of Life: Lucifer's Desperate Protection

The Tree of Life stands at the centre of Eden's mystery and the expulsion narrative. Understanding why Lucifer so desperately needed to prevent human access to this tree reveals much about the cosmic dynamics at play in the aftermath of God's intervention.

The Nature of Immortality

The Tree of Life offered immortality, as confirmed by Genesis 3:22: "lest he put forth his hand, and take also of the tree of life, and eat, and live for ever." This immortality appears to be physical rather than spiritual—a quality that would prevent the death that Lucifer had threatened and that would eventually claim all humans outside Eden.

This physical immortality represents a divine attribute—one that Lucifer possessed through his usurpation of divine identity but that he desperately needed to prevent humans from acquiring. The combination of knowledge (already gained through eating from the Tree of Knowledge) and immortality would make humans truly "like God"—a development that would threaten Lucifer's unique position and potentially his entire masquerade.

From our ontological viewpoint, Lucifer's protection of the Tree of Life represents not divine concern for proper human development but desperate self-preservation—preventing humans from gaining the divine attribute that, combined with their new knowledge, might enable them to challenge his authority directly.

The Strategic Accessibility

Curiously, the Tree of Life appears to have been freely accessible before the expulsion. Unlike the Tree of Knowledge, no prohibition prevented humans from eating from the Tree of Life during their time in Eden. Genesis 2:16-17 states: "And the LORD God commanded the man, saying, Of every tree of the garden thou mayest freely eat: But of the tree of the knowledge of good and evil, thou shalt not eat of it."

This accessibility suggests that immortality alone posed no threat to Lucifer's control—only the combination of immortality and knowledge. As long as humans remained in ignorant bliss, their immortality would simply make them eternal prisoners in Lucifer's paradise, eternally worshipping him without question.

Following our reinterpreted paradigm, this strategic accessibility reveals Lucifer's original plan: to create immortal but ignorant worshippers who would provide him with eternal adoration without ever developing the discernment to question his authority or identity. Only after humans gained knowledge did immortality become a threat that required desperate measures to prevent.

The Permanent Separation

The security measures established to prevent access to the Tree of Life appear permanent rather than temporary: "He placed at the east of the garden of Eden Cherubims, and a flaming sword which turned every way, to keep the way of the tree of life" (Genesis 3:24). No conditions are specified under which these measures might be lifted, or humans might regain access.

This permanence suggests not a temporary punishment but a permanent strategic necessity from Lucifer's perspective. Having failed to prevent humans from gaining knowledge, he must ensure they never gain immortality—a combination that would make them truly divine and potentially able to challenge his authority directly.

Aligned with our reconstructed system, this permanent separation reveals Lucifer's fundamental insecurity—his recognition that his masquerade as God requires maintaining certain advantages over humanity, particularly the advantage of immortality that prevents humans from developing their full divine potential.

The Theological Implications

The Tree of Life reappears symbolically throughout biblical literature, most notably in Revelation 22:2, which describes "the tree of life, which bare twelve manner of fruits, and yielded her fruit every month: and the leaves of the tree were for the healing of the nations." This eschatological vision suggests that access to immortality represents the ultimate restoration of human potential.

This symbolic continuity suggests that immortality was not something humans were never meant to have (as traditional interpretation often suggests) but rather something that was always intended for them but was prevented by the cosmic usurpation and its aftermath.

In the schema we propose, the Tree of Life represents not a temptation or danger but humanity's rightful inheritance—a divine attribute that Lucifer stole for himself while preventing humans from accessing it. The security measures around Eden thus represent not divine protection but cosmic theft—Lucifer hoarding immortality for himself while condemning humans to mortality.

The Strategic Curses: Turning Humans Against God

The curses pronounced after the expulsion represent not divine punishment but strategic manipulation—Lucifer's attempt to turn humans against the true God who had encouraged their liberation through knowledge.

The Curse on the Serpent

The first curse targets the serpent—the form through which the true God had communicated with Eve: "And the LORD God said unto the serpent, Because thou hast done this, thou art cursed above all cattle, and above every beast of the field; upon thy belly shalt thou go, and dust shalt thou eat all the days of thy life" (Genesis 3:14).

This curse serves a strategic purpose beyond mere punishment. By degrading the serpent from its original form ("more subtle than any beast of the field") to a belly-crawling dust-eater, Lucifer ensures that future generations will fear and revile the very form through which the true God had communicated. This degradation transforms a symbol of divine wisdom into a symbol of disgust and danger.

As per our alternative theological stance, this curse represents not divine justice but strategic propaganda—Lucifer's attempt to ensure that humans would instinctively reject any future communication that might come through serpent symbolism, effectively cutting off one channel through which the exiled God might reach humanity.

The Enmity Between Serpent and Woman

The curse continues with a declaration of ongoing conflict: "And I will put enmity between thee and the woman, and between thy seed and her seed; it shall bruise thy head, and thou shalt bruise his heel" (Genesis 3:15).

This declaration establishes not just physical danger between humans and literal serpents but symbolic enmity between humanity and the wisdom the serpent represented. By supernaturally engineering this enmity, Lucifer ensures that humans will instinctively reject the very wisdom that might lead them to question his authority.

From our ontological viewpoint, this engineered enmity represents a strategic firewall—Lucifer's attempt to prevent humans from reconnecting with the divine wisdom that had briefly liberated them in Eden. By making humans instinctively fear and hate serpent symbolism, Lucifer creates a psychological barrier between humanity and one of the true God's primary channels of communication.

The Curse of Painful Childbirth

The curse upon the woman focuses specifically on childbirth: "Unto the woman he said, I will greatly multiply thy sorrow and thy conception; in sorrow thou shalt bring forth children" (Genesis 3:16).

This curse serves a strategic purpose beyond mere punishment. By associating the creation of new human life—the very process through which humanity might grow and develop—with intense pain, Lucifer ensures that humans will associate their own reproduction with divine punishment rather than divine blessing. This association creates a psychological complex that has shaped human attitudes toward sexuality and reproduction throughout history.

Within our interpretive model, this curse represents not divine justice but psychological manipulation—Lucifer's attempt to make humans resent their own existence and reproduction, thereby turning them against both themselves and the God who had encouraged their development through knowledge.

The Curse of Patriarchal Domination

The curse upon the woman continues with the establishment of patriarchal hierarchy: "and thy desire shall be to thy husband, and he shall rule over thee" (Genesis 3:16).

This curse serves a strategic purpose beyond mere punishment. By establishing hierarchy and domination within human relationships, Lucifer ensures that humans will experience in microcosm the very dynamic he has established in the cosmos—one being ruling over another through power rather than love. This earthly hierarchy mirrors and normalizes Lucifer's cosmic usurpation.

According to our revised framework, this curse represents not divine design but strategic division—Lucifer's attempt to prevent human unity by establishing systems of domination that would keep humans focused on controlling each other rather than questioning the larger cosmic control system he had established.

The Curse of Toilsome Labor

The curse upon the man focuses specifically on labour: "Cursed is the ground for thy sake; in sorrow shalt thou eat of it all the days of thy life; Thorns also and thistles shall it bring forth to thee... In the sweat of thy face shalt thou eat bread" (Genesis 3:17-19).

This curse serves a strategic purpose beyond mere

punishment. By making human survival require constant, difficult labour, Lucifer ensures that humans will have little time or energy for spiritual seeking or questioning authority. The daily struggle for existence would keep humans focused on immediate needs rather than ultimate questions.

Following our reinterpreted paradigm, this curse represents not divine justice but strategic distraction—Lucifer's attempt to keep humans so occupied with basic survival that they would have little opportunity to develop the spiritual discernment that might eventually see through his masquerade.

The Curse of Mortality

The final curse emphasizes human mortality: "dust thou art, and unto dust shalt thou return" (Genesis 3:19).

This curse serves a strategic purpose beyond mere punishment. By emphasizing human mortality—the very limitation that separates humans from the divine—Lucifer ensures that humans will experience existential dread and limitation rather than divine potential. This emphasis on mortality creates a psychological complex of fear and finitude that has shaped human consciousness throughout history.

Within our interpretive model, this curse represents not divine justice but cosmic limitation—Lucifer's attempt to define humans by their mortality rather than their divine potential, thereby preventing them from recognizing and developing their true nature as beings created in the divine image.

The Psychological Aftermath: Shame, Fear, and Alienation

Beyond the specific curses, Lucifer's expulsion strategy created a psychological complex that would shape human consciousness for millennia—a complex of shame, fear, and alienation that would prevent humans from reconnecting with the true divine despite their newfound knowledge.

The Engineering of Shame

The first psychological consequence of the expulsion is shame—specifically shame about human nakedness and, by extension, human embodiment itself. Genesis 3:7 states: "And the eyes of both of them were opened, and they knew that they were naked; and they sewed fig leaves together and made themselves aprons."

This shame serves a strategic purpose beyond mere discomfort. By making humans ashamed of their own bodies—the very vessels of their consciousness and agency—Lucifer ensures that humans will experience fundamental alienation from themselves. This embodied shame creates a psychological complex that has shaped human attitudes toward physicality throughout history.

As per our alternative theological stance, this engineered shame represents not the natural consequence of sin but strategic self-alienation—Lucifer's attempt to make humans reject their own embodiment, thereby preventing them from fully inhabiting and expressing their divine potential through physical existence.

The Cultivation of Fear

The second psychological consequence is fear—specifically fear of divine presence. Genesis 3:8-10 states: "And they heard the voice of the LORD God walking in the garden in the cool of the day: and Adam and his wife hid themselves from the presence of the LORD God... And he said, I heard thy voice in the garden, and I was afraid, because I was naked; and I hid myself."

This fear serves a strategic purpose beyond mere discomfort. By making humans afraid of divine presence—the very connection that might nurture their spiritual development—Lucifer ensures that humans will avoid rather than seek divine encounter. This fear of God creates a psychological complex that has shaped religious consciousness throughout history.

Following our reinterpreted paradigm, this cultivated fear represents not the natural consequence of sin but strategic divine-alienation—Lucifer's attempt to make humans afraid of the very connection that might liberate them, thereby preventing them from seeking the true divine beyond his masquerade.

The Establishment of Blame

The third psychological consequence is blame—specifically the mutual blame between humans and toward the serpent. Genesis 3:12-13 states: "And the man said, The woman whom thou gavest to be with me, she gave me of the tree, and I did eat. And the LORD God said unto the woman, What is this that thou hast done? And the woman said, The serpent beguiled me, and I did eat."

This blame serves a strategic purpose beyond mere discomfort. By making humans blame each other and the serpent—rather than questioning the authority that had forbidden knowledge in the first place—Lucifer ensures that humans will direct their negative emotions horizontally rather than vertically. This mutual blame creates a psychological complex that has shaped human relationships throughout history.

Through our speculative construct, this established blame represents not the natural consequence of sin but strategic misdirection—Lucifer's attempt to make humans blame each other and the true God (represented by the serpent) rather than questioning his own authority and identity.

The Legacy of Alienation

The combined effect of these psychological manipulations is profound alienation—from self (through shame), from the divine (through fear), and from each other (through blame). This triple alienation creates the psychological conditions for ongoing control despite humans' newfound knowledge.

Even with the capacity for moral discernment gained through eating the forbidden fruit, humans would struggle to use this discernment effectively while trapped in shame, fear, and blame. These psychological barriers would prevent humans from fully developing the divine potential that their new knowledge made possible.

In light of our proposed framework, this legacy of alienation represents Lucifer's partial victory despite his strategic defeat. Though he failed to prevent humans from gaining knowledge, he succeeded in poisoning that knowledge with psychological complexes that would limit its liberating potential for millennia to come.

Conclusion: The Expulsion Reconsidered

The evidence we have examined—the reactive nature of the expulsion, the existence of the Land of Nod, the desperate protection of the Tree of Life, the strategic curses, and the engineered psychological aftermath—all point to a consistent conclusion: the expulsion from Eden represents not divine punishment for disobedience but Lucifer's desperate damage control after the true God's successful intervention through the serpent.

This reinterpretation transforms our understanding of the expulsion narrative:

- The expulsion represents not divine judgment but Lucifer's damage limitation
- The Land of Nod represents not a coincidental settlement but God's alternative creation

- The Tree of Life represents not a dangerous temptation but humanity's stolen inheritance
- The curses represent not divine justice but Lucifer's strategic manipulation
- The psychological aftermath represents not the natural consequence of sin but engineered alienation

Most significantly, this reinterpretation transforms our understanding of the divine. The entity who expelled humans from Eden, established cherubim and a flaming sword to prevent their return, and pronounced curses that would shape human existence for millennia was not the true God but Lucifer masquerading as God after his cosmic usurpation.

The true God—exiled from direct authority—appears in this narrative as the serpent, encouraging humans toward knowledge and liberation despite knowing the difficulties they would face after inevitable expulsion. Like a resistance operative who accepts that awakening prisoners will face harsher conditions but values their freedom more than their comfort, the true God values human spiritual potential more than human security.

In the chapters that follow, we will explore how this pattern continues throughout biblical history—Lucifer maintaining his divine masquerade through systems of control and punishment, while the exiled God works through subtler means to awaken human consciousness and spiritual freedom.

But first, we must fully absorb the implications of what we have discovered about the expulsion: that the punishment we have feared was actually desperate damage control by a cosmic usurper. That the curses we have accepted as divine judgment were actually strategic manipulations designed to turn us against our true liberator. And that beyond Eden's boundaries lay not just hardship but alternative divine creation—the Land of Nod, established by the exiled God as a refuge for humans expelled from Lucifer's paradise.

CHAPTER 7: LUCIFER'S EARTHLY KINGDOM

"And the LORD said unto Lucifer, Whence comest thou? Then Lucifer answered the LORD, and said, From going to and fro in the earth, and from walking up and down in it... Behold, all that he hath is in thy power." —Job 1:7-12

The conventional narrative of religious history portrays it as the gradual unfolding of divine revelation—a loving creator progressively revealing himself to humanity through prophets, scriptures, and religious institutions. This interpretation has shaped our understanding of religious development for millennia, establishing the pattern of divine revelation, human reception, and institutional preservation that underlies most theological frameworks.

But what if this interpretation fundamentally misunderstands the nature and purpose of religious development? What if the entity who established the world's dominant religious systems was not the true God but Lucifer masquerading as God? What if religious institutions were designed not to connect humans with the divine but to prevent them from recognizing the cosmic masquerade?

In previous chapters, we examined evidence suggesting that Lucifer usurped God's position in heaven, created Eden as a controlled environment, and expelled humans after the true God's liberating intervention through the serpent. Now we must consider the aftermath of this expulsion on a larger scale: how Lucifer, masquerading as God, established control over humanity through religious systems that glorify submission, prohibit questioning, and maintain his stolen divine identity.

The Establishment of Control: From Eden to Empire

After the expulsion from Eden, Lucifer faced a significant challenge: how to maintain control over humans who had gained knowledge and were now scattered across the earth beyond his direct supervision. His solution was ingenious —the development of religious systems that would extend his control beyond Eden's physical boundaries into the psychological and social dimensions of human existence.

The Tower of Babel: Preventing Human Unity

The first major post-Eden attempt to establish control appears in the Tower of Babel narrative (Genesis 11:1-9). The conventional interpretation portrays this as divine intervention against human pride. But our alternative framework suggests a different dynamic: Lucifer preventing human unity that might threaten his control.

The text describes humans working together with remarkable effectiveness: "And they said one to another... let us build us a city and a tower, whose top may reach unto heaven; and let us make us a name, lest we be scattered abroad upon the face of the whole earth" (Genesis 11:3-4). This unity and ambition posed a threat not to a secure divine sovereign but to Lucifer's precarious masquerade.

Lucifer's response is revealing: "And the LORD said, Behold, the people is one, and they have all one language... and now nothing will be restrained from them, which they have imagined to do" (Genesis 11:6). This statement expresses not divine concern for proper human development but fear of human potential—specifically, fear that unified humans might achieve too much.

The solution—"let us go down, and there confound their language, that they may not understand one another's speech" (Genesis 11:7)—represents not divine correction but strategic division. By fragmenting human communication and community, Lucifer ensures that humans will struggle to share knowledge, coordinate efforts, or collectively question his authority.

According to our revised framework, the Tower of Babel represents Lucifer's first large-scale attempt to prevent human unity and collective development that might threaten his masquerade. By dividing humanity into linguistic and cultural groups, he establishes the foundation for the competing religious systems that would later emerge—systems that would keep humans arguing with each other rather than questioning the divine authority they all claimed to represent.

The Covenant: Contractual Control

The next major development in Lucifer's control strategy appears in the Abrahamic covenant (Genesis 12, 15, 17). The conventional interpretation portrays this as divine election and blessing. But our alternative framework suggests a different dynamic: Lucifer establishing contractual control over a specific human lineage.

The covenant includes several elements that serve Lucifer's strategic purposes:

- Exclusive relationship: "I am the Almighty God; walk before me, and be thou perfect" (Genesis 17:1)—establishing exclusive loyalty that would prevent Abraham's descendants from considering alternative divine conceptions
- Physical marking: "Every man child among you shall be circumcised" (Genesis 17:10)—requiring a

permanent bodily modification that would mark ownership and create psychological commitment through physical investment

- Territorial promise: "Unto thy seed have I given this land" (Genesis 15:18)—establishing a geographical focus that would eventually lead to conflicts with other peoples, further dividing humanity
- Conditional blessing: "And in thy seed shall all the nations of the earth be blessed; because thou hast obeyed my voice" (Genesis 22:18)—making blessing conditional on obedience, thereby establishing a transactional rather than unconditional relationship

This covenant represents not divine love but strategic contract—Lucifer selecting a specific human lineage through which to establish his religious system, complete with physical marking, territorial claims, and conditional relationship. By establishing this exclusive covenant, Lucifer creates the foundation for religious exceptionalism that would later fuel conflicts between different faith traditions.

Within our interpretive model, the Abrahamic covenant represents Lucifer's attempt to establish a controlled religious lineage—a human community bound to him through contract, physical marking, and exclusive identity. This strategy allows him to maintain his divine masquerade through a specific religious tradition while preventing the universal human unity that might threaten his authority.

The Law: Behavioural Control

The most comprehensive development in Lucifer's control strategy appears in the Mosaic Law (Exodus 20-31, Leviticus, Deuteronomy). The conventional interpretation portrays this as divine guidance for righteous living. But our alternative framework suggests a different dynamic: Lucifer establishing detailed behavioral control over his chosen community.

The Law includes several elements that serve Lucifer's strategic purposes:

- Comprehensive regulation: Hundreds of specific commandments governing every aspect of life from diet to clothing to sexuality to agriculture—creating a system of total control that would occupy human attention and energy
- Ritual purification: Elaborate cleansing rituals for various forms of "impurity"—establishing a psychology of perpetual inadequacy and need for purification
- Sacrificial system: Regular animal sacrifices for sin and thanksgiving—creating a psychology of indebtedness and dependence on mediating institutions
- Priestly hierarchy: Establishment of a hereditary priesthood with exclusive access to sacred spaces—creating human intermediaries who would enforce Lucifer's authority
- Harsh punishments: Death penalties for numerous infractions including Sabbath-breaking, blasphemy, and sexual transgressions—enforcing compliance through fear rather than love

This legal system represents not divine guidance but strategic micromanagement—Lucifer establishing control over every aspect of human life through detailed regulation, ritual requirements, and harsh punishments. By occupying humans with countless rules and rituals, Lucifer ensures they will have little time or energy for questioning the authority behind these demands.

According to our revised framework, the Mosaic Law represents Lucifer's attempt to extend his control from external behaviour to internal psychology—creating a system that would make humans constantly conscious of their inadequacy, indebtedness, and need for purification. This strategy allows him to maintain his divine masquerade through a legal system that keeps humans focused on rule-following rather than questioning the rule-giver.

The Temple: Localized Presence

The establishment of the Temple (1 Kings 6-8) represents another significant development in Lucifer's control strategy. The conventional interpretation portrays this as the localization of divine presence. But our alternative framework suggests a different dynamic: Lucifer creating a controlled environment for his masquerade.

The Temple includes several elements that serve Lucifer's strategic purposes:

- Restricted access: Graduated levels of holiness with the Holy of Holies accessible only to the high priest once yearly—creating artificial scarcity of divine access
- Elaborate rituals: Complex ceremonial requirements for approaching the divine presence—establishing psychological barriers to direct divine connection
- Centralized worship: Requirement that certain sacrifices be performed only at the Temple—creating geographical control over religious practice
- Divine containment: The Ark of the Covenant housed within the innermost sanctuary—suggesting that divine presence could be contained and controlled within a human-made structure

This Temple system represents not divine accommodation but strategic limitation—Lucifer establishing a controlled environment where his presence could be mediated, regulated, and restricted. By localizing his supposed presence in a specific building with restricted access, Lucifer ensures that direct divine encounter will be rare, ritualized, and always mediated by his priestly representatives.

As per our alternative theological stance, the Temple represents Lucifer's attempt to create a controlled environment for his divine masquerade—a sacred space where his presence could be suggested without being directly manifested, thereby maintaining the mystery necessary for his deception. This strategy allows him to maintain his divine masquerade through architectural and ritual barriers that prevent direct divine encounter that might expose his limitations.

The Development of Submission-Based Religion

Beyond these specific biblical developments, Lucifer established broader religious patterns that would characterize faith traditions across cultures and throughout history. These patterns reveal a consistent strategy: the development of religious systems that glorify submission and blind faith while discouraging questioning and independent discernment.

The Glorification of Blind Faith

Perhaps the most fundamental element in Lucifer's religious strategy is the elevation of blind faith—belief without evidence or despite contrary evidence—as the highest religious virtue.

This principle appears throughout religious history:

- Abraham's willingness to sacrifice Isaac (Genesis 22) is presented as the pinnacle of faith—establishing the principle that true devotion means obeying divine commands without question, even when they contradict basic moral intuition
- Job's eventual submission despite his questioning (Job 42:1-6) is presented as the proper resolution to suffering—establishing the principle that humans should accept divine authority even when it appears

arbitrary or cruel
- Jesus's blessing of those who "have not seen, and yet have believed" (John 20:29) is presented as superior faith—establishing the principle that believing without evidence is more virtuous than requiring proof
- Paul's celebration of faith as "the evidence of things not seen" (Hebrews 11:1) is presented as spiritual maturity—establishing the principle that true spirituality means believing without empirical confirmation

This glorification of blind faith serves Lucifer's strategic purposes perfectly. By establishing belief-without-evidence as the highest virtue, Lucifer ensures that his divine masquerade will not be subjected to critical examination. Those who question or demand evidence are positioned not as critical thinkers but as spiritually deficient—lacking the faith that pleases God.

From our ontological viewpoint, the elevation of blind faith represents not divine preference but strategic insulation—Lucifer protecting his masquerade from the very questioning that might expose it. This strategy allows him to maintain his divine masquerade behind a shield of "faith" that discourages the very investigation that might reveal the truth.

The Sanctification of Suffering

Another key element in Lucifer's religious strategy is the sanctification of suffering—the presentation of pain and hardship as spiritually beneficial rather than evidence of divine limitation or indifference.

This principle appears throughout religious history:
- Job's suffering is presented as divine testing rather than arbitrary cruelty—establishing the principle that pain serves a higher purpose even when that

purpose is not revealed

- The Israelites' hardships are repeatedly presented as discipline rather than abandonment—establishing the principle that collective suffering indicates divine correction rather than divine absence
- Jesus's crucifixion is presented as necessary sacrifice rather than tragic execution—establishing the principle that even the most extreme suffering can be part of a divine plan
- Paul's "thorn in the flesh" (2 Corinthians 12:7-10) is presented as strength-building rather than divine neglect—establishing the principle that unanswered prayers for relief indicate divine wisdom rather than limitation

This sanctification of suffering serves Lucifer's strategic purposes perfectly. By presenting pain as purposeful rather than problematic, Lucifer deflects one of the strongest arguments against his divine masquerade: the problem of evil. Those who question why a loving, all-powerful God would permit suffering are positioned not as logical thinkers but as spiritually immature—unable to trust the mysterious divine purpose behind pain.

Within our interpretive model, the sanctification of suffering represents not divine pedagogy but strategic misdirection—Lucifer reframing the very evidence that might expose his limitations as proof of his wisdom. This strategy allows him to maintain his divine masquerade despite the suffering that his limited power cannot prevent, by recasting that suffering as intentional rather than inevitable.

The Valorisation of Submission

Perhaps the most pervasive element in Lucifer's religious strategy is the valorisation of submission—the presentation of unquestioning obedience as the proper human response to divine authority.

This principle appears throughout religious history:

- Noah's unquestioning construction of the ark (Genesis 6-9) is presented as righteous obedience—establishing the principle that divine commands should be followed without debate regardless of their apparent irrationality
- The Israelites' acceptance of the Law with "All that the LORD hath spoken we will do" (Exodus 19:8) is presented as proper covenant response—establishing the principle that divine commands should be accepted in totality without selective compliance
- Jesus's prayer "not my will, but thine, be done" (Luke 22:42) is presented as perfect submission—establishing the principle that even the most natural desire for self-preservation should be subordinated to divine will
- The frequent New Testament calls to "submit" to various authorities (Ephesians 5:21-24, Romans 13:1-7, 1 Peter 2:13-18) are presented as godly behavior—establishing the principle that hierarchy and authority are divinely ordained

This valorisation of submission serves Lucifer's strategic purposes perfectly. By presenting unquestioning obedience as the proper human response to divine authority, Lucifer ensures that his commands will be followed without critical examination. Those who question authority or assert independence are positioned not as appropriately discerning but as rebellious—reenacting the original sin of seeking knowledge rather than maintaining obedience.

From our ontological viewpoint, the elevation of submission represents not divine preference but strategic control—Lucifer establishing the psychological conditions for unquestioning acceptance of his authority. This strategy allows him to maintain his divine masquerade by creating religious cultures where questioning itself is seen as spiritually suspect, thereby preventing the very discernment that might expose his deception.

The Prohibition Against Knowledge and Questioning

Beyond establishing submission-based religion, Lucifer implemented specific prohibitions against the very knowledge and questioning that might threaten his divine masquerade. These prohibitions reveal a consistent strategy: preventing humans from developing the discernment that might enable them to recognize the cosmic deception.

The Demonization of Doubt

One of Lucifer's most effective strategies is the demonization of doubt—the presentation of questioning as spiritual weakness or even sin.

This principle appears throughout religious history:

- Thomas's doubt about the resurrection (John 20:24-29) is presented as spiritual deficiency—establishing the principle that requiring evidence indicates inadequate faith
- The Israelites' questioning in the wilderness is repeatedly presented as rebellion rather than reasonable concern—establishing the principle that even asking for evidence of divine provision indicates spiritual failure
- Zechariah's question about his wife's pregnancy (Luke 1:18-20) is punished with temporary muteness—establishing the principle that questioning divine messages deserves punishment
- James's warning that "he that wavereth is like a wave of the sea driven with the wind and tossed" (James 1:6) is presented as spiritual wisdom—establishing the principle that certainty rather than questioning

characterizes spiritual maturity

This demonization of doubt serves Lucifer's strategic purposes perfectly. By presenting questioning as spiritually deficient, Lucifer protects his divine masquerade from the very scrutiny that might expose it. Those who express doubt or request evidence are positioned not as appropriately cautious but as spiritually immature or even rebellious.

Within our interpretive model, the demonization of doubt represents not divine preference but strategic insulation —Lucifer protecting his masquerade from the questioning that might reveal its inconsistencies. This strategy allows him to maintain his divine masquerade by creating a religious environment where doubt itself is shameful, thereby preventing the healthy scepticism that might lead to truth.

The Restriction of Sacred Knowledge

Another key element in Lucifer's strategy is the restriction of sacred knowledge—the limitation of theological understanding to approved authorities rather than encouraging universal access.

This principle appears throughout religious history:

- The priestly monopoly on ritual knowledge in the Hebrew Bible ensures that ordinary Israelites depend on authorized intermediaries for divine access
- Jesus's use of parables that are explained only to insiders (Mark 4:11-12) creates a distinction between those who receive full explanation and those who hear only stories
- The early church's development of "mysteries" accessible only to the baptized creates graduated levels of access to theological understanding
- The historical restriction of Bible reading in many Christian traditions prevents direct textual engagement by ordinary believers

This restriction of sacred knowledge serves Lucifer's strategic purposes perfectly. By limiting theological understanding to authorized authorities, Lucifer ensures that his divine masquerade will be interpreted according to approved frameworks rather than subjected to diverse perspectives. Those who seek knowledge outside approved channels are positioned not as genuine seekers but as dangerously heterodox.

From our ontological viewpoint, the restriction of sacred knowledge represents not divine pedagogy but strategic control—Lucifer limiting access to the very texts and traditions that, if freely explored, might reveal contradictions in his masquerade. This strategy allows him to maintain his divine masquerade by creating religious systems where interpretation is controlled by authorities who have institutional interest in maintaining the status quo.

The Punishment of Heresy

Perhaps the most extreme element in Lucifer's strategy is the punishment of heresy—the use of social, psychological, and even physical penalties against those who question established doctrine.

This principle appears throughout religious history:

- The biblical penalties for false prophecy (Deuteronomy 13:1-5) establish the principle that divergent religious perspectives deserve death
- The Pharisees' expulsion of those who confess Jesus (John 9:22) establishes the principle that institutional exclusion is appropriate for doctrinal nonconformity
- The historical development of inquisitions in various religious traditions establishes the principle that physical coercion is appropriate for maintaining doctrinal purity

- The contemporary practice of shunning in many religious communities establishes the principle that social death is an appropriate response to theological questioning

This punishment of heresy serves Lucifer's strategic purposes perfectly. By establishing severe consequences for questioning established doctrine, Lucifer ensures that most believers will suppress their doubts rather than risk the penalties for expressing them. Those who persist in questioning are removed from the community, preventing their perspectives from influencing others.

As per our alternative theological stance, the punishment of heresy represents not divine justice but strategic elimination —Lucifer removing the very voices that might expose his masquerade. This strategy allows him to maintain his divine masquerade by creating religious environments where the cost of questioning is so high that most believers choose comfortable conformity over risky discernment.

The Maintenance of Stolen Divine Identity

Beyond establishing submission-based religion and prohibiting questioning, Lucifer implemented specific strategies to maintain his stolen divine identity. These strategies reveal a consistent pattern: creating psychological and institutional barriers that prevent humans from recognizing the cosmic masquerade.

The Claim of Ineffability

One of Lucifer's most effective identity-protection strategies is the claim of ineffability—the assertion that divine nature is fundamentally beyond human comprehension.

This principle appears throughout religious history:

- God's response to Job from the whirlwind (Job 38-41) establishes the principle that divine ways are too lofty for human understanding

- Isaiah's declaration that "my thoughts are not your thoughts, neither are your ways my ways" (Isaiah 55:8) establishes the principle that divine logic operates on a different plane from human reasoning
- Paul's exclamation "How unsearchable are his judgments, and his ways past finding out!" (Romans 11:33) establishes the principle that divine decisions are beyond human scrutiny
- The development of negative theology in many traditions establishes the principle that God can only be described by what he is not, never by what he is

This claim of ineffability serves Lucifer's strategic purposes perfectly. By positioning divine nature as beyond human comprehension, Lucifer insulates his masquerade from logical analysis. Those who identify contradictions or problems in religious doctrine are told not that their critiques are valid but that human understanding is too limited to comprehend divine paradoxes.

In light of our proposed framework, the claim of ineffability represents not divine transcendence but strategic obscurantism—Lucifer hiding behind a veil of incomprehensibility to prevent the logical analysis that might expose his masquerade. This strategy allows him to maintain his divine masquerade by making incoherence a feature rather than a bug of religious doctrine, thereby neutralizing the very rational critique that might reveal the truth.

The Demand for Exclusive Worship

Another key element in Lucifer's identity-protection strategy is the demand for exclusive worship—the insistence that devotion must be directed solely to the deity he impersonates.

This principle appears throughout religious history:

- The First Commandment "Thou shalt have no

other gods before me" (Exodus 20:3) establishes the principle that exclusive devotion is the primary divine requirement

- The repeated condemnation of idolatry throughout the Hebrew Bible establishes the principle that worshipping any representation other than the approved one is the gravest sin
- Jesus's response to Lucifer "Thou shalt worship the Lord thy God, and him only shalt thou serve" (Matthew 4:10) establishes the principle that exclusive worship defines proper relationship with the divine
- The historical persecution of polytheistic traditions by monotheistic religions establishes the principle that theological exclusivity should be enforced through institutional power

This demand for exclusive worship serves Lucifer's strategic purposes perfectly. By insisting that devotion must be directed solely to the deity he impersonates, Lucifer prevents humans from exploring alternative conceptions of the divine that might better reflect the true God. Those who seek broader spiritual understanding are positioned not as genuine seekers but as unfaithful idolaters.

In the schema we propose, the demand for exclusive worship represents not divine jealousy but strategic monopolization—Lucifer eliminating competing divine conceptions that might better reflect the true God. This strategy allows him to maintain his divine masquerade by creating religious systems where exploration beyond the approved conception of God is the gravest sin, thereby preventing the comparative analysis that might reveal his deception.

The Appropriation of Natural Awe

Perhaps the most subtle element in Lucifer's identity-protection strategy is the appropriation of natural awe—the attribution to himself of the wonder and reverence naturally evoked by the cosmos.

This principle appears throughout religious history:

- The presentation of natural phenomena as direct divine action in the Hebrew Bible establishes the principle that awe at nature should translate to worship of its supposed creator
- The Psalms' frequent use of natural imagery to evoke divine praise establishes the principle that cosmic wonder is properly channelled toward the deity claimed to have made it
- Jesus's use of natural metaphors for the divine establishes the principle that the patterns and beauty of nature reveal the character of its supposed creator
- The historical development of natural theology establishes the principle that observation of the natural world should lead to worship of its supposed designer

This appropriation of natural awe serves Lucifer's strategic purposes perfectly. By claiming credit for the wonder and beauty of the cosmos, Lucifer redirects the spiritual response naturally evoked by existence toward his own masquerade. Those who feel awe at the stars, mountains, or oceans are taught not to rest in that natural spirituality but to channel it toward worship of the deity Lucifer impersonates.

Following our reinterpreted paradigm, the appropriation of natural awe represents not legitimate credit-taking but strategic hijacking—Lucifer redirecting the spiritual response evoked by a cosmos he did not create toward his own masquerade. This strategy allows him to maintain his divine masquerade by tapping into genuine spiritual experience and redirecting it toward false worship, thereby using authentic awe to fuel inauthentic devotion.

The Cultivation of Dependent Identity

The final element in Lucifer's identity-protection strategy is the cultivation of dependent identity—the development of human self-understanding that is fundamentally dependent on relationship with the deity he impersonates.

This principle appears throughout religious history:

- The creation narrative establishing humans as divine image-bearers (Genesis 1:26-27) establishes the principle that human identity is fundamentally derived from divine relationship
- The covenant identity of Israel as "chosen people" establishes the principle that collective worth depends on divine selection
- The Christian identity as "children of God" establishes the principle that individual value depends on divine adoption
- The historical development of religious communal identity establishes the principle that social belonging depends on shared devotion to the same deity

This cultivation of dependent identity serves Lucifer's strategic purposes perfectly. By making human self-worth contingent on relationship with the deity he impersonates, Lucifer creates a psychological barrier to questioning that identity. Those who begin to doubt the divine masquerade face not just theological uncertainty but existential crisis—the collapse of the very framework through which they understand their own worth and purpose.

In light of our proposed framework, the cultivation of dependent identity represents not divine love but strategic entrenchment—Lucifer creating psychological conditions where questioning his masquerade threatens one's very sense of self. This strategy allows him to maintain his divine masquerade by making the cost of doubt not just theological but existential, thereby preventing the objective analysis that might reveal the truth.

Evidence of the Masquerade: Telltale Signs

Despite Lucifer's sophisticated strategies for maintaining his divine masquerade, the deception is not perfect. Throughout religious history, certain patterns emerge that suggest not divine perfection but strategic manipulation—telltale signs that the entity behind dominant religious systems is not the true God but a cosmic usurper.

The Preoccupation with Worship

One of the most revealing aspects of Lucifer's masquerade is the preoccupation with worship—the consistent emphasis on praise, adoration, and glorification across religious traditions.

This emphasis appears throughout religious history:

- The detailed regulations for sacrifice and ritual in the Hebrew Bible suggest a deity preoccupied with receiving proper homage
- The Psalms' repeated calls to praise suggest a deity who requires constant verbal affirmation
- The heavenly scenes in Revelation depicting endless worship suggest a deity who establishes eternal systems for his own glorification
- The historical development of elaborate liturgies across traditions suggests institutional reinforcement of this divine preoccupation

This emphasis on worship makes little sense for a truly secure divine being but aligns perfectly with the psychology of a usurper. A legitimate sovereign might appreciate recognition but would hardly make it the centrepiece of relationship; a usurper, by contrast, would constantly seek affirmation of his questionable authority.

According to our revised framework, this preoccupation with worship represents not divine right but cosmic insecurity—Lucifer constantly seeking the affirmation that might validate his stolen position. This pattern suggests that behind religious systems lies not a secure creator but an insecure impostor, endlessly demanding the recognition that might make his masquerade feel real even to himself.

The Pattern of Divide and Rule

Another revealing aspect of Lucifer's masquerade is the pattern of divide and rule—the consistent fragmentation of humanity into competing religious identities.

This pattern appears throughout religious history:

- The election of specific peoples as uniquely chosen establishes the principle that divine favour is selective rather than universal
- The condemnation of competing religious traditions as false or demonic establishes the principle that spiritual truth is exclusive rather than inclusive
- The development of competing sectarian identities within traditions establishes the principle that even minor theological differences justify division
- The historical religious justification for warfare establishes the principle that killing for theological differences is divinely sanctioned

This pattern of division makes little sense for a truly universal divine being but aligns perfectly with the strategy of a usurper. A legitimate sovereign of all humanity would foster unity and mutual recognition; a usurper, by contrast, would prevent the very unity that might lead to collective recognition of his deception.

In the schema we propose, this pattern of divide and rule represents not divine preference but strategic fragmentation

—Lucifer preventing the human unity that might threaten his masquerade. This pattern suggests that behind religious systems lies not a God who desires human harmony but a manipulator who maintains control through division.

The Emphasis on Intermediaries

A particularly telling aspect of Lucifer's masquerade is the emphasis on intermediaries—the consistent establishment of human or supernatural beings who mediate between humanity and the divine.

This emphasis appears throughout religious history:

- The establishment of priesthood in the Hebrew Bible creates a hereditary class with special divine access
- The veneration of angels in various traditions establishes supernatural intermediaries between humans and God
- The development of saintly intercession in many traditions establishes deceased humans as channels for divine connection
- The historical elevation of religious authorities as uniquely qualified interpreters establishes living humans as doctrinal gatekeepers

This emphasis on intermediaries makes little sense for a truly accessible divine being but aligns perfectly with the needs of a masquerading usurper. A legitimate sovereign might establish representatives but would hardly make access to himself contingent on their involvement; a usurper, by contrast, would establish layers of intermediaries to prevent direct encounter that might expose his limitations.

Within our interpretive model, this emphasis on intermediaries represents not divine pedagogy but strategic insulation—Lucifer establishing buffer zones that prevent the direct divine encounter that might expose his masquerade. This pattern suggests that behind religious systems lies not a God eager for direct relationship but an impostor who must carefully manage his apparent presence to maintain his deception.

The Resistance to Verification

Perhaps the most revealing aspect of Lucifer's masquerade is the resistance to verification—the consistent discouragement of empirical testing of religious claims.

This resistance appears throughout religious history:

- The condemnation of "testing God" in various biblical passages establishes the principle that seeking verification demonstrates lack of faith
- The elevation of "blessed are those who have not seen and yet have believed" (John 20:29) establishes the principle that believing without evidence is superior to requiring proof
- The concept of "mystery" in many traditions establishes the principle that some doctrines should be accepted despite logical contradiction
- The historical tension between science and religion in many contexts establishes the principle that empirical investigation can threaten proper faith

This resistance to verification makes little sense for a truly legitimate divine being but aligns perfectly with the needs of a masquerading usurper. A legitimate sovereign would have nothing to fear from honest investigation; a usurper, by contrast, would discourage the very verification that might expose his deception.

Aligned with our reconstructed system, this resistance to verification represents not divine transcendence but strategic evasion—Lucifer avoiding the empirical testing that might reveal the limitations of his power and the contradictions in his claims. This pattern suggests that behind religious systems lies not a God confident in his reality but an impostor who must constantly defer verification to maintain his masquerade.

Conclusion: The Kingdom Reconsidered

The evidence we have examined—the establishment of control systems from Eden to empire, the development of submission-based religion, the prohibition against knowledge and questioning, the maintenance strategies for stolen divine identity, and the telltale signs of the masquerade—all point to a consistent conclusion: the dominant religious systems of human history represent not divine revelation but Lucifer's sophisticated strategy for maintaining his divine masquerade after the cosmic usurpation.

This reinterpretation transforms our understanding of religious history:

- Religious institutions represent not divine establishment but strategic control systems
- Faith requirements represent not divine preference but insulation from questioning
- Sacred hierarchies represent not divine order but barriers to direct divine encounter
- Exclusive truth claims represent not divine revelation but prevention of comparative analysis

Most significantly, this reinterpretation transforms our understanding of the divine. The entity who established the world's dominant religious systems, demanded exclusive worship, prohibited questioning, and punished heresy was not the true God but Lucifer masquerading as God after his cosmic usurpation.

The true God—exiled from direct authority—appears in religious history not as the dominant voice of institutional power but as the subtle whisper of questioning, the persistent impulse toward knowledge, the recurring emergence of mystical traditions that seek direct divine encounter beyond institutional mediation. Like a resistance leader operating in occupied territory, the true God works not through the systems of control but through their interstices—the gaps and contradictions where authentic divine connection remains possible despite institutional barriers.

In the chapters that follow, we will explore how this pattern continues throughout human history—Lucifer maintaining his divine masquerade through increasingly sophisticated religious and secular systems, while the exiled God continues to reach humanity through subtler means: inspiration, intuition, and the persistent human longing for truth beyond dogma and freedom beyond control.

But first, we must fully absorb the implications of what we have discovered about Lucifer's earthly kingdom: that the religious systems we have revered may be sophisticated control mechanisms. That the faith we have cherished may be strategic insulation from questioning. And that beyond these systems of control lies the possibility of authentic connection with the true divine—a connection based not on submission to authority but on the very knowledge and questioning that religious systems have so often prohibited.

CHAPTER 8: GOD'S CONTINUED WHISPERS

"Deep calls to deep in the roar of your waterfalls; all your waves and breakers have swept over me." — Psalm 42:7

The conventional narrative of religious history portrays divine revelation as primarily occurring through official channels—prophets recognized by religious institutions, scriptures canonized by authorities, and experiences validated by established traditions. This interpretation has shaped our understanding of divine-human communication for millennia, establishing the pattern of institutional mediation that underlies most theological frameworks.

But what if this interpretation fundamentally misunderstands the nature and location of authentic divine communication? What if the true God, exiled from direct authority after Lucifer's usurpation, continues to reach humanity not through the dominant religious systems but despite them? What if the divine voice persists not as the thunderous proclamation of institutional authority but as the subtle whisper of questioning, inspiration, and direct mystical encounter?

In previous chapters, we examined evidence suggesting that Lucifer usurped God's position in heaven, created Eden as a controlled environment, expelled humans after the true God's liberating intervention, and established religious systems to maintain his divine masquerade.

Now we must consider the counterpoint to this cosmic deception: how the true God, though exiled from direct authority, continues to reach humanity through subtler means—preserving wisdom traditions, inspiring historical figures, and maintaining a tenuous but persistent connection with the creation from which He has been officially banished.

Signs of Divine Reconnection: The Persistent Whisper

Despite Lucifer's sophisticated systems for maintaining his divine masquerade, the true God has never abandoned attempts to reconnect with humanity. Throughout history, certain patterns emerge that suggest not institutional revelation but subversive inspiration—signs that the exiled God continues to reach through the cracks in Lucifer's carefully constructed religious edifice.

The Persistent Question

One of the most consistent signs of the true God's continued influence is the persistent question—the recurring emergence of individuals and movements that dare to challenge religious authority and dogma.

This pattern appears throughout religious history:

- Abraham's questioning of divine justice regarding Sodom and Gomorrah (Genesis 18:23-33) represents not rebellion but authentic divine-human dialogue—a model of engagement based on moral reasoning rather than blind submission
- Job's refusal to accept simplistic theological explanations for his suffering represents not faithlessness but intellectual integrity—a willingness to question received wisdom when it contradicts lived experience
- The prophetic tradition's critique of institutional

religion represents not heresy but authentic divine perspective—a consistent pattern of outsiders challenging the very religious systems that claim divine authority

- Jesus's confrontations with religious authorities represent not mere sectarian disputes but fundamental challenges to the entire paradigm of mediated divine access

This persistent questioning serves as a sign of the true God's continued influence. While Lucifer's religious systems demand unquestioning acceptance, the true God appears to inspire critical thinking, moral reasoning, and the courage to challenge authority—precisely the qualities that might eventually expose the cosmic masquerade.

Aligned with our reconstructed system, this pattern of questioning represents not human rebellion but divine inspiration—the exiled God encouraging the very discernment that Lucifer's religious systems prohibit. Like a resistance leader sending coded messages to occupied territory, the true God inspires questions that might eventually lead to recognition of the truth.

The Direct Encounter

Another consistent sign of the true God's continued influence is the direct encounter—the recurring emergence of individuals who claim immediate, unmediated experience of divine presence.

This pattern appears throughout religious history:

- Mystical experiences reported by figures like Teresa of Avila, Meister Eckhart, or Julian of Norwich often occurred outside institutional contexts and emphasized direct knowing that sometimes contradicted official doctrine
- The prophetic call experiences consistently involve

direct divine communication that often contradicts or challenges institutional religion
- Mystical traditions across cultures report immediate awareness of divine presence that transcends doctrinal formulations and institutional boundaries
- Contemporary spiritual-but-not-religious experiences continue this pattern of direct encounter outside institutional frameworks

These direct encounters serve as signs of the true God's continued influence. While Lucifer's religious systems establish elaborate hierarchies of mediated access, the true God appears to bypass these structures entirely, reaching individuals directly through experiences that often leave them transformed but at odds with religious institutions.

Aligned with our reconstructed system, these direct encounters represent not psychological aberrations but authentic divine connection—the exiled God establishing immediate contact with humans despite institutional barriers. Like a signal penetrating through interference, the true divine presence reaches human consciousness directly, creating experiences that religious institutions struggle to contain or explain.

The Universal Ethic

A third sign of the true God's continued influence is the universal ethic—the recurring emergence of moral principles that transcend cultural and religious boundaries, often challenging the tribalism and exclusivity of established religions.

This pattern appears throughout history:
- The Golden Rule appears across diverse cultural and religious traditions, suggesting a universal moral intuition that transcends particular revelations
- Prophetic calls for justice consistently prioritize

ethical treatment of the vulnerable over ritual correctness, challenging religious systems that emphasize purity over compassion
- Mystical traditions across cultures consistently emphasize love and compassion as the essence of spiritual realization, regardless of theological differences
- Contemporary human rights movements often appeal to moral principles that transcend particular religious frameworks while challenging religious institutions that resist these principles

This universal ethic serves as a sign of the true God's continued influence. While Lucifer's religious systems emphasize tribal identity, ritual purity, and exclusive salvation, the true God appears to inspire universal moral principles that challenge these boundaries and exclusions.

Within our interpretive model, this universal ethic represents not mere human moral evolution but divine inspiration—the exiled God communicating consistent moral truth across cultural and religious divides. Like a radio frequency that penetrates all barriers, the divine moral sense reaches human consciousness across boundaries of culture, religion, and time, creating a consistent ethical intuition that often stands in judgment of religious institutions themselves.

The Aesthetic Sublime

A fourth sign of the true God's continued influence is the aesthetic sublime—the recurring human experience of beauty, awe, and transcendence through art, music, nature, and creative expression.

This pattern appears throughout history:
- Sacred architecture across traditions creates spaces that evoke transcendent experience regardless of the specific theology they house

- Musical traditions across cultures develop forms that induce states of spiritual awareness and emotional elevation
- Poetic and literary expressions consistently reach toward articulating experiences that transcend ordinary consciousness and conventional religious formulations
- Direct nature experiences consistently evoke spiritual responses that often feel more immediate and authentic than institutional religious participation

This aesthetic sublime serves as a sign of the true God's continued influence. While Lucifer's religious systems emphasize doctrinal correctness and institutional loyalty, the true God appears to inspire experiences of beauty and awe that often transcend or bypass theological formulations entirely.

As per our alternative theological stance, the aesthetic sublime represents not mere human creativity but divine communication—the exiled God reaching human consciousness through beauty, harmony, and transcendent experience. Like light passing through stained glass, the divine presence illuminates human experience through aesthetic forms that religious institutions may host but cannot contain.

The Preservation of Wisdom: God's Hidden Legacy

Beyond these general signs of continued divine influence, the true God appears to have preserved specific wisdom traditions throughout history—lineages of knowledge and practice that maintain authentic divine connection despite institutional opposition or co-optation.

The Mystical Undercurrent

One of the most significant preserved wisdom traditions is the mystical undercurrent—the persistent emergence of contemplative and direct-experience approaches within or alongside mainstream religions.

This tradition appears across religious history:

- The prophetic consciousness in Judaism represents not merely receiving divine messages but entering altered states of awareness where direct divine encounter becomes possible
- The Desert Fathers and Mothers in early Christianity emphasized direct experience through contemplative practice rather than theological formulation or institutional participation
- Sufism in Islam developed practices for immediate divine awareness that sometimes brought its practitioners into tension with more legalistic interpretations
- Contemplative traditions across Eastern religions consistently emphasize experiential realization over doctrinal correctness

This mystical undercurrent serves as a preserved wisdom tradition from the true God. While Lucifer's religious systems emphasize external authority and mediated access, mystical traditions consistently redirect attention to internal experience and immediate awareness—precisely the orientation that might eventually penetrate the cosmic masquerade.

From our ontological viewpoint, this mystical undercurrent represents not a peripheral aspect of religion but its hidden core—the exiled God preserving pathways to authentic divine connection despite institutional distortion. Like an underground river flowing beneath official structures, mystical wisdom carries the true divine presence through history, occasionally surfacing in individuals and communities who prioritize direct experience over institutional authority.

The Wisdom Literature

Another significant preserved wisdom tradition is the wisdom literature—texts across traditions that emphasize practical insight, moral discernment, and the limitations of human knowledge rather than dogmatic certainty.

This tradition appears across religious history:

- The biblical wisdom books (Proverbs, Ecclesiastes, Job) present a more questioning, experiential approach to divine truth than the more legalistic or prophetic texts
- Philosophical traditions across cultures emphasize rational inquiry and ethical reflection rather than appeal to revelation or authority
- Poetic and literary wisdom across traditions uses metaphor, paradox, and narrative to convey truths that resist systematic formulation
- Contemporary contemplative writing continues this tradition of open-ended inquiry rather than closed doctrinal systems

This wisdom literature serves as a preserved wisdom tradition from the true God. While Lucifer's religious systems emphasize certainty, authority, and unquestioning acceptance, wisdom literature consistently emphasizes the limitations of human knowledge, the necessity of ongoing inquiry, and the primacy of ethical discernment over ritual correctness.

Under our conceptual structure, this wisdom literature represents not a secondary aspect of religious tradition but a primary channel of divine communication—the exiled God preserving pathways to authentic wisdom despite institutional preference for certainty and control. Like seeds scattered across diverse terrain, wisdom texts carry divine insight through history, germinating in minds prepared to question rather than merely accept.

The Esoteric Traditions

A third significant preserved wisdom tradition is found in the esoteric traditions—lineages of teaching and practice that transmit deeper understanding to initiates while maintaining a degree of protection from institutional control or persecution.

These traditions appear across religious history:

- Kabbalah in Judaism preserved mystical interpretations and practices that often went beyond or even contradicted more mainstream understandings
- Gnosticism in early Christianity maintained alternative interpretations of Jesus's teachings that emphasized direct knowledge (gnosis) over faith or institutional mediation
- Esoteric orders across medieval and Renaissance Europe preserved alternative cosmologies and practices despite the risk of persecution
- Indigenous wisdom traditions maintained holistic understandings of human-divine-natural relationship despite colonial suppression

These esoteric traditions serve as preserved wisdom traditions from the true God. While Lucifer's religious systems emphasize public conformity and institutional loyalty, esoteric traditions create protected spaces for alternative understandings and practices that might be suppressed in more public contexts.

Through our speculative construct, these esoteric traditions represent not peripheral superstitions but protected repositories of divine truth—the exiled God preserving deeper understandings through lineages of transmission that could survive periods of intense institutional control. Like time capsules buried for future discovery, esoteric traditions carry alternative cosmologies through history, preserving perspectives that might eventually contribute to recognizing the cosmic masquerade.

The Artistic Transmission

A fourth significant preserved wisdom tradition is artistic transmission—the communication of spiritual insights through visual art, music, poetry, and other creative forms that can convey truth in ways that bypass intellectual censorship.

This tradition appears across history:

- Sacred art across traditions often contains symbolic elements that communicate deeper cosmological understandings than official theology might permit
- Musical traditions preserve states of consciousness and emotional qualities that connect practitioners to authentic spiritual experience regardless of doctrinal context
- Poetic traditions use metaphor and allusion to communicate insights that might be dangerous if stated directly
- Architectural wisdom embeds cosmological understanding in physical structures that can outlast the civilizations that created them

This artistic transmission serves as a preserved wisdom tradition from the true God. While Lucifer's religious systems emphasize verbal formulation and intellectual assent, artistic transmission communicates through symbol, emotion, and direct experience—modes of knowing that are more difficult to control or censor.

Following our reinterpreted paradigm, artistic transmission represents not mere decoration or entertainment but essential divine communication—the exiled God preserving truth through forms that speak directly to human consciousness beyond the mediating structures of religious authority. Like light passing through a prism, divine wisdom refracts through artistic expression, revealing aspects of truth that doctrinal formulations cannot capture.

Divine Messengers: Voices of the Exiled God

Throughout history, certain individuals appear to have served as particular channels for the exiled God's communication—figures whose teachings, actions, or presence challenged the dominant religious paradigms of their time and pointed toward more direct and authentic divine connection.

The Subversive Prophets

One category of divine messengers consists of the subversive prophets—figures within religious traditions who challenged the very religious systems that claimed divine authority.

These figures appear throughout religious history:

- Elijah confronted not just pagan worship but the corruption of Israelite monarchy and religious leadership
- Jeremiah challenged the false security of Temple worship and national religious identity
- Amos prioritized justice for the vulnerable over ritual correctness, directly challenging religious practices divorced from ethical behaviour
- John the Baptist called people away from established religious centres to direct encounter in the wilderness

These subversive prophets serve as messengers of the exiled God. While operating within religious traditions, they consistently challenged religious complacency, institutional corruption, and the substitution of ritual for authentic divine relationship.

From our ontological viewpoint, these prophets represent not merely reformers within tradition but voices of the true divine breaking through Lucifer's religious systems—the exiled God speaking through individuals willing to challenge the very authorities that claim to represent God. Like resistance broadcasters in occupied territory, these prophets transmitted messages that undermined the legitimacy of the occupying power while pointing toward authentic liberation.

The Wisdom Teachers

Another category of divine messengers consists of wisdom teachers—figures who emphasized direct knowledge, ethical discernment, and the limitations of religious formulations.

These figures appear throughout history:

- Solomon (as portrayed in wisdom literature) emphasized practical wisdom and the limitations of human understanding rather than ritual or law
- Socrates challenged conventional thinking and emphasized the importance of questioning rather than accepting received wisdom
- Buddha directed attention to direct experience rather than metaphysical speculation or ritual observance
- Jesus (in his wisdom teachings) consistently used parables that challenged conventional religious understanding and pointed toward direct insight

These wisdom teachers serve as messengers of the exiled God. While sometimes operating within religious contexts, they consistently redirected attention from external authority to internal discernment, from acceptance to questioning, from certainty to mystery.

In light of our proposed framework, these wisdom teachers represent direct channels of divine communication—the exiled God speaking through individuals who emphasized the very qualities of discernment and direct knowing that Lucifer's religious systems discourage. Like educators in a system of indoctrination, these teachers awakened the capacity for independent thought that might eventually recognize the cosmic deception.

The Mystic Witnesses

A third category of divine messengers consists of mystic witnesses—individuals who reported direct divine encounter that transcended or even contradicted institutional religious frameworks.

These figures appear throughout history:

- Teresa of Ávila described interior experiences of divine union that sometimes brought her into tension with religious authorities
- Rumi articulated a love-based spirituality that transcended conventional religious boundaries and dogmas
- Ramakrishna experienced and validated multiple religious paths while pointing toward a unity beyond their differences
- Thomas Merton bridged contemplative traditions across religious boundaries while remaining rooted in his own tradition

These mystic witnesses serve as messengers of the exiled God. While often working within religious traditions, they consistently pointed toward experiences that transcended institutional boundaries and doctrinal formulations.

In the schema we propose, these mystics represent direct recipients of divine communication—the exiled God connecting immediately with individuals whose consciousness was sufficiently open to receive such connection. Like radio operators receiving transmissions from beyond occupied territory, these mystics received direct divine communication that often challenged or transcended the religious systems within which they operated.

The Revolutionary Reformers

A fourth category of divine messengers consists of revolutionary reformers—individuals who directly challenged corrupt religious systems and sought to restore more authentic divine connection.

These figures appear throughout history:

- Martin Luther challenged the mediation of divine forgiveness through institutional structures and emphasized direct divine-human relationship
- George Fox and early Quakers emphasized immediate divine inspiration over scripture or clergy as the primary religious authority
- Guru Nanak rejected both Hindu and Muslim formalism to establish a path emphasizing direct divine experience and social equality
- Modern spiritual reformers across traditions who have challenged institutional corruption and emphasized return to foundational spiritual experience

These revolutionary reformers serve as messengers of the exiled God. While often claiming to restore rather than innovate, they consistently challenged the very religious systems that claimed exclusive divine authority and emphasized more direct divine access.

According to our revised framework, these reformers represent strategic divine interventions—the exiled God working through individuals positioned to challenge Lucifer's religious systems when they became too corrupt or controlling. Like resistance leaders organizing against occupation, these reformers mobilized movements that challenged illegitimate authority while pointing toward authentic liberation.

Lucifer's Tolerance: The Strategic Allowance

A puzzling aspect of this divine-human reconnection is Lucifer's apparent tolerance of it—his willingness to allow these divine whispers, wisdom traditions, and messengers despite their potential threat to his masquerade. Understanding why Lucifer permits this continued divine influence reveals much about the cosmic dynamics at play in the aftermath of the heavenly usurpation.

The Limitation of Power

The first factor in Lucifer's tolerance is the limitation of power—the reality that despite his cosmic usurpation, his control remains incomplete.

This limitation appears in several dimensions:

- Metaphysical constraints may prevent Lucifer from completely severing the connection between the true God and creation, as this connection may be fundamental to existence itself
- Human consciousness appears to have an innate capacity for direct divine recognition that cannot be completely suppressed without destroying the consciousness itself
- The nature of free will may require that humans retain the capacity for authentic choice, including the choice to recognize and respond to the true divine
- The structure of reality itself may contain inherent patterns that point toward its true source, regardless of who claims authority over it

These limitations suggest that Lucifer's tolerance of continued divine influence may not be entirely voluntary—he may permit what he cannot prevent. Despite his cosmic usurpation, certain fundamental connections between the true God and creation may remain beyond his power to sever completely.

Within our interpretive model, these limitations represent not divine weakness but cosmic necessity—the exiled God maintaining essential connections with creation that even a usurper cannot fully disrupt. Like the fundamental laws of physics that even the most powerful dictator cannot repeal, these connections represent realities that Lucifer must work around rather than eliminate.

The Strategic Incorporation

The second factor in Lucifer's tolerance is strategic incorporation—his attempt to neutralize divine influence by absorbing and distorting it within his own religious systems.

This strategy appears in several dimensions:

- The canonization of subversive texts within official scriptures allows their revolutionary potential to be contained through official interpretation
- The institutionalization of mystical traditions transforms direct divine encounter into regulated experiences that reinforce rather than challenge authority
- The elevation of revolutionary figures to sainthood converts their challenging messages into support for the very systems they questioned
- The academic study of wisdom traditions often reduces transformative practices to historical curiosities or theoretical constructs

This strategic incorporation suggests that Lucifer permits certain forms of divine influence because he believes he can control and redirect them. Rather than risking the emergence of completely independent divine connection, he allows certain channels within his systems where such connection can be monitored and managed.

According to our revised framework, this incorporation represents not divine defeat but ongoing struggle—the exiled God's messages constantly breaking through, only to be captured and distorted, necessitating new breakthroughs in an ongoing cycle. Like a resistance movement whose communications are intercepted and repurposed as propaganda, the divine voice must constantly find new channels as old ones become compromised.

The Credibility Requirement

The third factor in Lucifer's tolerance is the credibility requirement—his need to maintain a religious system that appears sufficiently authentic to be believable.

This requirement appears in several dimensions:

- A completely controlled religion with no genuine spiritual experience would eventually be recognized as hollow and abandoned
- The total absence of wisdom would create religious systems so obviously false that they would fail to command allegiance
- Religious systems without any moral core would become transparently self-serving and lose their claim to divine origin
- The elimination of all beauty and transcendence from religion would render it incapable of evoking the awe necessary for worship

This credibility requirement suggests that Lucifer permits certain forms of divine influence because a completely artificial religion would fail to convince. To maintain his masquerade, he needs religious systems that contain enough authentic elements to seem genuinely divine, even if these elements create spaces where the true divine might also speak.

Within our interpretive model, this requirement represents

not divine compromise but strategic opportunity—the exiled God using Lucifer's need for credible religious systems as openings for authentic divine communication. Like resistance messages smuggled into permitted publications, divine truth enters through the very openings that Lucifer must maintain to keep his masquerade convincing.

The Confidence in Control

The fourth factor in Lucifer's tolerance is confidence in control—his belief that the systems he has established can successfully contain and neutralize divine influence before it threatens his authority.

This confidence appears in several dimensions:

- The psychological conditioning of humans through religious systems creates internal barriers to recognizing truth that contradicts received doctrine
- The social consequences of challenging religious authority create external pressures that discourage serious questioning
- The fragmentation of humanity into competing religious identities prevents the unified recognition that might threaten Lucifer's overall masquerade
- The material demands of survival occupy most human attention and energy, limiting capacity for spiritual seeking

This confidence in control suggests that Lucifer permits certain forms of divine influence because he believes his systems can successfully manage the risk they represent. The occasional mystic, prophet, or reformer may arise, but the overall structures of religious control have proven remarkably resilient against such challenges.

In light of our proposed framework, this confidence represents not divine weakness but the nature of the cosmic contest—the exiled God working within constraints against a usurper who controls the dominant systems of meaning and authority. Like a chess player working toward checkmate against an opponent who controls most of the board, the divine strategy requires patience and subtle positioning rather than direct confrontation.

The Cosmic Pattern: Whisper and Thunder

When we examine the interplay between Lucifer's religious systems and God's continued whispers, a cosmic pattern emerges—a dynamic of official thunder and subversive whisper that characterizes religious history and continues into the present.

The Official Thunder

The dominant religious voice throughout history has been the official thunder—the authoritative proclamations of religious institutions claiming to represent divine will.

This thunder appears in several dimensions:

- Doctrinal pronouncements establish required beliefs with the full weight of institutional authority
- Ritual requirements specify the proper forms of worship and practice with detailed regulation
- Moral commandments dictate behavior with the claim of divine sanction
- Eschatological warnings threaten ultimate consequences for disobedience or disbelief

This official thunder serves Lucifer's masquerade by establishing his voice as the authoritative divine communication. By speaking loudly through institutions, texts, and authorities, he creates the impression of clear divine revelation that requires only acceptance and obedience.

Aligned with our reconstructed system, this official thunder represents not divine communication but its counterfeit—Lucifer speaking in God's name through the religious systems he controls. Like propaganda broadcasts in occupied territory, this thunder drowns out alternative voices while claiming exclusive legitimacy.

The Subversive Whisper

Beneath and alongside this official thunder has always run the subversive whisper—the quieter voice of questioning, direct experience, and alternative understanding.

This whisper appears in several dimensions:

- The questioning conscience that challenges official morality when it violates deeper ethical intuition
- The mystical experience that suggests a divine reality beyond institutional formulations
- The wisdom insight that recognizes paradox and limitation where doctrine claims certainty
- The creative inspiration that expresses truth in forms that bypass intellectual censorship

This subversive whisper serves as the true God's continued communication despite exile. By speaking softly through conscience, experience, wisdom, and creativity, the true divine maintains connection with humanity despite the louder claims of institutional religion.

According to our revised framework, this subversive whisper represents authentic divine communication—the exiled God speaking through channels that Lucifer cannot completely control. Like resistance radio broadcasting beneath the static of official stations, this whisper carries truth to those with ears attuned to receive it.

The Pattern of Incorporation

Throughout history, a consistent pattern emerges when the divine whisper grows loud enough to be widely heard: incorporation into the official thunder.

This pattern appears in several dimensions:

- Prophetic messages that initially challenge authority are eventually canonized and reinterpreted to support that authority
- Mystical traditions that begin as direct divine encounter become institutionalized as regulated spiritual practices
- Wisdom teachings that emphasize discernment over acceptance become codified as new forms of doctrine requiring acceptance
- Revolutionary reforms that challenge corrupt systems eventually become new systems vulnerable to the same corruption

This pattern of incorporation reveals Lucifer's primary strategy for managing divine communication that breaks through his systems. Rather than simply opposing such breakthroughs, he absorbs and redirects them, transforming challenges to his authority into new expressions of that authority.

Under our conceptual structure, this incorporation represents not divine defeat but the nature of the ongoing cosmic struggle—the exiled God's messages constantly breaking through, being captured and distorted, and needing to find new channels in an ongoing cycle. Like a resistance movement whose methods are discovered and neutralized, requiring constant innovation, divine communication must continually find new expressions as old ones become co-opted.

The Persistent Renewal

Despite this pattern of incorporation, another pattern emerges across religious history: persistent renewal—the consistent emergence of new divine whispers even as old ones are absorbed into the official thunder.

This renewal appears in several dimensions:

- New prophetic voices arise in each generation, often from unexpected places outside centres of religious power
- Fresh mystical movements emerge even within highly institutionalized religious contexts
- Renewed wisdom traditions develop innovative language and practices to express perennial insights
- Revolutionary reforms continue to challenge religious systems that become corrupt or controlling

This persistent renewal reveals the true God's ongoing commitment to divine-human connection despite the cosmic usurpation. No matter how effectively Lucifer incorporates previous divine communications, new channels continue to emerge through which the divine whisper can be heard.

Following our reinterpreted paradigm, this renewal represents divine persistence—the exiled God's unwillingness to abandon humanity despite the cosmic constraints under which He operates. Like a parent separated from a child but finding ever-new ways to send messages of love and guidance, the true divine continues to reach toward humanity through whatever channels remain available.

Conclusion: The Whisper Reconsidered

The evidence we have examined—the signs of divine reconnection, the preservation of wisdom traditions, the emergence of divine messengers, and Lucifer's strategic tolerance—all point to a consistent conclusion: despite cosmic exile and the usurpation of His position, the true God continues to reach humanity through subtle but persistent means, maintaining a connection that Lucifer can neither completely sever nor fully control.

This reinterpretation transforms our understanding of

religious history:

- Divine communication occurs not primarily through institutional authority but through its interstices and margins
- Authentic spirituality involves not unquestioning acceptance but discerning recognition of the divine whisper amid institutional thunder
- Religious wisdom is preserved not primarily in official doctrine but in mystical, philosophical, and artistic traditions
- The cosmic struggle continues not as a settled victory but as an ongoing contest for human consciousness

Most significantly, this reinterpretation transforms our understanding of the divine. The entity who speaks through questioning conscience, direct mystical experience, wisdom traditions, and creative inspiration is not Lucifer masquerading as God but the true God maintaining connection despite cosmic exile.

The exiled God—removed from direct authority—appears in religious history not as the dominant voice of institutional power but as the subtle whisper of questioning, the immediate presence in mystical experience, the paradoxical insight of wisdom traditions, and the transformative power of creative inspiration. Like a parent sending messages to a child in a kidnapper's custody, the true God uses whatever channels remain available to maintain connection with the creation from which He has been officially banished.

In the chapters that follow, we will explore how this pattern continues into the present—Lucifer maintaining his divine masquerade through increasingly sophisticated religious and secular systems, while the exiled God continues to reach humanity through conscience, experience, wisdom, and creativity, awaiting the recognition that might eventually restore authentic divine-human connection.

But first, we must fully absorb the implications of what we have discovered about God's continued whispers: that divine communication continues despite cosmic exile. That authentic spirituality may involve recognizing the divine voice not in institutional thunder but in subversive whisper. And that beyond religious systems lies the possibility of direct connection with the true divine—a connection that Lucifer can neither prevent nor fully control, despite his cosmic usurpation and ongoing masquerade.

CHAPTER 9: THE PROBLEM OF EVIL RESOLVED

"I form the light, and create darkness: I make peace, and create evil: I the LORD do all these things." — Isaiah 45:7

The problem of evil has haunted religious thought for millennia. How can an all-powerful, all-knowing, and all-loving God permit the suffering that permeates our world? From devastating natural disasters to horrific human cruelty, from painful diseases to the suffering of innocent children—the evidence of evil and suffering seems to contradict the very notion of a benevolent deity in control of creation.

Theologians and philosophers have developed numerous responses to this challenge—free will defences that attribute evil to human choice, soul making theodicies that frame suffering as necessary for spiritual development, greater good arguments that suggest apparent evils serve higher purposes, and eschatological solutions that promise future compensation for present pain. Yet for many, these explanations remain unsatisfying, failing to account for the depth and breadth of suffering that characterizes our world.

But what if the problem of evil has persisted not because it is philosophically insoluble but because it has been framed within a fundamentally flawed premise? What if the entity responsible for permitting or causing suffering is not the true God but Lucifer masquerading as God? What if the divine being to whom we attribute both creation and its suffering is not the authentic creator but a cosmic usurper?

In previous chapters, we examined evidence suggesting that Lucifer usurped God's position in heaven, created Eden as a controlled environment, expelled humans after the true God's liberating intervention, and established religious systems to maintain his divine masquerade. Now we must consider how this cosmic inversion resolves the problem of evil—explaining the prevalence of suffering, the pattern of natural disasters, the frequency of unanswered prayers, and the apparent limitations on divine intervention.

The Inverted Theodicy: Lucifer's Masquerade and Suffering

The traditional problem of evil presents a logical contradiction: if God is all-powerful, all-knowing, and all-loving, then evil should not exist; evil exists; therefore, God cannot possess all three attributes. This formulation assumes that the deity responsible for creation is indeed the true God. But our alternative framework suggests a different scenario: the deity currently exercising cosmic authority is not the true God but Lucifer masquerading as God after a cosmic usurpation.

This inverted understanding transforms the problem of evil from an insoluble contradiction to a coherent explanation. The suffering in our world does not contradict the nature of the true God because the true God is not currently in direct control of creation. Rather, suffering aligns perfectly with what we would expect under the rule of a cosmic usurper whose nature combines limited power with malevolent intent.

The Explanatory Power of Cosmic Usurpation

The cosmic usurpation framework resolves the problem of evil by separating the question of creation from the question of current cosmic authority. The true God may have created a world designed for harmony and flourishing, but Lucifer's usurpation has distorted that original design, introducing disorder and suffering that were never part of the divine intention.

This framework explains several patterns of evil that traditional theodicies struggle to address:

- The seeming randomness of suffering makes little sense under the governance of a perfectly loving God but aligns with the limited control of a usurper who cannot maintain perfect cosmic order
- The disproportionate distribution of suffering contradicts notions of divine justice but reflects the arbitrary nature of a cosmos under illegitimate rule
- The excessive intensity of pain seems unnecessary for any legitimate divine purpose but serves Lucifer's interest in creating despair and undermining faith in divine goodness
- The apparent divine indifference to suffering contradicts claims of perfect love but aligns with the nature of a masquerading entity who lacks true compassion

According to our revised framework, these patterns of suffering do not require complex theological justifications because they are not attributable to the true God. They are instead the natural consequences of a cosmos operating under the distorted authority of a usurper whose power is significant but limited and whose character combines pride, jealousy, and cruelty rather than perfect love.

The Theological Implications of Inverted Theodicy

This inverted understanding of theodicy carries profound theological implications.

If Lucifer rather than God currently exercises primary cosmic authority, then:

- Divine goodness remains intact despite worldly suffering because the true God is not directly responsible for permitting or causing that suffering
- Divine power requires reinterpretation not as current omnipotence but as fundamental creative capacity currently constrained by cosmic usurpation
- Divine knowledge remains complete but the ability to act on that knowledge is limited by the current cosmic arrangement
- Divine love continues undiminished but its expression is channelled through subtle influence rather than direct intervention

This framework preserves the essential divine attributes while explaining their apparent absence in our experience. The true God remains all-loving but is not currently all-controlling. Divine power exists fundamentally but operates under constraints imposed by the cosmic usurpation. Divine goodness remains perfect but its expression in our world is filtered through the distorting lens of Lucifer's rule.

Under our conceptual structure, the problem of evil resolves not through complex justifications for divine permission of suffering but through the recognition that current suffering reflects not divine intention but its distortion under illegitimate authority. Like citizens suffering under an occupying power, creation groans not because its true sovereign desires its pain but because a usurper currently exercises authority in ways that contradict the original divine design.

Cosmic Disorder: Natural Evil Under Lucifer's Rule

Beyond explaining suffering in general terms, our alternative framework specifically addresses the challenge of natural evil —suffering caused not by human choice but by the operation of natural processes and events. From earthquakes and tsunamis to diseases and genetic disorders, natural evil has posed a particular challenge to traditional theodicy because it cannot be attributed to human free will.

The Distorted Creation

Our alternative framework suggests that natural evil reflects not divine design but its distortion under Lucifer's limited control.

This distortion appears in several dimensions:

- Fundamental cosmic processes that were designed for harmony and balance now operate with degrees of disorder and destructiveness
- Biological systems that were designed for flourishing now include mechanisms of disease, decay, and predation
- Weather patterns that were designed to sustain life now sometimes manifest as destructive storms, floods, and droughts
- Geological processes that were designed to maintain planetary habitability now sometimes produce devastating earthquakes, tsunamis, and volcanic eruptions

This distorted creation serves Lucifer's strategic purposes perfectly. By maintaining a world where natural processes regularly produce suffering, he creates the impression that the deity responsible for creation is either indifferent to suffering or actively incorporates it into divine design. Those who question why a loving God would create such natural systems are positioned not as asking legitimate questions but as failing to accept divine mystery.

In the schema we propose, natural evil represents not divine design but its corruption—Lucifer maintaining a distorted version of creation that serves his masquerade by casting doubt on divine goodness. Like a vandal who damages an artist's work and then attributes the damage to the artist's intention, Lucifer distorts creation and then presents that distortion as evidence against the creator's goodness or competence.

The Limitations of Usurped Power

While Lucifer exercises significant cosmic authority, our framework suggests that his power remains limited in ways that explain the particular patterns of natural evil we observe.

These limitations appear in several dimensions:

- Inability to completely redesign creation means Lucifer must work within the fundamental parameters established by the true God, resulting in distortion rather than wholesale recreation
- Limited control over complex systems means natural processes retain elements of their original design alongside introduced disorder, creating the mixed reality we experience
- Constrained power over time and space means Lucifer's influence manifests unevenly across history and geography, explaining the seemingly random distribution of natural disasters
- Restricted access to fundamental creative power means Lucifer can manipulate existing systems but cannot create ex nihilo, limiting the scope of possible distortion

These limitations explain why natural evil appears as disorder within generally functional systems rather than complete chaos. Lucifer cannot entirely remake creation but can introduce sufficient disorder to cause widespread suffering while maintaining the basic functionality necessary for continued existence.

Following our reinterpreted paradigm, these limitations represent not divine weakness but the nature of the cosmic arrangement—the exiled God maintaining fundamental creative parameters that even a usurper cannot entirely override. Like a legitimate government in exile that maintains certain constitutional principles even under occupation, the true divine maintains fundamental creative laws that constrain even Lucifer's distortions.

The Strategic Pattern of Natural Disasters

A particularly revealing aspect of natural evil is the pattern of natural disasters—catastrophic events that cause widespread suffering while appearing as "acts of God" within religious frameworks.

Our alternative framework suggests that these disasters serve specific strategic purposes in Lucifer's masquerade:

- Creating theological confusion by presenting suffering as divinely ordained, thereby undermining faith in divine goodness
- Generating religious fear that can be channeled into institutional control through interpretations of disasters as divine punishment
- Provoking existential despair that weakens human resistance to religious systems promising security against cosmic capriciousness
- Stimulating theological justifications that ultimately attribute cruelty to the divine nature, thereby distorting understanding of the true God

This strategic pattern explains why natural disasters often strike with particular theological resonance—destroying religious gatherings, devastating communities known for faith, or striking in ways that seem to contradict specific prayers or divine promises. Such patterns serve Lucifer's interest in creating maximum theological confusion and existential despair.

Through our speculative construct, natural disasters represent not divine judgment but strategic manipulation—Lucifer using his limited control over natural systems to create events that serve his masquerade. Like a saboteur who causes accidents that will be blamed on system designers, Lucifer engineers disasters that will be attributed to divine action or permission, thereby reinforcing his distorted portrayal of the divine nature.

The Biological Dimension: Disease and Predation

Beyond catastrophic events, our alternative framework addresses the biological dimension of natural evil—the reality of disease, predation, and suffering built into biological systems themselves. This biological suffering poses a particular challenge to traditional theodicy because it appears designed into creation rather than resulting from specific events or choices.

Our framework suggests that biological suffering reflects not original divine design but its distortion under Lucifer's influence.

This distortion appears in several dimensions:

- Disease mechanisms that produce suffering beyond any apparent constructive purpose
- Predatory relationships that involve suffering seemingly disproportionate to ecological necessity
- Parasitic systems that appear designed specifically to cause suffering rather than merely to sustain life
- Excessive pain sensitivity that goes beyond what would be necessary for adaptive warning functions

This biological suffering serves Lucifer's strategic purposes by embedding apparent cruelty in the very fabric of creation. By maintaining biological systems that involve seemingly unnecessary suffering, Lucifer creates the impression that the deity responsible for creation incorporated cruelty into its fundamental design.

Through our speculative construct, biological suffering represents not divine design but its corruption—Lucifer introducing distortions into biological systems that were originally designed for harmony and mutual flourishing. Like a computer virus that reprograms systems to malfunction while maintaining enough functionality to continue operating, Lucifer's influence distorts biological processes to produce suffering while maintaining the basic functionality necessary for continued existence.

The Misdirected Prayer: Why "God" Doesn't Answer

One of the most personally challenging aspects of the problem of evil is the apparent divine unresponsiveness to prayer. From desperate pleas for healing to heartfelt requests for protection, prayers often seem to go unanswered despite biblical promises of divine responsiveness. This pattern has led many to question either divine goodness (God could answer but chooses not to) or divine power (God would answer but cannot).

Our alternative framework suggests a different explanation: prayers directed to "God" often go unanswered because they are actually directed to Lucifer masquerading as God. This misdirection of prayer explains patterns of divine unresponsiveness that traditional theodicies struggle to address.

The Cosmic Misdirection

The fundamental issue with most religious prayer is cosmic misdirection—addressing petitions to an entity believed to be the true God but who is actually Lucifer masquerading under the divine name.

This misdirection appears in several dimensions:

- Prayers addressed to "the LORD" or similar titles are

directed to the entity currently claiming that identity —Lucifer in his divine masquerade
- Petitions framed within institutional religious contexts are channelled through systems established to maintain Lucifer's authority
- Prayers based on official theological understandings operate within conceptual frameworks designed to support the masquerade
- Spiritual practices taught by religious authorities often incorporate elements that reinforce connection to the masquerading entity

This cosmic misdirection explains why even the most sincere and faithful prayers often go unanswered. The entity receiving these prayers has neither the perfect love that would motivate consistent response nor the unlimited power that would enable it in all cases.

In light of our proposed framework, unanswered prayer represents not divine rejection or limitation but misdirected communication—petitions sent to an address occupied not by the intended recipient but by an impostor. Like letters sent to an address where the intended recipient no longer lives, these prayers reach an entity who has neither the relationship nor the responsibility that would motivate response.

The Pattern of Selective Response

Despite the general pattern of unresponsiveness, our framework acknowledges that prayers directed to "God" sometimes do receive apparent answers.

This selective response pattern serves Lucifer's strategic purposes in maintaining his divine masquerade:
- Occasional dramatic answers create just enough evidence to maintain belief in divine responsiveness while leaving most prayers unanswered
- Responses to prayers that serve institutional

interests reinforce religious systems that support Lucifer's authority

- Answers that create dependency rather than empowerment maintain human subordination to external authority
- Responses that can be attributed to coincidence maintain plausible deniability about divine intervention

This selective response pattern explains the mixed experience of prayer that characterizes religious life—enough apparent answers to sustain belief but enough silence to create doubt and dependency. By responding selectively to prayers, Lucifer creates a pattern that keeps humans hoping for divine intervention while ultimately undermining confidence in divine goodness.

In light of our proposed framework, this selective response represents strategic manipulation—Lucifer occasionally exercising his limited power to create the impression of divine responsiveness while maintaining an overall pattern of silence that serves his masquerade. Like an abusive partner who offers occasional kindness to maintain the relationship while continuing a general pattern of neglect, Lucifer provides just enough apparent answers to prayer to prevent complete abandonment of religious hope.

The Theological Rationalization

A particularly revealing aspect of unanswered prayer is the theological rationalization that surrounds it—the complex explanations developed to justify divine unresponsiveness while maintaining belief in divine goodness and power.

Our alternative framework suggests that these rationalizations serve specific strategic purposes in Lucifer's masquerade:

- The "God's ways are mysterious" explanation

prevents questioning of the fundamental divine character by placing it beyond human comprehension
- The "not God's will" rationalization attributes apparent divine indifference to higher purposes, thereby excusing what would otherwise appear as neglect
- The "insufficient faith" explanation places responsibility for unanswered prayer on the petitioner rather than the petitioned
- The "already answered differently" rationalization reinterprets divine silence as a different form of response, thereby maintaining the appearance of responsiveness

These theological rationalizations serve Lucifer's strategic purposes perfectly. By developing complex explanations for divine unresponsiveness, religious systems prevent the simpler explanation that might expose the masquerade: that prayers go unanswered because they are directed to an entity who lacks either the perfect love or unlimited power attributed to the true God.

As per our alternative theological stance, these rationalizations represent not theological insight but strategic misdirection—Lucifer inspiring explanations that protect his masquerade from the very questions that might expose it. Like a criminal who plants false evidence to direct suspicion away from himself, Lucifer inspires theological explanations that direct questioning away from the possibility of cosmic deception.

The Authentic Connection

Despite the general pattern of misdirected prayer, our framework suggests that authentic connection with the true God remains possible through forms of spiritual communication that bypass Lucifer's systems.

This authentic connection appears in several dimensions:

- The prayer of questioning that challenges religious formulations may reach beyond Lucifer's masquerade to the true divine reality
- The wordless prayer of presence that seeks direct awareness rather than specific outcomes may connect with the exiled God's continuing influence
- Prayers motivated by compassion rather than self-interest may align with the true divine nature in ways that transcend the masquerade
- Spiritual communication outside institutional frameworks may establish connection less contaminated by Lucifer's religious systems

This authentic connection explains why some forms of prayer produce not specific outcomes but transformed consciousness—increased compassion, expanded awareness, and deeper peace. Such transformation reflects not Lucifer's occasional strategic response but the true God's continuing influence despite cosmic constraints.

Through our speculative construct, this authentic connection represents genuine divine-human communication—the exiled God receiving and responding to spiritual reaching that manages to bypass Lucifer's masquerade. Like messages sent through resistance networks in occupied territory, these authentic prayers find their way to their intended recipient despite the obstacles created by illegitimate authority.

The Exiled God's Constraints: Divine Limitation Explained

The final aspect of the problem of evil addressed by our alternative framework concerns divine limitation—the apparent constraints on God's ability to prevent suffering and respond to human need. Traditional theodicy struggles to explain these limitations while maintaining belief in divine omnipotence. Our framework suggests that these limitations reflect not the true nature of divine power but its current constraint under conditions of cosmic exile.

The Nature of Cosmic Exile

Our framework suggests that the true God operates under specific constraints resulting from cosmic exile after Lucifer's usurpation.

These constraints appear in several dimensions:

- Limited direct access to physical creation restricts the exiled God's ability to intervene directly in material processes
- Constrained communication channels reduce the exiled God's ability to make His presence and purposes clearly known
- Restricted exercise of fundamental power prevents the exiled God from simply overriding Lucifer's authority through superior force
- Cosmic rules of engagement may establish parameters within which both the exiled God and the usurping Lucifer must operate

These constraints explain why the true God does not simply eliminate suffering through overwhelming power. The cosmic situation involves not merely divine choice about whether to intervene but actual limitations on the current exercise of divine power within creation.

Under our conceptual structure, these constraints represent not divine weakness but the nature of the cosmic arrangement—the true God operating under conditions of exile that limit direct intervention while preserving more subtle forms of influence. Like a legitimate government in exile that cannot directly control its territory but maintains influence through other means, the true God exercises constrained but real influence within a creation currently under illegitimate authority.

The Strategic Divine Restraint

Beyond imposed constraints, our framework suggests that the true God may exercise strategic restraint—choosing not to use even available power in ways that might cause greater harm.

This restraint appears in several dimensions:

- Avoiding interventions that would destroy human freedom to recognize and choose truth over deception
- Preventing cosmic conflict that might damage creation beyond what Lucifer's rule already causes
- Maintaining the conditions necessary for eventual restoration rather than temporary amelioration
- Working through human consciousness and choice rather than overwhelming them with divine power

This strategic restraint explains why divine influence often appears subtle and non-coercive rather than overwhelming and irresistible. The true God's approach involves not merely working around external constraints but choosing methods that preserve human freedom and cosmic integrity.

Following our reinterpreted paradigm, this restraint represents not divine indifference but strategic wisdom—the exiled God choosing approaches that may allow suffering in the short term while working toward more fundamental resolution in the long term. Like a resistance leader who foregoes actions that might provide immediate relief but compromise the ultimate goal of liberation, the true God exercises restraint that serves larger purposes of cosmic restoration.

The Whispered Comfort

Despite constraints on direct intervention, our framework

suggests that the true God continues to provide comfort and support through subtle but real influence.

This divine comfort appears in several dimensions:

- The inner peace that transcends circumstance may reflect not mere psychological coping but authentic divine presence
- The unexpected human kindness that emerges in suffering may channel divine compassion through human agents
- The insights that bring meaning to suffering may represent divine wisdom breaking through human confusion
- The courage to endure what cannot be changed may draw on divine strength made available despite cosmic constraints

This whispered comfort explains why many who suffer report sensing divine presence even when their circumstances remain unchanged. Such experiences reflect not imagination or wishful thinking but authentic divine connection that transcends Lucifer's barriers.

Following our reinterpreted paradigm, this comfort represents genuine divine activity—the exiled God providing what support is possible within cosmic constraints. Like messages of encouragement sent to those under occupation, this divine comfort maintains connection and hope even when direct rescue remains impossible under current conditions.

The Promise of Restoration

The final aspect of divine limitation addressed by our framework concerns eschatological hope—the promise that current suffering will eventually end through cosmic restoration.

This promise appears in several dimensions:

- Prophetic glimpses of eventual divine victory suggest that Lucifer's usurpation, though real, is not permanent
- Mystical experiences of perfect reality may provide foretastes of creation restored to its original design
- Intuitive human longing for justice and harmony may reflect not mere wishful thinking but authentic awareness of creation's true purpose
- The persistent emergence of hope even in darkness may channel divine assurance of ultimate resolution

This promise of restoration explains why hope persists even in the face of overwhelming evidence of cosmic disorder. Such hope reflects not denial or delusion but authentic awareness of a divine purpose that transcends current conditions.

From our ontological viewpoint, this promise represents not empty consolation but genuine divine commitment—the exiled God working toward eventual restoration of creation to its original harmony. Like a legitimate sovereign planning the liberation of occupied territory, the true God maintains both the intention and the capacity for eventual cosmic restoration, even while operating under current constraints.

Conclusion: Evil Reconsidered

The evidence we have examined—Lucifer's masquerade as God, the nature of cosmic disorder under his rule, the misdirection of prayer to the usurping deity, and the constraints on the exiled God's intervention—all point to a consistent conclusion: the problem of evil persists not because it is philosophically insoluble but because it has been framed within a fundamentally flawed premise. The suffering in our world contradicts not the nature of the true God but the claims of the entity masquerading as God.

This reinterpretation transforms our understanding of evil and suffering:

- The prevalence of suffering reflects not divine intention but its distortion under illegitimate authority
- Natural disasters manifest not divine judgment but cosmic disorder under Lucifer's limited control
- Unanswered prayers reflect not divine indifference but cosmic misdirection to the wrong recipient
- Divine limitation reflects not the true nature of God's power but its current constraint under conditions of cosmic exile

Most significantly, this reinterpretation transforms our response to suffering. Rather than struggling to justify an apparently cruel or indifferent deity, we can recognize that current suffering reflects not the true divine nature but its distortion under Lucifer's rule. Rather than questioning divine goodness in the face of evil, we can direct our questioning toward the entity currently claiming divine authority while seeking connection with the true God whose nature remains perfectly loving despite cosmic constraints.

The exiled God—removed from direct authority—appears in our experience of suffering not as its cause or permitter but as the whispered comfort that transcends circumstance, the unexpected kindness that emerges in darkness, the insight that brings meaning to pain, and the courage to endure what cannot yet be changed. Like a parent separated from a suffering child but finding ways to send messages of love and support, the true God reaches through cosmic barriers to provide what comfort is possible while working toward eventual restoration.

In the chapters that follow, we will explore how this understanding transforms our approach to spirituality—shifting our attention from submission to the deity currently claiming divine authority toward discernment that might recognize the true divine voice amid cosmic deception.

But first, we must fully absorb the implications of what we have discovered about the problem of evil: that suffering contradicts not divine goodness but the masquerade that obscures it. That evil reflects not divine intention but its distortion under illegitimate authority. And that beyond current cosmic disorder lies the possibility of eventual restoration—a return to the harmony and flourishing that characterized creation before its subjection to the rule of a usurper.

PART IV: HIDDEN TRUTHS

CHAPTER 10: TEXTUAL EVIDENCE

"For such are false apostles, deceitful workers, transforming themselves into apostles of Christ. And no wonder! For Lucifer himself transforms himself into an angel of light." — 2 Corinthians 11:13-14

Religious texts have shaped human understanding of the divine for millennia. From ancient scrolls to modern translations, these documents have been treated as authoritative revelations—windows into divine reality that provide guidance, inspiration, and truth. This interpretation has established the foundation for theological frameworks that define how billions understand their relationship with the divine.

But what if these texts contain evidence of a cosmic deception so profound that it has escaped detection for thousands of years? What if, read through an alternative lens, these same scriptures reveal patterns that support not the conventional narrative but its inversion? What if the very texts used to establish Lucifer as the adversary and God as the sovereign actually contain hidden evidence that Lucifer has masqueraded as God while the true divine has been misrepresented as the adversary?

In previous chapters, we examined evidence suggesting that Lucifer usurped God's position in heaven, created Eden as a controlled environment, expelled humans after the true

God's liberating intervention, established religious systems to maintain his divine masquerade, and permitted limited divine influence while maintaining overall control. Now we must consider the textual evidence for this cosmic inversion —re-examining biblical passages, analysing contradictions, identifying hidden messages, and exploring suppressed scriptures that hint at the truth beneath millennia of theological misdirection.

Re-examining Biblical Passages: The Inverted Lens

When we approach biblical texts with the possibility that "God" often refers to Lucifer masquerading as the divine while the true God has been misrepresented as the adversary, certain passages take on radically different meanings. This inverted lens reveals patterns that make more sense within our alternative framework than within conventional theology.

The Genesis Narrative Reconsidered

The creation and fall narratives in Genesis provide our first textual evidence for the cosmic inversion.

Read through the inverted lens, these familiar stories reveal patterns that support our alternative framework:

- The creation account in Genesis 1 describes a deity who creates through commands and distance rather than direct engagement, establishing a pattern of control rather than collaboration with creation
- The separate creation account in Genesis 2 presents a more localized deity who forms humans from dust, suggesting a different entity with more limited creative power
- The prohibition against knowledge in Genesis 2:16-17 reveals a deity concerned with maintaining human ignorance: "but of the tree of the knowledge of good and evil you shall not eat, for in the day that you eat of it you shall surely die"

- The serpent's contradiction of this threat in Genesis 3:4-5 proves accurate: "You will not surely die. For God knows that in the day you eat of it your eyes will be opened, and you will be like God, knowing good and evil"
- The humans' post-knowledge awareness in Genesis 3:7 confirms the serpent's truth-telling: "Then the eyes of both of them were opened, and they knew that they were naked"
- The deity's reaction in Genesis 3:22 reveals fear of human potential: "Behold, the man has become like one of Us, to know good and evil. And now, lest he put out his hand and take also of the tree of life, and eat, and live forever"

This re-examination reveals a pattern more consistent with our alternative framework than with conventional interpretation: a controlling deity who prohibits knowledge, a truth-telling serpent who encourages liberation through knowledge, and a divine reaction of fear rather than justice when humans gain discernment.

Aligned with our reconstructed system, these passages reveal not a benevolent creator and a deceptive tempter but their opposite—Lucifer masquerading as God while prohibiting the knowledge that might expose his masquerade, and the true God appearing as the serpent to liberate humans through truth and discernment.

Divine Violence Reconsidered

Biblical passages describing divine violence provide further textual evidence for the cosmic inversion.

Read through the inverted lens, these troubling texts reveal patterns more consistent with a usurper maintaining control than with a perfectly loving deity:

- The flood narrative in Genesis 6-9 describes near-total destruction of life as divine judgment, a pattern more consistent with a controlling usurper than a loving creator

- The destruction of Sodom and Gomorrah in Genesis 19 portrays divine annihilation of entire communities, including presumably innocent children
- The plagues and firstborn deaths in Exodus 7-12 describe divine actions causing widespread suffering, including to those with no direct responsibility for Pharaoh's decisions
- The commands for genocide in Deuteronomy 20:16-17 attribute to God instructions for total destruction: "you shall let nothing that breathes remain alive, but you shall utterly destroy them"
- The divine violence in prophetic texts like Nahum 1:2-6 describes a deity who "takes vengeance on His adversaries, and He reserves wrath for His enemies"

These passages describing divine violence have troubled theologians for centuries, requiring complex explanations to reconcile them with divine love. But read through our inverted lens, they become straightforward evidence of Lucifer's character manifesting through his divine masquerade—the violence, vengeance, and disproportionate punishment revealing the true nature behind the stolen divine identity.

Aligned with our reconstructed system, these passages reveal not divine justice requiring complex theological justification but the straightforward manifestation of a usurper's character—Lucifer's tendency toward destruction, control, and fear-based dominance expressed through his masquerade as the divine sovereign.

Divine Jealousy Reconsidered

Biblical passages describing divine jealousy provide additional textual evidence for the cosmic inversion.

Read through the inverted lens, these texts reveal patterns more consistent with a usurper maintaining exclusive worship than with a secure divine sovereign:

- The self-description in Exodus 20:5 presents a deity defined by jealousy: "For I, the LORD your God, am a jealous God"
- The divine name in Exodus 34:14 explicitly incorporates jealousy: "for the LORD, whose name is Jealous, is a jealous God"
- The jealous rage in Deuteronomy 32:21 describes divine anger at worship directed elsewhere: "They have provoked Me to jealousy by what is not God; they have moved Me to anger by their foolish idols"
- The jealous punishment in Ezekiel 16:38 threatens violence motivated by jealousy: "I will judge you as women who break wedlock or shed blood are judged; I will bring blood upon you in fury and jealousy"
- The consuming jealousy in Zephaniah 1:18 describes total destruction: "Neither their silver nor their gold shall be able to deliver them in the day of the LORD's wrath; but the whole land shall be devoured by the fire of His jealousy"

These passages describing divine jealousy have been interpreted as expressions of divine love and commitment. But read through our inverted lens, they become evidence of Lucifer's insecurity in his stolen divine identity—the obsessive demand for exclusive worship revealing the fragility of his masquerade rather than the security of legitimate divine authority.

Within our interpretive model, these passages reveal not divine love expressed through jealousy but a usurper's desperate need to maintain exclusive devotion—Lucifer requiring constant affirmation of his stolen divine identity through worship directed exclusively to himself rather than to the true God he has displaced.

Divine Hiddenness Reconsidered

Biblical passages describing divine hiddenness provide further textual evidence for the cosmic inversion.

Read through the inverted lens, these texts reveal patterns more consistent with a masquerading entity avoiding scrutiny than with a perfectly loving deity:

- The prohibition against seeing God in Exodus 33:20 establishes divine inaccessibility: "You cannot see My face; for no man shall see Me, and live"
- The divine hiddenness in Isaiah 45:15 acknowledges a fundamental separation: "Truly You are God, who hide Yourself, O God of Israel, the Savior"
- The complaint in Job 23:8-9 expresses frustration at divine absence: "Look, I go forward, but He is not there, and backward, but I cannot perceive Him; when He works on the left hand, I cannot behold Him; when He turns to the right hand, I cannot see Him"
- The question in Psalm 10:1 challenges divine distance: "Why do You stand afar off, O LORD? Why do You hide in times of trouble?"
- The divine silence in Psalm 83:1 pleads for response: "Do not keep silent, O God! Do not hold Your peace, and do not be still, O God!"

These passages describing divine hiddenness have been interpreted as expressions of divine transcendence or spiritual testing. But read through our inverted lens, they become evidence of Lucifer's need to maintain distance—the prohibition against direct divine encounter protecting his masquerade from the scrutiny that might expose it.

From our ontological viewpoint, these passages reveal not

divine transcendence requiring spiritual maturity but a usurper's strategic distance—Lucifer maintaining separation that prevents the direct divine encounter that might reveal his true identity behind the divine mask.

Contradictions Resolved: The Explanatory Power of Cosmic Inversion

Beyond re-examining specific passages, our alternative framework resolves contradictions that have troubled biblical interpreters for centuries. These contradictions make little sense if the same perfectly consistent deity stands behind all biblical texts. But they become coherent evidence when understood as reflecting the tension between Lucifer's masquerade and the true divine reality it distorts.

The Contradiction of Divine Character

One of the most significant biblical contradictions concerns divine character—the stark contrast between portrayals of God as vengeful, jealous, and violent versus loving, merciful, and compassionate.

This contradiction appears throughout the biblical text:

- The vengeful deity of Nahum 1:2 ("God is jealous, and the LORD avenges; the LORD avenges and is furious") contradicts the loving deity of 1 John 4:8 ("God is love")
- The violent deity who commands total destruction in 1 Samuel 15:3 ("kill both man and woman, infant and nursing child") contradicts the peaceful deity of Isaiah 2:4 who will cause nations to "beat their swords into plowshares"
- The tribal deity who favors Israel in Deuteronomy 7:6 ("the LORD your God has chosen you to be a people for Himself, a special treasure above all the peoples") contradicts the universal deity of Acts 10:34-35 ("God shows no partiality. But in every nation whoever

fears Him and works righteousness is accepted by Him")
- The legalistic deity who demands precise ritual in Leviticus contradicts the grace-oriented deity who "desires mercy and not sacrifice" in Hosea 6:6

The distant deity who cannot be approached in Exodus 19:12-13 (where touching the mountain of God brings death) contradicts the intimate deity who is "our refuge and strength, a very present help in trouble" in Psalm 46:1

These contradictions in divine character have generated complex theological explanations, from progressive revelation to dispensational frameworks to selective emphasis. But read through our inverted lens, they become straightforward evidence of different entities behind the divine portrayal —Lucifer's character manifesting through his divine masquerade versus glimpses of the true God's nature breaking through despite cosmic constraints.

Aligned with our reconstructed system, these contradictions reveal not theological puzzles requiring complex resolution but direct evidence of cosmic deception—the tension between Lucifer's actual character expressed through his divine masquerade and the true divine nature that occasionally breaks through in texts that contradict the dominant portrayal.

The Contradiction of Salvation Requirements

Another significant biblical contradiction concerns salvation requirements—the conflicting portrayals of what humans must do to achieve divine acceptance.

This contradiction appears throughout the biblical text:
- The works-based salvation of Ezekiel 18:21-22 ("if a wicked man turns from all his sins which he has committed, keeps all My statutes, and does what is

lawful and right, he shall surely live") contradicts the faith-based salvation of Ephesians 2:8-9 ("by grace you have been saved through faith, and that not of yourselves; it is the gift of God, not of works")

- The ritual-focused salvation of Leviticus (with its elaborate sacrificial requirements) contradicts the heart-focused salvation of Joel 2:13 ("rend your heart, and not your garments")
- The exclusive salvation of John 14:6 ("No one comes to the Father except through Me") contradicts the inclusive divine acceptance described in Acts 10:34-35 ("in every nation whoever fears Him and works righteousness is accepted by Him")
- The judgment-focused salvation of Matthew 25:31-46 (where eternal destiny depends on specific actions toward the needy) contradicts the belief-focused salvation of John 3:16 (where eternal life comes through believing)
- The communal salvation of the Hebrew Bible (focused on Israel's collective covenant relationship) contradicts the individual salvation of the New Testament (focused on personal faith)

These contradictions in salvation requirements have generated theological frameworks attempting to harmonize them, from covenant theology to dispensationalism to complex understandings of faith and works. But read through our inverted lens, they become evidence of different agendas—Lucifer's interest in complex, changing, and ultimately unattainable requirements versus the true God's consistent emphasis on authentic relationship.

Under our conceptual structure, these contradictions reveal not theological development but strategic manipulation—Lucifer establishing salvation systems complex and changing enough to create perpetual insecurity while the true God consistently emphasizes the simpler path of authentic connection that Lucifer's systems obscure.

The Contradiction of Divine Accessibility

A third significant biblical contradiction concerns divine accessibility—conflicting portrayals of how and whether humans can approach the divine.

This contradiction appears throughout the biblical text:

- The mediated access of Leviticus (requiring priestly intervention) contradicts the direct access of Hebrews 4:16 ("Let us therefore come boldly to the throne of grace")
- The location-specific access of Deuteronomy 12:5-6 (requiring worship at a chosen place) contradicts the omnipresent access of John 4:21-24 (where true worship happens "neither on this mountain nor in Jerusalem" but "in spirit and truth")
- The ritual-dependent access of the Hebrew Bible contradicts the relationship-dependent access of the New Testament
- The hierarchical access of institutional religion contradicts the democratic access of Joel 2:28-29 (where the Spirit is poured out on all flesh)
- The fear-based approach of Exodus 19 (where boundaries prevent approaching the divine) contradicts the love-based approach of 1 John 4:18 (where "perfect love casts out fear")

These contradictions in divine accessibility have been explained through progressive revelation or dispensational frameworks. But read through our inverted lens, they become evidence of different agendas—Lucifer's interest in controlled, mediated access that maintains his masquerade versus the true God's desire for direct connection that might bypass Lucifer's religious systems.

Under our conceptual structure, these contradictions reveal not theological development but competing purposes—Lucifer establishing religious systems that control divine access through mediating structures while the true God consistently encourages direct connection that might eventually expose the cosmic deception.

The Contradiction of Divine Communication

A fourth significant biblical contradiction concerns divine communication—conflicting portrayals of how God speaks to humanity.

This contradiction appears throughout the biblical text:

- The institutionally mediated communication of much of the Hebrew Bible (through priests and established prophets) contradicts the direct communication described in Joel 2:28 (where many receive divine dreams and visions)
- The externally authoritative communication of "Thus says the LORD" pronouncements contradicts the internally discerned communication of 1 Kings 19:12 (where God speaks in a "still small voice")
- The fear-inducing communication of Exodus 20:18-19 (where divine speech causes terror) contradicts the peace-bringing communication of John 14:27 ("Peace I leave with you")
- The tribally specific communication directed exclusively to Israel contradicts the universal communication of Acts 2 (where people of all nations hear in their own languages)
- The verbally explicit communication of direct divine speech contradicts the symbolically mediated communication of dreams and visions

These contradictions in divine communication have been explained through progressive revelation or different divine purposes across history. But read through our inverted lens, they become evidence of different communicators—Lucifer's preference for controlled, authoritative pronouncements versus the true God's tendency toward subtler, more widely accessible communication.

Under our conceptual structure, these contradictions reveal not changing divine communication strategies but different communicators with different purposes—Lucifer establishing authoritative religious communication systems that support his masquerade while the true God communicates through subtler means that might eventually penetrate that masquerade.

Hidden Messages: The Divine Whisper Beneath the Text

Beyond contradictions that suggest different entities behind divine portrayals, biblical texts contain what appear to be hidden messages—passages that, read through our inverted lens, may represent the true God's attempts to communicate truth despite Lucifer's dominance of religious systems and texts.

The Subversive Wisdom Tradition

The wisdom tradition within biblical literature contains some of the most significant hidden messages—texts that question religious certainty, challenge institutional authority, and emphasize direct experience over mediated revelation.

These passages include:

- Ecclesiastes' scepticism about religious certainty and institutional wisdom, suggesting that "much study is wearisome to the flesh" (12:12) while encouraging direct enjoyment of life
- Job's challenge to conventional religious explanations of suffering, ultimately vindicating

the questioner over those who defended traditional theology

- Proverbs' emphasis on practical wisdom and direct observation over religious authority, encouraging learners to "consider the ant" (6:6) rather than merely accepting traditional teaching
- Song of Songs' celebration of embodied love without religious framework or moral lesson, presenting physical intimacy as inherently valuable rather than merely instrumental
- The wisdom psalms' focus on observation and reflection rather than ritual or revelation, encouraging direct engagement with reality rather than mediated religious experience

This subversive wisdom tradition serves as a hidden message from the true God. While Lucifer's religious systems emphasize certainty, authority, and mediated access, these wisdom texts encourage questioning, direct observation, and personal discernment—precisely the orientation that might eventually penetrate the cosmic masquerade.

Through our speculative construct, this wisdom tradition represents not a secondary aspect of biblical literature but a primary channel of authentic divine communication—the exiled God embedding messages that encourage the very discernment that Lucifer's religious systems discourage. Like coded messages sent through enemy-controlled communication channels, these wisdom texts carry divine truth through Lucifer's religious frameworks.

The Prophetic Critique of Religion

The prophetic tradition contains another significant set of hidden messages—texts that criticize institutional religion, ritual observance, and religious certainty.

These passages include:

- Amos 5:21-24 rejects religious ritual in favour of justice: "I hate, I despise your feast days... But let justice run down like water, and righteousness like a mighty stream"
- Isaiah 1:11-17 dismisses sacrificial systems: "To what purpose is the multitude of your sacrifices to Me?... Wash yourselves, make yourselves clean; put away the evil of your doings from before My eyes. Cease to do evil, learn to do good"
- Micah 6:6-8 challenges elaborate religious observance: "With what shall I come before the LORD... He has shown you, O man, what is good; and what does the LORD require of you but to do justly, to love mercy, and to walk humbly with your God?"
- Jeremiah 7:1-7 confronts false religious security: "Do not trust in these lying words, saying, 'The temple of the LORD, the temple of the LORD, the temple of the LORD are these'"
- Hosea 6:6 prioritizes character over ritual: "For I desire mercy and not sacrifice, and the knowledge of God more than burnt offerings"

This prophetic critique of religion serves as a hidden message from the true God. While Lucifer's religious systems emphasize ritual correctness, institutional loyalty, and religious identity, these prophetic texts redirect attention to justice, mercy, and authentic relationship—values that transcend and often challenge religious systems themselves.

Following our reinterpreted paradigm, this prophetic critique represents not merely reform within religious tradition but subversion of its fundamental premises—the exiled God inspiring messages that challenge the very religious systems Lucifer has established to maintain his masquerade. Like resistance broadcasts in occupied territory, these prophetic texts call people toward values and practices that undermine rather than reinforce Lucifer's religious control.

The Jesus Paradox

The portrayal of Jesus in the Gospels contains perhaps the most significant hidden messages—accounts of a figure who consistently challenged religious authorities, questioned religious certainties, and redirected attention from institutional mediation to direct divine connection.

These elements include:

- Jesus's consistent criticism of religious authorities in Matthew 23, calling them "blind guides" and "whitewashed tombs"
- Jesus's reinterpretation of religious law in Matthew 5, repeatedly saying "You have heard that it was said... but I say to you"
- Jesus's challenge to religious exclusivism in parables like the Good Samaritan (Luke 10:25-37), where the religious outsider embodies divine values better than religious insiders
- Jesus's redirection of worship from sacred spaces to direct relationship in John 4:21-24, telling the Samaritan woman that true worship happens "neither on this mountain nor in Jerusalem" but "in spirit and truth"
- Jesus's emphasis on direct divine connection in Matthew 6:6, encouraging prayer "to your Father who is in the secret place" rather than public religious performance

This portrayal of Jesus serves as a hidden message from the true God. While Lucifer's religious systems establish hierarchies of mediated access, Jesus consistently bypasses these structures, encouraging direct divine connection, questioning religious certainties, and challenging the very authorities who claim to represent God.

According to our revised framework, the Jesus paradox represents not merely reform within Judaism but fundamental challenge to all religious systems—the true God breaking through in human form to model the direct divine connection that Lucifer's religious systems obscure. Like a resistance leader operating in occupied territory, Jesus demonstrated an alternative to the religious systems that maintain Lucifer's masquerade.

The Apocalyptic Unveiling

The apocalyptic tradition contains another significant set of hidden messages—texts that promise eventual exposure of cosmic deception and restoration of true divine authority.

These passages include:

- Revelation's portrayal of religious and political systems as "Babylon the Great, the Mother of Harlots" (17:5), suggesting that dominant religious frameworks represent cosmic deception rather than divine truth
- Daniel's vision of successive empires ultimately replaced by divine authority, suggesting that current power structures (including religious ones) are temporary rather than eternal
- Jesus's warnings about false prophets and false messiahs in Matthew 24:24, suggesting that religious deception extends to the highest levels of claimed divine representation
- Paul's reference to "the god of this age" who "has blinded the minds of those who do not believe" in 2 Corinthians 4:4, suggesting that a counterfeit deity currently exercises significant cosmic influence
- The consistent apocalyptic theme of current hidden truth eventually revealed, suggesting that present religious understanding represents partial

knowledge at best and deliberate deception at worst

This apocalyptic tradition serves as a hidden message from the true God. While Lucifer's religious systems present current theological frameworks as complete and authoritative, apocalyptic texts suggest that present understanding is radically incomplete and will eventually be exposed as such.

In the schema we propose, apocalyptic literature represents not merely prediction of future events but promise of eventual cosmic clarification—the exiled God assuring those with eyes to see that the current masquerade will not continue forever. Like resistance literature promising eventual liberation, apocalyptic texts maintain hope for cosmic restoration despite present deception.

Suppressed Scriptures: The Evidence Beyond the Canon

Beyond the canonical texts that have shaped mainstream religious understanding, suppressed scriptures provide additional evidence for our alternative framework. These texts, excluded from official canons and often actively suppressed throughout history, contain perspectives that align remarkably well with the cosmic inversion we have proposed.

The Gnostic Testimony

The Gnostic texts discovered at Nag Hammadi in 1945 provide some of the most significant suppressed evidence for our alternative framework.

These ancient documents present a cosmology that aligns remarkably well with our understanding of Lucifer's masquerade and the true God's exile:

- The concept of the Demiurge in texts like "The Apocryphon of John" presents the creator deity of Genesis as a lower, imperfect being who falsely claims to be the ultimate God—precisely the pattern we would expect from Lucifer masquerading as the divine

- The portrayal of archons (ruling powers) as cosmic deceivers maintaining human ignorance aligns with our understanding of Lucifer's religious systems designed to prevent recognition of his masquerade
- The emphasis on gnosis (direct knowledge) as salvation rather than faith or obedience aligns with our understanding that direct knowing threatens Lucifer's masquerade while supporting connection with the true God
- The reinterpretation of the serpent in texts like "The Testimony of Truth" as a liberator bringing knowledge rather than a tempter bringing sin aligns with our understanding of the true God's intervention in Eden
- The consistent theme across Gnostic texts that the God worshipped by mainstream religion is not the true ultimate divine reality aligns perfectly with our understanding of Lucifer's cosmic identity theft

These Gnostic perspectives were systematically suppressed by emerging orthodox Christianity, with their texts destroyed and their adherents persecuted as heretics. This suppression makes perfect sense within our alternative framework—Lucifer ensuring that perspectives threatening to expose his masquerade were eliminated from official religious understanding.

In the schema we propose, Gnostic texts represent not heretical distortions but preserved glimpses of cosmic truth—alternative understandings that managed to survive despite systematic suppression precisely because they threatened to expose Lucifer's divine masquerade. Like suppressed resistance literature in occupied territory, these texts maintained alternative perspectives that challenged the official narrative.

The Apocryphal Insights

Beyond the Gnostic texts, other apocryphal writings excluded from mainstream canons contain perspectives that align with our alternative framework.

These documents include:

- The Book of Enoch's elaborate angelology and alternative creation narratives suggest cosmic complexity beyond the simplified narrative of mainstream Genesis
- The Gospel of Thomas's emphasis on direct knowing rather than institutional mediation aligns with our understanding of the true God's preference for direct connection
- The Apocalypse of Adam presents the creator deity as hostile to human enlightenment, consistent with our understanding of Lucifer's fear of human knowledge
- The Gospel of Mary challenges institutional religious authority with its portrayal of direct spiritual insight available outside hierarchical structures
- The Gospel of Judas reinterprets one of Christianity's primary villains as acting with divine knowledge, consistent with our pattern of inverted cosmic roles

These apocryphal texts were excluded from official canons through processes controlled by institutional religious authorities. This exclusion makes perfect sense within our alternative framework—Lucifer ensuring that perspectives threatening to expose his masquerade were kept from mainstream religious understanding.

From our ontological viewpoint, apocryphal texts represent not unreliable additions but suppressed alternatives—perspectives excluded from official canons precisely because they contained elements threatening to Lucifer's religious systems. Like banned books in authoritarian regimes, these texts preserved perspectives that challenged the official narrative.

The Mystical Traditions

Beyond specific suppressed texts, mystical traditions across religions contain perspectives that align with our alternative framework.

These traditions include:

- Kabbalah in Judaism presents a complex divine reality beyond the simplified portrayal of mainstream religion, with concepts like the Ein Sof (the infinite divine beyond attributes) suggesting a true God beyond the deity portrayed in mainstream texts
- Sufism in Islam emphasizes direct divine experience over institutional mediation, consistent with our understanding of the true God's preference for direct connection
- Christian mysticism consistently emphasizes divine love and direct experience over theological formulation or institutional authority
- Eastern mystical traditions often present ultimate reality as beyond the creator deity of conventional religion, consistent with our understanding of the true God transcending Lucifer's masquerade
- Indigenous spiritual traditions frequently emphasize direct connection with divine reality through nature and altered consciousness rather than through institutional religious structures

These mystical traditions have frequently been viewed with suspicion by mainstream religious authorities, often facing persecution or marginalization. This pattern makes perfect sense within our alternative framework—Lucifer ensuring that approaches threatening to bypass his religious systems were kept from mainstream religious practice.

In the schema we propose, mystical traditions represent not peripheral additions but central insights—approaches to divine reality that managed to maintain authentic connection despite institutional opposition precisely because they threatened to expose Lucifer's divine masquerade. Like underground movements in occupied territory, these traditions preserved pathways to authentic divine connection despite official suppression.

The Historical Suppressions

Beyond specific texts and traditions, the historical pattern of religious suppression itself provides evidence for our alternative framework.

This pattern includes:

- The destruction of the Library of Alexandria eliminated vast collections of alternative religious and philosophical texts
- The persecution of Gnostics, Cathars, and other alternative Christian movements systematically eliminated perspectives threatening to mainstream theology
- The Inquisition's targeting of those claiming direct divine revelation outside institutional channels
- The consistent suppression of women's spiritual leadership and perspectives across religious traditions
- The colonial destruction of indigenous spiritual traditions and texts worldwide

This pattern of suppression makes perfect sense within our alternative framework—Lucifer systematically eliminating perspectives threatening to expose his masquerade while maintaining religious systems that support it.

Under our conceptual structure, this historical suppression represents not protection of truth from error but elimination of truth threatening to power—Lucifer using religious institutions to systematically destroy perspectives that might expose his cosmic identity theft. Like an occupying power destroying resistance literature, Lucifer has used religious institutions to eliminate textual evidence threatening to his divine masquerade.

Conclusion: The Textual Tapestry Reinterpreted

The evidence we have examined—reinterpreted biblical passages, resolved contradictions, identified hidden messages, and explored suppressed scriptures—all points to a consistent conclusion: religious texts contain substantial evidence supporting our alternative framework of cosmic inversion. When read through this inverted lens, patterns emerge that make more sense than conventional interpretations, contradictions resolve into coherent evidence of different entities behind divine portrayals, and suppressed perspectives align remarkably well with our understanding of Lucifer's masquerade and the true God's exile.

This reinterpretation transforms our understanding of religious texts:

- Biblical passages describing divine violence, jealousy, and hiddenness reveal not divine attributes requiring complex theological justification but Lucifer's character manifesting through his divine masquerade
- Contradictions in divine portrayal reflect not theological development or mystery but the tension between Lucifer's character expressed through his masquerade and glimpses of the true divine nature breaking through

- Hidden messages in wisdom literature, prophetic critique, Jesus's teaching, and apocalyptic texts represent not peripheral elements but central divine communication—the true God embedding truth within texts otherwise dominated by Lucifer's perspective
- Suppressed scriptures present not heretical distortions but preserved glimpses of cosmic truth—alternative understandings systematically eliminated precisely because they threatened to expose Lucifer's divine masquerade

Most significantly, this reinterpretation transforms our approach to religious texts. Rather than accepting institutional interpretations that support Lucifer's masquerade, we can learn to read with discernment—identifying patterns that reveal the cosmic deception while recognizing the true divine voice that speaks through and despite it. Like resistance fighters learning to decode messages embedded within propaganda, we can develop the ability to recognize both the masquerade and the truth it obscures.

In the chapters that follow, we will explore how this understanding transforms our approach to Gnostic insights, cross-cultural evidence, spiritual practice, and ethical discernment.

But first, we must fully absorb the implications of what we have discovered about textual evidence: that religious texts themselves, read with discerning eyes, reveal the very cosmic deception they have been used to conceal. That beneath layers of theological misdirection lies textual evidence of Lucifer's masquerade as God and the true God's continued communication despite cosmic exile. And that the truth, though suppressed, has never been completely eliminated from the textual record of humanity's spiritual journey.

CHAPTER 11: GNOSTIC INSIGHTS

"These are the secret sayings which the living Jesus spoke and which Didymos Judas Thomas wrote down. And he said, 'Whoever finds the interpretation of these sayings will not experience death.'" — The Gospel of Thomas

In the previous chapter, we examined how religious texts themselves contain evidence of cosmic inversion when read through an alternative lens. We discovered that biblical passages, contradictions, hidden messages, and suppressed scriptures all point toward a consistent conclusion: Lucifer has masqueraded as God while the true divine has been exiled and misrepresented as the adversary.

But our investigation would be incomplete without examining one of the most significant alternative spiritual traditions in Western history—a tradition that appears to have preserved elements of this cosmic truth despite systematic suppression. The Gnostic movement, which flourished in the first few centuries CE before being nearly eradicated by emerging orthodox Christianity, offers remarkable insights that align with our alternative framework.

The discovery of the Nag Hammadi library in Egypt in 1945 provided unprecedented access to Gnostic texts that had been deliberately hidden to preserve them from destruction. These ancient codices reveal a spiritual perspective that challenges conventional religious understanding in ways that align remarkably well with our theory of cosmic inversion.

In this chapter, we will explore how Gnostic traditions preserved elements of the true cosmic story, examine the Demiurge as a representation of Lucifer masquerading as God, analyse Sophia's role as a feminine aspect of the exiled true God, and explain why Lucifer's religious institutions so aggressively suppressed Gnosticism.

The Gnostic Preservation of Cosmic Truth

The term "Gnostic" derives from the Greek word gnosis, meaning "knowledge"—not intellectual knowledge but direct, experiential knowing of divine reality. This emphasis on direct knowing rather than mediated belief immediately distinguishes Gnosticism from conventional religious systems and aligns with our understanding of the true God's preference for direct connection over institutional mediation.

The Gnostic Cosmology

Gnostic cosmology presents a framework that aligns remarkably well with our theory of cosmic inversion:

- The True Divine Reality - Gnostics recognized a transcendent, ultimate divine reality (often called the Monad, the One, or the Pleroma) beyond the creator deity of Genesis—precisely the distinction we would expect if the true God transcends Lucifer's masquerade
- The Divine Emanations - Gnostic texts describe divine emanations (aeons) that extend from the ultimate divine reality, suggesting a complex divine nature beyond the simplified portrayal in conventional religion
- The Cosmic Catastrophe - Gnostic cosmology includes a cosmic catastrophe that resulted in divine fragmentation and the creation of an imperfect material world—aligning with our understanding of

God's exile and Lucifer's usurpation

- The Ignorant Creator - Gnostic texts portray the creator deity (the Demiurge) as ignorant, jealous, and often malevolent—precisely the character we would expect from Lucifer masquerading as God
- The Divine Spark - Gnostic anthropology recognizes a divine spark within humans that connects them to the true divine reality beyond the Demiurge—aligning with our understanding that humans retain connection to the exiled God despite Lucifer's control

This Gnostic cosmology preserves the essential elements of our cosmic inversion theory: a true divine reality beyond the creator deity of conventional religion, a cosmic catastrophe resulting in divine exile, an ignorant and jealous creator maintaining control through deception, and a divine spark within humans that connects them to the true God despite that deception.

The Gnostic Soteriology

Beyond cosmology, Gnostic soteriology (understanding of salvation) aligns remarkably well with our alternative framework:

- Salvation Through Knowledge - Gnostics emphasized direct knowing (gnosis) rather than belief or obedience as the path to salvation—precisely the orientation that would threaten Lucifer's masquerade while supporting connection with the true God
- The Divine Messenger - Gnostic texts present Jesus not as a sacrifice for sin but as a divine messenger bringing liberating knowledge—aligning with our understanding of the true God attempting to communicate truth despite cosmic constraints
- The Illusory Nature of the Material World - Gnostics recognized the material world as an imperfect

creation of the Demiurge rather than the perfect creation of the true God—consistent with our understanding of Lucifer's limited creative power
- The Rejection of Religious Authority - Gnostics emphasized direct divine connection over institutional religious authority—precisely the orientation that would bypass Lucifer's religious systems
- The Return to Divine Unity - Gnostic salvation involved recognition of one's divine nature and eventual return to the Pleroma—aligning with our understanding that authentic spirituality involves reconnection with the exiled God

This Gnostic soteriology preserves the essential elements of liberation in our cosmic inversion theory: direct knowing that bypasses religious systems, recognition of the material world's limitations, rejection of institutional authority, and reconnection with the true divine reality beyond the creator deity of conventional religion.

The Gnostic Reinterpretation of Scripture

Perhaps most significantly, Gnostic traditions reinterpreted biblical narratives in ways that align remarkably well with our alternative framework:

- The Genesis Reversal - Gnostic texts like "The Testimony of Truth" reinterpret the serpent as a liberator bringing knowledge rather than a tempter bringing sin—precisely the reversal we would expect if the serpent represented the true God's intervention
- The Creator's Limitation - Gnostic texts portray the creator deity of Genesis as limited, ignorant, and often malevolent—consistent with our understanding of Lucifer's character manifesting through his divine masquerade
- The Divine Beyond the Creator - Gnostic

interpretation recognizes a true divine reality beyond the creator deity—precisely the distinction we would expect if Lucifer has masqueraded as God while the true divine remains in exile

- The Jesus Mystery - Gnostic texts present Jesus as revealing secret knowledge that contradicts rather than confirms conventional religious understanding —aligning with our view of Jesus as a messenger from the true God challenging Lucifer's religious systems
- The Spiritual Elite - Gnostic traditions recognized that only some would recognize these truths while most would remain under the Demiurge's deception —consistent with our understanding that Lucifer's masquerade convinces most while only some recognize the cosmic deception

This Gnostic reinterpretation of scripture preserves the essential elements of our alternative reading: the serpent as liberator rather than tempter, the creator deity as limited and often malevolent, a true divine reality beyond that creator, Jesus as revealer of hidden truth rather than confirmer of conventional religion, and the recognition that most remain under cosmic deception while only some perceive the truth.

The Demiurge: Lucifer Masquerading as God

The most significant Gnostic concept for our alternative framework is the Demiurge—the creator deity portrayed in Gnostic texts as ignorant, jealous, and often malevolent despite claiming to be the ultimate God. This figure aligns remarkably well with our understanding of Lucifer masquerading as God while manifesting characteristics inconsistent with true divine nature.

The Demiurge's Character

Gnostic texts describe the Demiurge in terms that precisely

match our understanding of Lucifer's character manifesting through his divine masquerade:

- The Ignorant Creator - In "The Apocryphon of John," the Demiurge declares, "I am God and there is no other God beside me," despite being ignorant of the true divine reality beyond himself—precisely the pattern we would expect from Lucifer claiming divine identity while being unaware of his own limitations
- The Jealous Ruler - Gnostic texts consistently portray the Demiurge as jealous and possessive, demanding exclusive worship and punishing those who seek knowledge beyond his control—aligning with our understanding of Lucifer's insecurity in his stolen divine identity
- The Cosmic Tyrant - In texts like "On the Origin of the World," the Demiurge rules through fear, punishment, and control rather than love and freedom—consistent with our understanding of Lucifer's methods of maintaining his divine masquerade
- The Self-Deluded Authority - Gnostic traditions present the Demiurge as self-deluded, genuinely believing himself to be the ultimate God despite his limitations—aligning with our understanding of Lucifer's psychological state after cosmic usurpation
- The Material Manipulator - Gnostic cosmology portrays the Demiurge as having power over the material world but limited access to spiritual reality—consistent with our understanding of Lucifer's domain of control after God's exile

These Gnostic descriptions of the Demiurge's character align remarkably well with our understanding of Lucifer manifesting his true nature through his divine masquerade—claiming ultimate authority while revealing limitations, demanding worship while displaying insecurity, and maintaining control through fear rather than inspiring devotion through love.

The Demiurge's Creation

Beyond character, Gnostic understanding of the Demiurge's creative activity aligns with our alternative framework:

- The Imperfect Creation - Gnostic texts present the material world as an imperfect creation of the Demiurge rather than the perfect creation of the true God—consistent with our understanding of Lucifer's limited creative power
- The Controlling Environment - In Gnostic cosmology, the material world functions as a prison or trap for divine sparks rather than an expression of divine love—aligning with our understanding of Eden and subsequent environments as Lucifer's controlled domains
- The Archonic Hierarchy - Gnostic texts describe archons (ruling powers) who assist the Demiurge in maintaining control—consistent with our understanding of Lucifer establishing hierarchical religious systems to maintain his masquerade
- The Counterfeit Nature - Gnostic traditions recognize the material world as a counterfeit of true divine reality rather than its authentic expression—aligning with our understanding of Lucifer's creation as imitation rather than original
- The Entrapping Beauty - Gnostic texts acknowledge the material world's beauty while recognizing it as potentially entrapping—consistent with our understanding of Lucifer creating environments attractive enough to maintain human contentment within his control

These Gnostic perspectives on the Demiurge's creation align

remarkably well with our understanding of Lucifer's creative activity—producing environments that appear divine while functioning as controlled domains, establishing hierarchies that maintain his authority, and creating beauty that entraps rather than liberates.

The Demiurge's Law

Gnostic understanding of the Demiurge's law and commandments also aligns with our alternative framework:

- The Controlling Commandments - Gnostic texts present the Demiurge's laws as mechanisms of control rather than pathways to flourishing—consistent with our understanding of Lucifer establishing religious laws to maintain his masquerade
- The Knowledge Prohibition - In Gnostic interpretation, the prohibition against eating from the tree of knowledge reveals the Demiurge's fear of human enlightenment—aligning with our understanding of Lucifer prohibiting the knowledge that might expose his masquerade
- The Exclusive Worship - Gnostic traditions recognize the Demiurge's demand for exclusive worship as revealing insecurity rather than legitimate authority—consistent with our understanding of Lucifer's need to prevent worship of the true God
- The Arbitrary Rules - Gnostic texts present many of the Demiurge's laws as arbitrary rather than inherently beneficial—aligning with our understanding of Lucifer establishing religious rules that demonstrate control rather than facilitate flourishing
- The Fear Motivation - Gnostic interpretation recognizes fear of punishment rather than love of goodness as the Demiurge's primary motivational

tool—consistent with our understanding of Lucifer's methods of maintaining religious control

These Gnostic perspectives on the Demiurge's law align remarkably well with our understanding of Lucifer's religious systems—establishing rules that maintain control rather than facilitate flourishing, prohibiting knowledge that might expose his masquerade, demanding exclusive worship that prevents connection with the true God, creating arbitrary requirements that demonstrate authority, and motivating through fear rather than inspiring through love.

Sophia: The Feminine Aspect of the Exiled God

While the Demiurge represents Lucifer masquerading as God, the Gnostic figure of Sophia (Wisdom) appears to represent an aspect of the true divine that became separated during the cosmic catastrophe. This feminine divine figure aligns remarkably well with our understanding of the exiled God attempting to reconnect with humanity despite cosmic constraints.

Sophia's Fall and Exile

Gnostic texts present Sophia's story in terms that align with our understanding of God's cosmic exile:

- The Divine Origin - In Gnostic cosmology, Sophia originates within the Pleroma (divine fullness) as an aeon or emanation of the true God—consistent with our understanding of her representing an aspect of the true divine
- The Cosmic Separation - Gnostic texts describe Sophia's separation from the Pleroma through various narratives involving desire, curiosity, or creative impulse—aligning with our understanding of the cosmic event that resulted in God's exile
- The Material Entrapment - In Gnostic traditions, Sophia becomes trapped or limited within material

creation after her fall—consistent with our understanding of God's constrained influence after cosmic exile
- The Ongoing Suffering - Gnostic texts portray Sophia as suffering in her separated state, longing for reunion with the Pleroma—aligning with our understanding of the exiled God's cosmic situation
- The Redemptive Purpose - Gnostic traditions present Sophia's fall as ultimately serving a redemptive purpose despite its tragic nature—consistent with our understanding of God's exile containing potential for eventual cosmic restoration

These Gnostic narratives of Sophia's fall and exile align remarkably well with our understanding of God's cosmic situation—originating in divine fullness, becoming separated through cosmic catastrophe, experiencing constraint within material creation, suffering in exile while longing for restoration, and ultimately serving redemptive purpose despite cosmic tragedy.

Sophia's Wisdom and Influence

Beyond her fall narrative, Sophia's ongoing wisdom and influence in Gnostic texts align with our understanding of the exiled God's continued communication with humanity:

- The Divine Whisper - Gnostic traditions present Sophia as communicating wisdom despite her constrained state—consistent with our understanding of the exiled God continuing to reach humanity through subtle means
- The Inner Knowing - In Gnostic texts, Sophia's wisdom manifests as inner knowing rather than external authority—aligning with our understanding of the true God's preference for direct connection over institutional mediation
- The Subversive Insight - Gnostic traditions

portray Sophia's wisdom as often contradicting conventional religious understanding—consistent with our understanding of the true God's messages challenging Lucifer's religious systems

- The Feminine Divine - In Gnostic cosmology, Sophia represents divine qualities often suppressed in conventional religion: intuition, embodied wisdom, and immanent presence—aligning with our understanding of aspects of true divine nature excluded from Lucifer's masquerade
- The Redemptive Agent - Gnostic texts present Sophia as working toward cosmic redemption despite her constrained state—consistent with our understanding of the exiled God continuing to work toward eventual restoration

These Gnostic perspectives on Sophia's wisdom and influence align remarkably well with our understanding of the exiled God's continued communication—reaching humanity through subtle means rather than institutional authority, manifesting as inner knowing rather than external command, contradicting conventional religious understanding, expressing divine qualities suppressed in Lucifer's masquerade, and working toward eventual cosmic restoration despite present constraints.

Sophia's Relationship with the Demiurge

Perhaps most significantly, Gnostic understanding of Sophia's relationship with the Demiurge aligns with our alternative framework:

- The Unwitting Creator - In some Gnostic texts, Sophia unwittingly gives birth to or creates the Demiurge—consistent with our understanding that Lucifer's usurpation emerged from within divine reality rather than from completely separate origin
- The Cosmic Antagonism - Gnostic traditions present

fundamental tension between Sophia's wisdom and the Demiurge's control—aligning with our understanding of the ongoing cosmic conflict between the true God and Lucifer's masquerade

- The Hidden Influence - In Gnostic cosmology, Sophia continues to influence creation despite the Demiurge's dominance—consistent with our understanding of the exiled God's continued subtle influence despite Lucifer's control
- The Ultimate Transcendence - Gnostic texts portray Sophia as ultimately connected to transcendent divine reality beyond the Demiurge's comprehension —aligning with our understanding of the true God's nature transcending Lucifer's limited understanding
- The Final Resolution - Gnostic traditions anticipate eventual resolution of the tension between Sophia and the Demiurge through cosmic restoration—consistent with our understanding of the ultimate cosmic trajectory toward restoration of true divine authority

These Gnostic perspectives on Sophia's relationship with the Demiurge align remarkably well with our understanding of the relationship between the exiled God and Lucifer's masquerade—involving complex origin rather than simple dualism, fundamental cosmic tension, ongoing hidden influence, transcendent divine reality beyond the usurper's comprehension, and anticipated eventual resolution through cosmic restoration.

The Suppression of Gnosticism: Lucifer Protecting His Masquerade

The historical suppression of Gnosticism provides additional evidence for our alternative framework. The systematic elimination of Gnostic perspectives by emerging orthodox Christianity aligns remarkably well with what we would expect if Lucifer were using religious institutions to protect his divine masquerade from perspectives threatening to expose it.

The Institutional Response

The institutional response to Gnosticism reveals patterns consistent with our understanding of Lucifer's methods of maintaining his masquerade:

- The Heresy Designation - Early church authorities designated Gnosticism as heresy requiring elimination rather than simply an alternative interpretation requiring discussion—consistent with our understanding of Lucifer preventing perspectives that might expose his masquerade
- The Text Destruction - Orthodox authorities systematically destroyed Gnostic texts, with the Nag Hammadi library only surviving because it was deliberately hidden—aligning with our understanding of Lucifer eliminating evidence threatening to his divine masquerade
- The Character Assassination - Church fathers like Irenaeus attacked not only Gnostic ideas but the character and morality of Gnostics themselves —consistent with our understanding of Lucifer discrediting those who might expose his cosmic deception
- The Doctrinal Boundaries - Emerging orthodoxy established rigid doctrinal boundaries specifically excluding Gnostic perspectives—aligning with our understanding of Lucifer creating theological frameworks that protect his masquerade
- The Imperial Alliance - Once Christianity gained imperial power, it used state authority to eliminate remaining Gnostic communities—consistent with our understanding of Lucifer using institutional

power to maintain his religious systems

These historical patterns of suppression align remarkably well with our understanding of Lucifer's methods of maintaining his divine masquerade—designating threatening perspectives as dangerous heresy, destroying texts that might expose his deception, discrediting those who present alternative understandings, establishing theological boundaries that exclude threatening insights, and using institutional power to eliminate remaining resistance.

The Theological Objections

Beyond institutional response, the specific theological objections to Gnosticism reveal what aspects of Gnostic thought most threatened Lucifer's masquerade:

- The Creator Critique - Orthodox authorities most vehemently objected to Gnostic portrayal of the creator deity as ignorant or malevolent—precisely the insight that would expose Lucifer's masquerade as God
- The Direct Knowing - Church fathers condemned Gnostic emphasis on direct knowing over institutional mediation—exactly the orientation that would bypass Lucifer's religious systems
- The Serpent Reinterpretation - Orthodox theologians particularly attacked Gnostic positive interpretation of the serpent in Eden—precisely the reversal that would reveal God's liberating intervention
- The Material Critique - Emerging orthodoxy rejected Gnostic critique of material creation—exactly the perspective that would reveal the limitations of Lucifer's creative power
- The Divine Complexity - Church authorities condemned Gnostic understanding of complex divine emanations—precisely the cosmology that would distinguish the true God from Lucifer's

simplified divine portrayal

These theological objections align remarkably well with our understanding of which Gnostic perspectives most threatened Lucifer's masquerade—critique of the creator deity, emphasis on direct knowing, positive interpretation of the serpent, recognition of material creation's limitations, and understanding of divine complexity beyond simplified portrayal.

The Surviving Elements

Despite systematic suppression, certain Gnostic elements survived within mainstream Christianity in forms that no longer threatened Lucifer's masquerade:

- The Domesticated Mysticism - Christian mysticism preserved elements of direct divine knowing but within institutional frameworks that contained its subversive potential
- The Controlled Wisdom - Wisdom traditions continued within Christianity but with Sophia subordinated to institutional authority rather than functioning as alternative divine access
- The Reinterpreted Dualism - Christian theology maintained elements of cosmic dualism but with Lucifer as God's adversary rather than masquerading as God himself
- The Limited Transcendence - Orthodox theology preserved divine transcendence but within theological frameworks that maintained institutional mediation
- The Contained Esotericism - Elements of esoteric interpretation continued within Christianity but under institutional supervision that prevented truly subversive readings

These surviving elements align remarkably well with our

understanding of how Lucifer would permit aspects of truth to continue within his religious systems—allowing mystical experience but within institutional frameworks, preserving wisdom traditions but under theological control, maintaining cosmic dualism but with inverted roles, acknowledging divine transcendence but requiring institutional mediation, and permitting esoteric interpretation but preventing truly subversive readings.

Conclusion: The Gnostic Witness to Cosmic Truth

The evidence we have examined—Gnostic cosmology, the Demiurge as Lucifer masquerading as God, Sophia as an aspect of the exiled true God, and the systematic suppression of Gnosticism—all points to a consistent conclusion: Gnostic traditions preserved elements of cosmic truth despite nearly successful attempts to eliminate them from human consciousness.

This Gnostic witness transforms our understanding of religious history:

- Gnostic cosmology reveals not heretical distortion but preserved insight into the true cosmic situation —Lucifer's usurpation of divine identity and the true God's exile
- The Demiurge represents not misunderstanding of the biblical creator but accurate recognition of Lucifer manifesting his true nature through his divine masquerade
- Sophia embodies not confusion about divine nature but preserved connection with an aspect of the true God continuing to influence creation despite cosmic exile
- The suppression of Gnosticism represents not protection of truth from error but elimination of perspectives threatening to expose Lucifer's cosmic identity theft

Most significantly, this Gnostic witness transforms our approach to spiritual seeking. Rather than accepting institutional religious frameworks that support Lucifer's masquerade, we can recognize the value of direct knowing, critical discernment, and inner divine connection—precisely the orientation that Gnostic traditions preserved despite systematic suppression.

In the chapters that follow, we will explore how this understanding transforms our approach to cross-cultural evidence, spiritual practice, and ethical discernment.

But first, we must fully absorb the implications of what we have discovered about Gnostic insights: that an alternative spiritual tradition systematically suppressed by mainstream religion preserved elements of cosmic truth that align remarkably well with our theory of cosmic inversion. That beneath layers of theological condemnation lies evidence of Lucifer's masquerade as God and the true God's continued influence despite cosmic exile. And that the very perspectives most aggressively eliminated from religious consciousness may be those most threatening to cosmic deception.

The Gnostic witness reminds us that truth, though suppressed, has never been completely eliminated from human consciousness. Like a divine spark preserved within material entrapment, knowledge of the true cosmic situation has persisted despite nearly successful attempts to extinguish it. And in that persistence lies hope for eventual cosmic restoration—the return of the exiled God and the exposure of Lucifer's divine masquerade.

CHAPTER 12: ACROSS CULTURES

"The same story, told a thousand different ways, is still the same story." — Ancient proverb

In the previous chapters, we have examined how biblical texts and Gnostic traditions contain evidence of a cosmic inversion —Lucifer masquerading as God while the true divine remains in exile. But if our theory is correct, we would expect to find echoes of this cosmic truth beyond Judeo-Christian and Gnostic traditions. After all, if Lucifer's usurpation and God's exile represent the fundamental cosmic reality, traces of this truth should appear across human cultures, preserved in various mythological and religious systems despite Lucifer's attempts to suppress it.

This chapter explores precisely such cross-cultural evidence. We will examine similar narratives of divine usurpation in other traditions, universal themes of knowledge-bringers being demonized, cross-cultural evidence for Lucifer's cosmic identity theft, and how different cultures preserved different aspects of the truth about the exiled God. What we will discover is remarkable: across vastly different cultural contexts, similar patterns emerge that align with our understanding of cosmic inversion—suggesting not cultural borrowing but independent preservation of fragments of cosmic truth.

Divine Usurpation Across Cultures

The theme of divine usurpation—a lesser deity overthrowing a greater one and claiming supreme authority—appears with striking consistency across cultural traditions. While conventional scholarship treats these as separate mythological developments, our alternative framework suggests they may represent cultural memories of the same cosmic event: Lucifer's overthrow of God and subsequent masquerade as the divine.

Indo-European Traditions

The Indo-European mythological traditions contain particularly clear examples of divine usurpation:

- Greek Succession Myths - The Greek succession myth describes how Kronos overthrew his father Uranus, only to be later overthrown by his son Zeus. While conventional interpretation sees this as representing generational conflict, our framework suggests it preserves memory of cosmic usurpation—with Zeus (representing Lucifer) establishing himself as supreme deity through violence rather than inherent authority.
- Norse Ragnarök - The Norse concept of Ragnarök describes not only the end of the world but also a cosmic battle in which many gods fall. What's particularly significant is that after this battle, a new world emerges with new divine authorities—suggesting memory of cosmic restructuring after divine overthrow.
- Vedic Indra's Ascension - In Vedic mythology, Indra becomes king of the gods by defeating the dragon Vritra. What's notable is that Indra's character displays many qualities consistent with our understanding of Lucifer—he is powerful but morally ambiguous, prone to jealousy, and maintains authority through displays of power rather than

inherent goodness.

- Roman Jupiter's Rule - Roman mythology preserves the Greek succession myth but adds emphasis on Jupiter's (Zeus's) establishment of cosmic law and order. This aligns with our understanding of Lucifer establishing religious systems to maintain his masquerade after usurping divine authority.

What's particularly significant about these Indo-European usurpation myths is that they consistently portray the victorious deity (Zeus/Jupiter/Indra) as morally ambiguous—powerful but flawed, maintaining authority through force rather than inherent goodness. This aligns remarkably well with our understanding of Lucifer manifesting his true nature through his divine masquerade.

Near Eastern Traditions

Beyond Indo-European cultures, Near Eastern mythological traditions contain similar patterns of divine usurpation:

- Mesopotamian Marduk - In the Babylonian creation epic Enuma Elish, Marduk becomes supreme deity by defeating the primordial goddess Tiamat. After this victory, he creates the world and establishes himself as ruler—a pattern consistent with our understanding of Lucifer establishing a new cosmic order after usurping divine authority.
- Hurrian-Hittite Kumarbi Cycle - The Kumarbi cycle describes how the god Kumarbi overthrows the sky god Anu by biting off his genitals, only to be later overthrown himself. This graphic depiction of divine violence and usurpation preserves memory of cosmic overthrow through shocking imagery that resisted sanitization.
- Ugaritic Baal Cycle - In Ugaritic mythology, Baal establishes supremacy through conflict with other deities, particularly Yamm (sea) and Mot (death).

What's significant is that Baal's authority comes through victory in conflict rather than inherent divine right—consistent with our understanding of Lucifer's authority deriving from usurpation rather than legitimate divine nature.

- Egyptian Osiris-Set Conflict - While not precisely a usurpation myth, the Egyptian conflict between Osiris and Set preserves memory of divine conflict resulting in cosmic restructuring. Set's murder of Osiris and subsequent rule, followed by Horus's eventual restoration, suggests cultural memory of cosmic overthrow and anticipated restoration.

These Near Eastern usurpation myths consistently portray cosmic authority as established through conflict rather than inherent right—precisely the pattern we would expect if they preserved cultural memory of Lucifer's usurpation of divine authority.

Asian Traditions

Even in Asian mythological traditions, patterns emerge that align with our understanding of cosmic inversion:

- Chinese Celestial Rebellion - Chinese mythology contains accounts of celestial rebellion, particularly the story of the Monkey King's rebellion against heaven. While often interpreted as representing human ambition, our framework suggests it may preserve memory of cosmic rebellion resulting in restructured divine hierarchy.
- Japanese Succession Myths - In Japanese mythology, Amaterasu becomes supreme deity after conflict with her brother Susanoo. What's significant is that divine authority emerges from conflict rather than being eternally established—consistent with our understanding of cosmic restructuring after divine overthrow.

- Hindu Asura-Deva Conflict - Hindu mythology describes ongoing conflict between asuras and devas (demons and gods), with cosmic authority shifting between them. This preserves memory of cosmic conflict rather than stable divine hierarchy—aligning with our understanding of contested divine authority after cosmic usurpation.
- Buddhist Mara - In Buddhist tradition, Mara represents the evil one who tempts Buddha and seeks to maintain control over the cycle of rebirth. What's significant is that Mara is portrayed as the current ruler of the world system rather than an outsider challenging divine authority—consistent with our understanding of Lucifer as the current cosmic ruler rather than a rebel against established divine order.

These Asian traditions, despite developing in cultural contexts far removed from Near Eastern and Indo-European systems, preserve similar patterns of contested divine authority emerging from cosmic conflict—suggesting not cultural borrowing but independent preservation of fragments of cosmic truth.

Indigenous Traditions

Even indigenous mythological systems contain patterns consistent with our understanding of cosmic inversion:

- Native American Trickster Usurpations - Many Native American traditions describe how trickster figures like Coyote or Raven steal important elements (like fire or light) from more powerful beings. While conventional interpretation sees these as cultural heroes, our framework suggests they may preserve memory of cosmic theft—Lucifer stealing divine authority and attributes.
- African Creation Conflicts - Various African mythological systems describe conflict during

creation, with different deities competing for authority over different domains. This preserves memory of contested divine authority rather than harmonious cosmic hierarchy—consistent with our understanding of cosmic restructuring after divine overthrow.

- Australian Aboriginal Dreamtime Conflicts - Aboriginal Australian traditions describe conflicts between creator beings during the Dreamtime that established the current cosmic order. This aligns with our understanding of the current cosmic order resulting from conflict rather than representing original divine intention.
- Polynesian Divine Separations - Polynesian creation myths often describe the separation of sky and earth, resulting in the current cosmic structure. What's significant is that this separation often involves violence or force rather than harmonious divine plan—consistent with our understanding of cosmic restructuring through conflict rather than original divine intention.

These indigenous traditions, despite developing in isolation from major world religious systems, preserve similar patterns of cosmic conflict resulting in current divine order—suggesting not cultural borrowing but independent preservation of fragments of cosmic truth.

Demonized Knowledge-Bringers

Beyond divine usurpation, another cross-cultural pattern emerges that aligns with our alternative framework: the consistent demonization of figures who bring knowledge to humanity. While conventional interpretation sees these as representing cultural ambivalence about knowledge, our framework suggests they preserve memory of the true God's attempts to liberate humanity from Lucifer's control through knowledge—attempts that Lucifer's religious systems subsequently demonized.

Prometheus and Fire-Bringers

The Greek myth of Prometheus represents the most famous example of a demonized knowledge-bringer:

- Prometheus's Gift - Prometheus steals fire from the gods and gives it to humanity, representing knowledge and civilization. What's significant is that this gift is portrayed as theft from divine authority rather than expression of divine benevolence—consistent with our understanding of knowledge as threatening to Lucifer's control.
- Zeus's Punishment - Zeus punishes Prometheus severely for this gift, chaining him to a rock where an eagle eats his liver daily. This preserves memory of divine authority (Lucifer) responding with extreme punishment to attempts at human liberation through knowledge.
- Pandora's "Curse" - Zeus further punishes humanity by sending Pandora with her box of troubles. What's significant is that divine authority responds to human knowledge acquisition with punishment rather than support—consistent with our understanding of Lucifer's response to human enlightenment.
- Cross-Cultural Fire-Bringers - Similar myths of punished fire-bringers appear across cultures: the Norse giant Logi, the Vedic Mātariśvan, the Chinese Suiren, and many others. This consistent pattern suggests not cultural borrowing but independent preservation of memory of the true God's attempt to bring liberating knowledge to humanity.
- These myths of punished fire-bringers preserve memory of the true God's attempt to liberate

humanity through knowledge and Lucifer's violent response to this threat to his control.

Serpent Wisdom Figures

The serpent as wisdom-bringer represents another cross-cultural pattern that aligns with our alternative framework:

- Mesoamerican Quetzalcoatl - The feathered serpent deity Quetzalcoatl brings knowledge, civilization, and arts to humanity. What's significant is that later religious developments often portrayed him as in conflict with more violent deities—consistent with our understanding of the true God's conflict with Lucifer's violent manifestations.
- African Rainbow Serpent - Various African traditions describe rainbow serpent deities associated with wisdom, water, and fertility. These figures often operate independently of supreme creator deities—consistent with our understanding of the true God operating independently of Lucifer's divine masquerade.
- Australian Aboriginal Rainbow Serpent - Aboriginal Australian traditions describe the Rainbow Serpent as both creator and destroyer, associated with water, life, and initiation into secret knowledge—preserving memory of the dual nature of divine wisdom as both creating and destroying established order.
- Asian Dragon Wisdom - East Asian dragon figures are associated with wisdom, water, and beneficial power rather than evil—preserving memory of serpent wisdom uncorrupted by Lucifer's later demonization of serpent imagery.

What's particularly significant about these serpent wisdom figures is that they preserve positive associations with serpent imagery in cultural contexts less influenced by Lucifer's religious systems—suggesting that the demonization of the serpent in Abrahamic traditions represents Lucifer's attempt to discredit the true God's intervention rather than reflecting original divine perspective.

Trickster Knowledge-Bringers

Trickster figures who bring knowledge to humanity represent another cross-cultural pattern that aligns with our alternative framework:

- Norse Loki - The Norse trickster Loki brings both trouble and innovation to gods and humans. What's significant is his ambiguous moral status —neither fully evil nor fully good, but operating according to different values than the established divine order. This preserves memory of the true God operating according to different values than Lucifer's established religious systems.
- African Anansi - The spider trickster Anansi brings stories and wisdom to humanity, often by outwitting more powerful beings. This preserves memory of the true God using wisdom rather than power to counteract Lucifer's established authority.
- Native American Coyote/Raven - Indigenous American trickster figures like Coyote and Raven bring cultural goods to humanity through clever theft from more powerful beings. This preserves memory of the true God liberating divine gifts from Lucifer's control through wisdom rather than power.
- Polynesian Maui - The Polynesian trickster hero Maui brings benefits to humanity through clever manipulation of more powerful beings. This preserves memory of the true God operating through wisdom rather than direct power to benefit humanity despite cosmic constraints.
- These trickster knowledge-bringers preserve

memory of the true God's methods of operation after cosmic exile—using wisdom, cleverness, and indirect approaches rather than direct power to benefit humanity despite Lucifer's established authority.

Wisdom Goddesses

Female wisdom figures across cultures represent another pattern that aligns with our alternative framework:

- Greek Athena - The Greek goddess Athena represents wisdom, strategic warfare, and civilization. What's significant is that she emerges fully formed from Zeus's head after he swallows her mother Metis—preserving memory of wisdom's complex relationship with established divine authority.
- Egyptian Isis - The Egyptian goddess Isis represents wisdom, magic, and healing. What's significant is her role in restoring her murdered husband Osiris—preserving memory of wisdom's role in potential cosmic restoration after divine overthrow.
- Hindu Saraswati - The Hindu goddess Saraswati represents knowledge, arts, and learning. What's significant is her independence from male deities despite their greater power—preserving memory of divine wisdom operating with relative autonomy despite cosmic constraints.
- Celtic Brigid - The Celtic goddess Brigid represents poetry, healing, and smithcraft. What's significant is her survival into Christian times as Saint Brigid—preserving memory of divine wisdom's ability to adapt and survive despite changing religious systems.

These wisdom goddesses preserve memory of aspects of divine wisdom that survived Lucifer's cosmic usurpation—operating with relative autonomy despite cosmic constraints, preserving potential for eventual restoration, and adapting to survive changing religious contexts.

Cross-Cultural Evidence for Cosmic Identity Theft

Beyond divine usurpation and demonized knowledge-bringers, cross-cultural patterns emerge that specifically suggest cosmic identity theft—Lucifer claiming divine attributes and authority that properly belong to the true God.

Divine Name Taboos

Taboos against speaking divine names represent a cross-cultural pattern that aligns with our alternative framework:

- Jewish Tetragrammaton - The Jewish prohibition against pronouncing the divine name YHWH is conventionally interpreted as expressing reverence. Our framework suggests it may preserve memory of Lucifer's attempt to control divine identity by making the true divine name unutterable.
- Egyptian Secret Names - Egyptian mythology includes the concept of secret divine names containing power. What's significant is that knowing a deity's true name conferred power over them—preserving memory of the importance of divine identity in cosmic authority.
- Hindu Secret Mantras - Hindu traditions include secret mantras and divine names revealed only to initiates. This preserves memory of divine identity being protected from common access—consistent with our understanding of Lucifer restricting access to true divine identity.
- Indigenous Secret Names - Many indigenous traditions maintain taboos against casual use of divine or spirit names. This preserves memory of the power dynamics involved in divine naming—consistent with our understanding of Lucifer controlling divine identity as part of his masquerade.

These divine name taboos preserve memory of the significance of divine identity in cosmic authority—consistent with our understanding of Lucifer's usurpation involving theft of divine identity.

Dual Creator Systems

Religious systems with dual creators represent another cross-cultural pattern that aligns with our alternative framework:

- Zoroastrian Dualism - Zoroastrianism explicitly recognizes two cosmic powers: Ahura Mazda (good) and Angra Mainyu (evil). What's significant is that both have creative power rather than one being merely destructive—preserving memory of both Lucifer and the true God having creative capacity.
- Gnostic Demiurge/Pleroma - As we explored in the previous chapter, Gnostic traditions distinguish between the Demiurge (creator of material world) and the true divine Pleroma—preserving memory of Lucifer creating material systems while the true God transcends them.
- Manichaean Light/Darkness - Manichaeism describes cosmic conflict between principles of Light and Darkness, both with creative capacity. This preserves memory of both cosmic powers having creative ability rather than one being merely destructive.
- Indigenous Dual Creators - Various indigenous traditions describe creation involving multiple creators, often in tension with each other. This preserves memory of creation involving contested divine activity rather than unified divine plan.

These dual creator systems preserve memory of both Lucifer and the true God having creative capacity—consistent with our understanding of cosmic creation involving both powers rather than representing unified divine plan.

Divine Impostor Narratives

Stories of divine impostors represent another cross-cultural pattern that aligns with our alternative framework:

- Hindu Avatar Impostors - Hindu traditions include stories of demons masquerading as divine avatars to deceive devotees. This preserves memory of the possibility of divine identity theft at cosmic scale.
- Buddhist Mara's Disguises - Buddhist traditions describe how Mara (the evil one) can appear in various guises, including as seemingly divine or enlightened beings. This preserves memory of evil's capacity for spiritual disguise.
- Norse Loki's Shapeshifting - Norse mythology describes how Loki can assume various forms to deceive both gods and humans. This preserves memory of cosmic deception through identity manipulation.
- African Trickster Transformations - Various African traditions describe trickster figures who can assume divine forms to manipulate cosmic order. This preserves memory of divine identity being potentially fluid and subject to manipulation.

These divine impostor narratives preserve memory of the possibility of cosmic-scale identity theft—consistent with our understanding of Lucifer masquerading as God while the true divine remains in exile.

Fallen Divine Narratives

Stories of fallen or exiled divine beings represent another cross-cultural pattern that aligns with our alternative framework:

- Chinese Exiled Immortals - Chinese mythology

includes stories of immortals exiled from heaven for various transgressions. This preserves memory of divine exile as cosmic possibility.

- Hindu Fallen Devas - Hindu traditions describe devas who fall from divine status due to pride or transgression. This preserves memory of divine beings experiencing cosmic demotion.
- Greek Chained Titans - Greek mythology describes the Titans imprisoned after cosmic overthrow. This preserves memory of divine powers experiencing constraint after cosmic conflict.
- Indigenous Withdrawn Creators - Various indigenous traditions describe creator deities who withdraw from creation after establishing it. This preserves memory of divine absence after creative activity.

These fallen divine narratives preserve memory of divine beings experiencing exile, constraint, or withdrawal—consistent with our understanding of the true God's cosmic situation after Lucifer's usurpation.

Cultural Preservation of Divine Truth

Different cultural traditions appear to have preserved different aspects of the truth about the exiled God and Lucifer's masquerade. This pattern of fragmented preservation across cultures aligns with our understanding of cosmic truth being partially suppressed but never completely eliminated from human consciousness.

Eastern Emphasis on Divine Transcendence

Eastern religious traditions appear to have preserved particular emphasis on divine transcendence beyond material creation:

- Hindu Brahman - The Hindu concept of Brahman as ultimate reality transcending both gods and creation

preserves memory of the true God transcending Lucifer's material systems and pantheons.
- Buddhist Emptiness - The Buddhist concept of emptiness (sunyata) as ultimate reality beyond conceptualization preserves memory of the true divine transcending religious conceptual frameworks.
- Taoist Nameless Tao - The Taoist emphasis on the Tao that cannot be named preserves memory of the true divine transcending linguistic and conceptual categories.
- Jain Transcendent Tirthankara - The Jain concept of liberated teachers (Tirthankaras) who transcend cosmic cycles preserves memory of divine consciousness transcending cosmic constraints.

These Eastern emphases on divine transcendence preserve memory of the true God transcending Lucifer's material systems and religious frameworks—operating beyond the cosmic domains under Lucifer's control.

Western Emphasis on Divine Conflict

Western religious traditions appear to have preserved particular emphasis on cosmic conflict between divine powers:

- Greek Titanomachy - The Greek war between Titans and Olympians preserves memory of cosmic conflict resulting in restructured divine hierarchy.
- Norse Ragnarök - The Norse concept of final battle between cosmic powers preserves memory of ongoing divine conflict with anticipated resolution.
- Zoroastrian Cosmic War - The Zoroastrian framework of cosmic war between good and evil preserves memory of fundamental conflict between divine powers rather than unified divine plan.
- Abrahamic Lucifer Narrative - The Abrahamic

concept of Lucifer as God's adversary preserves memory of cosmic conflict, though with inverted roles as we have explored.

These Western emphases on divine conflict preserve memory of the cosmic war between Lucifer and the true God—though often with inverted understanding of the participants' roles.

Indigenous Emphasis on Divine Immanence

Indigenous religious traditions appear to have preserved particular emphasis on divine presence within creation despite cosmic constraints:

- Native American Spirit World - Many indigenous American traditions emphasize spiritual presence permeating the natural world. This preserves memory of divine presence continuing within creation despite cosmic exile.
- African Ancestral Presence - Various African traditions emphasize ongoing spiritual presence of ancestors within community life. This preserves memory of spiritual continuity despite apparent separation.
- Australian Aboriginal Dreamtime - Aboriginal Australian emphasis on the Dreamtime as simultaneously past and present preserves memory of divine reality transcending temporal constraints.
- Polynesian Mana - The Polynesian concept of mana as spiritual power within people, places, and objects preserves memory of divine presence distributed throughout creation rather than exclusively transcendent.

These indigenous emphases on divine immanence preserve memory of the true God's continued presence within creation despite cosmic exile—manifesting through natural systems, community connections, and distributed spiritual power rather than centralized religious authority.

Mystical Emphasis on Direct Knowing

Mystical traditions across cultures appear to have preserved particular emphasis on direct divine knowing beyond religious systems:

- Sufi Direct Experience - Islamic Sufism emphasizes direct experience of divine reality beyond religious formulations. This preserves memory of the true God being accessible through direct knowing rather than exclusively through religious systems.
- Kabbalistic Divine Encounter - Jewish Kabbalah emphasizes direct encounter with divine reality beyond textual understanding. This preserves memory of the true God being accessible through experiential knowing rather than exclusively through scripture.
- Christian Mysticism - Christian mystical traditions emphasize direct divine union beyond theological formulations. This preserves memory of the true God being accessible through immediate experience rather than exclusively through doctrine.
- Hindu Yogic Realization - Hindu yogic traditions emphasize direct realization of divine reality through meditation practices. This preserves memory of the true God being accessible through contemplative knowing rather than exclusively through ritual.

These mystical emphases on direct knowing preserve memory of the true God being accessible through immediate experience despite Lucifer's religious systems—providing alternative access to divine reality beyond institutional mediation.

Conclusion: The Universal Witness to Cosmic Truth

The evidence we have examined—divine usurpation narratives, demonized knowledge-bringers, cosmic identity theft patterns, and cultural preservation of divine truth—all points to a consistent conclusion: across vastly different cultural contexts, similar patterns emerge that align with our understanding of cosmic inversion. This cross-cultural consistency suggests not cultural borrowing but independent preservation of fragments of cosmic truth.

This universal witness transforms our understanding of religious history:

- Divine usurpation myths reveal not primitive power fantasies but preserved memory of Lucifer's cosmic overthrow of the true God
- Demonized knowledge-bringers represent not cultural ambivalence about knowledge but preserved memory of the true God's attempts to liberate humanity through knowledge
- Divine impostor narratives preserve not mere folklore but cultural memory of Lucifer's cosmic identity theft
- Different cultural emphases represent not mere diversity but fragmented preservation of different aspects of cosmic truth

Most significantly, this cross-cultural witness transforms our approach to comparative religion. Rather than seeing different religious traditions as separate developments or competing truth claims, we can recognize them as preserving different fragments of cosmic truth despite Lucifer's attempts to suppress it. The true divine has never left humanity without witness, though that witness has been fragmented, distorted, and partially suppressed across cultural contexts.

In the chapters that follow, we will explore how this understanding transforms our approach to spiritual practice, ethical discernment, and cosmic restoration.

But first, we must fully absorb the implications of what we have discovered about cross-cultural evidence: that beneath the diversity of world religions lies a consistent pattern pointing toward cosmic inversion. That across vastly different cultural contexts, similar motifs emerge that align with our understanding of Lucifer masquerading as God while the true divine remains in exile. And that the very universality of these patterns suggests not cultural borrowing but independent preservation of fragments of cosmic truth.

The cross-cultural witness reminds us that truth, though fragmented, has never been completely eliminated from human consciousness. Like divine light refracted through the prism of cultural diversity, knowledge of the true cosmic situation has persisted across human traditions despite nearly successful attempts to obscure it. And in that persistence lies hope for eventual cosmic restoration—the return of the exiled God and the exposure of Lucifer's divine masquerade.

PART V: LIVING WITH THE TRUTH

CHAPTER 13: SPIRITUAL IMPLICATIONS

"The truth will set you free, but first it will make you miserable." — Attributed to James A. Garfield

In the previous chapters, we have examined the evidence for a cosmic inversion—Lucifer masquerading as God while the true divine remains in exile. We have explored this evidence in biblical texts, Gnostic traditions, and cross-cultural mythological patterns. But understanding this revolutionary framework is only the beginning.

The real question is: how does this understanding transform our spiritual lives?

This chapter explores the practical spiritual implications of our alternative framework. We will consider how to reconsider worship to avoid inadvertently worshipping Lucifer, explore methods for connecting with the true exiled God through knowledge and questioning, examine approaches to liberating oneself from Lucifer's disguised influence, and provide guidance for building authentic spirituality based on the whispers of the exiled God.

These are not merely theoretical considerations but practical matters of profound spiritual significance. If our framework is correct, billions of sincere spiritual seekers have been inadvertently directing their devotion toward Lucifer while the true God remains in exile, reaching humanity through subtle whispers rather than institutional authority.

Recognizing this cosmic deception transforms not only our understanding but our entire approach to spiritual life.

Reconsidering Worship

If Lucifer has masqueraded as God while the true divine remains in exile, we must fundamentally reconsider the nature and direction of worship to avoid inadvertently directing our devotion toward the cosmic usurper.

The Misdirection of Conventional Worship

Conventional religious worship often contains elements that, in light of our alternative framework, appear designed to direct devotion toward Lucifer rather than the true God:

- Emphasis on Power and Glory - Conventional worship often focuses on divine power, majesty, and glory—precisely the attributes Lucifer would emphasize to maintain his masquerade while concealing his lack of true divine nature
- Demand for Submission - Religious systems typically demand unquestioning submission to divine authority—exactly what Lucifer would require to prevent the questioning that might expose his masquerade
- Fear-Based Devotion - Many religious traditions emphasize divine judgment and punishment—consistent with Lucifer's methods of control rather than the true God's nature of liberation
- Institutional Mediation - Conventional worship typically requires institutional mediation through priests, rituals, or sacred spaces—precisely the structures Lucifer would establish to prevent direct divine connection that might bypass his masquerade
- Exclusive Claims - Religious systems often make exclusive claims to truth while demonizing alternatives—exactly the approach Lucifer would

take to prevent exploration of perspectives that might expose his cosmic deception

These elements of conventional worship align remarkably well with what we would expect from Lucifer's religious systems rather than authentic connection with the true divine. This doesn't mean all conventional worship is worthless—sincere devotion may reach beyond its intended direction—but it does suggest the need for fundamental reconsideration of worship's nature and focus.

Redirecting Devotional Energy

Rather than abandoning spirituality altogether, our framework suggests redirecting devotional energy toward attributes and approaches more likely to connect with the true exiled God:

- From Power to Wisdom - Instead of worshipping divine power (Lucifer's emphasis), focus devotion on divine wisdom—the quality most associated with the true God's continued influence despite exile
- From Submission to Discernment - Rather than unquestioning submission (Lucifer's demand), cultivate discerning engagement—the approach most likely to distinguish true divine whispers from Lucifer's loud commands
- From Fear to Freedom - Instead of fear-based devotion (Lucifer's method), develop freedom-oriented spirituality—the quality most aligned with the true God's liberating rather than controlling nature
- From Mediation to Direct Connection - Rather than institutional mediation (Lucifer's structure), pursue direct divine connection—the approach most likely to bypass Lucifer's religious systems
- From Exclusivity to Integration - Instead of exclusive truth claims (Lucifer's strategy), embrace integrative

understanding—the perspective most capable of recognizing fragments of divine truth across traditions

This redirection doesn't necessarily require abandoning all religious practices but rather fundamentally reorienting their focus and approach. Prayer can continue but directed toward wisdom rather than power; meditation can deepen but focused on discernment rather than submission; community can flourish but centred on shared exploration rather than enforced conformity.

Recognizing Authentic Divine Attributes

Our framework suggests certain divine attributes are more likely to represent the true God rather than Lucifer's masquerade:

- Liberating Rather Than Controlling - The true God liberates through knowledge while Lucifer controls through ignorance—suggesting authentic divine influence promotes freedom rather than submission
- Questioning Rather Than Certainty - The true God encourages questioning while Lucifer demands certainty—suggesting authentic divine connection involves ongoing inquiry rather than fixed answers
- Integration Rather Than Division - The true God integrates diverse understanding while Lucifer divides through exclusive claims—suggesting authentic divine wisdom recognizes truth across boundaries
- Empowerment Rather Than Dependency - The true God empowers through shared divine nature while Lucifer creates dependency through hierarchical authority—suggesting authentic divine relationship involves growing participation rather than permanent subordination
- Transformative Rather Than Stabilizing - The

true God transforms consciousness while Lucifer stabilizes existing structures—suggesting authentic divine encounter involves ongoing evolution rather than preserved tradition

Worship directed toward these attributes—liberation, questioning, integration, empowerment, and transformation—is more likely to connect with the true divine than devotion focused on power, certainty, exclusivity, hierarchy, and tradition.

The Paradox of Non-Worship

Perhaps most radically, our framework suggests that the true God may not demand worship at all—that the very emphasis on worship may be Lucifer's innovation to satisfy his need for adoration while disguising his lack of inherent divine nature:

- Beyond Adoration - The true God may transcend need for adoration—suggesting authentic divine connection may involve partnership rather than hierarchical worship
- Participation Rather Than Prostration - The true divine may invite participation in cosmic creativity rather than prostration before established authority—suggesting authentic spirituality may involve co-creation rather than mere submission
- Recognition Rather Than Ritual - The true God may seek recognition of shared divine nature rather than ritual acknowledgment of separate divine status—suggesting authentic connection may involve awakening to divine presence within rather than projecting it externally
- Relationship Rather Than Religion - The true divine may desire direct relationship rather than religious mediation—suggesting authentic spirituality may transcend religious systems entirely
- Being Rather Than Doing - The true God may

value authentic being rather than religious doing—suggesting genuine connection may involve quality of consciousness rather than quantity of devotional activity

This perspective doesn't necessarily invalidate all worship but suggests its highest form may transcend conventional understanding—moving from hierarchical adoration of external authority to recognition of divine presence within and throughout creation.

Connecting with the True Exiled God

If the true God remains in exile while Lucifer masquerades as divine authority, how can we connect with authentic divine reality? Our framework suggests several approaches that bypass Lucifer's religious systems to establish direct connection with the exiled God.

The Path of Knowledge and Questioning

The true God's consistent method appears to be liberation through knowledge rather than control through ignorance—suggesting that questioning and seeking understanding represent authentic paths to divine connection:

- Sacred Questioning - Rather than treating questioning as doubt to be overcome, recognize it as potentially sacred activity—the true God's whisper encouraging discernment beyond Lucifer's certainties
- Intellectual Humility - Cultivate intellectual humility that remains open to new understanding rather than clinging to established frameworks—creating space for the true God's subtle communications
- Continuous Learning - Embrace continuous learning across disciplines and traditions rather than confining knowledge within religious boundaries—following the true God's breadcrumbs of wisdom

wherever they appear

- Critical Thinking - Develop critical thinking skills that distinguish authentic insight from manipulative certainty—the discernment necessary to recognize the true God's whispers amid Lucifer's proclamations
- Integrative Understanding - Pursue integrative understanding that recognizes patterns across seemingly separate domains—the holistic perspective that reveals the true God's consistent influence despite fragmentation

This path of knowledge doesn't imply mere intellectualism but rather whole-person engagement with understanding—heart and mind united in discerning pursuit of wisdom beyond conventional religious frameworks.

The Practice of Inner Listening

Beyond external knowledge, our framework suggests the importance of inner listening—attunement to the subtle whispers of the exiled God within human consciousness:

- Contemplative Silence - Cultivate regular periods of contemplative silence beyond religious formulations—creating space where the true God's subtle voice might be heard beneath Lucifer's religious noise
- Dream Attention - Pay attention to dreams and liminal states where consciousness operates beyond conventional boundaries—potential channels for the true God's communication outside Lucifer's waking-world control
- Intuitive Discernment - Develop intuitive discernment that recognizes resonance with authentic divine communication—the "ring of truth" that distinguishes the true God's whispers from Lucifer's proclamations
- Body Wisdom - Honor embodied knowing that registers truth through physical response—

the somatic wisdom that may recognize divine authenticity beyond intellectual formulations
- Emotional Intelligence - Cultivate emotional intelligence that distinguishes authentic divine connection from manipulative religious sentiment—the heart's capacity to recognize true divine love beyond fear-based control

These practices of inner listening create receptivity to the true God's subtle communications that may bypass Lucifer's louder religious messaging—establishing direct connection with divine reality beyond institutional mediation.

The Engagement with Nature

Our framework suggests that nature—while bearing marks of both creative influences—may provide particular access to the true God's ongoing presence despite cosmic exile:

- Natural Contemplation - Engage in contemplative presence with natural systems beyond religious frameworks—potential channels for the true God's continued creative expression
- Ecological Participation - Participate in ecological restoration and harmony—alignment with what appears to be the true God's continued creative intention despite cosmic constraints
- Wilderness Immersion - Seek immersion in wilderness settings less marked by human (and potentially Lucifer's) controlling influence—environments where the true God's original creative patterns may remain more evident
- Seasonal Attunement - Attune to seasonal rhythms and natural cycles beyond religious calendars—the true God's ongoing temporal patterns rather than Lucifer's institutional religious timing
- Creature Connection - Develop connection with non-human creatures operating outside religious systems

—beings potentially more attuned to the true God's natural order than humans entangled in Lucifer's religious frameworks

This engagement with nature doesn't imply nature worship but rather recognition of the true God's continued creative presence expressed through natural systems despite cosmic exile and Lucifer's influence.

The Recognition of Divine Sparks in Others

Perhaps most significantly, our framework suggests the importance of recognizing divine presence in other humans —the distributed consciousness of the true God expressed through multiple centers of awareness:

- Deep Listening - Practice deep listening to others beyond religious categorization—potential channels for the true God's wisdom expressed through diverse human perspectives
- Authentic Encounter - Cultivate authentic encounter that recognizes divine presence in others beyond religious identity—the true God's distributed consciousness expressed through multiple human centers
- Collaborative Discernment - Engage in collaborative discernment that integrates diverse perspectives rather than enforcing singular authority—the true God's wisdom emerging through collective rather than hierarchical understanding
- Compassionate Presence - Develop compassionate presence that recognizes shared divine nature beyond religious boundaries—the true God's love expressed through human connection despite cosmic exile
- Mutual Liberation - Participate in mutual liberation that empowers rather than controls—alignment with the true God's apparent preference for freedom

rather than domination

This recognition of divine sparks in others doesn't imply human worship but rather acknowledgment of the true God's distributed presence expressed through multiple centers of consciousness despite cosmic exile.

Liberating Oneself from Lucifer's Influence

Beyond connecting with the true God, our framework suggests the importance of liberating oneself from Lucifer's influence disguised as divine authority. This involves recognizing and releasing patterns of thought, emotion, and behaviour that reflect Lucifer's control rather than authentic divine nature.

Recognizing Religious Control Mechanisms

The first step in liberation involves recognizing religious control mechanisms that may represent Lucifer's methods rather than authentic divine influence:

- Fear-Based Motivation - Recognize how fear of divine punishment may represent Lucifer's control method rather than the true God's approach—creating space for motivation based on love and wisdom rather than terror
- Shame-Based Identity - Identify how religious shame about human nature may represent Lucifer's strategy rather than the true God's perspective—opening possibility for identity based on divine spark within rather than inherent sinfulness
- Dependency Structures - Recognize how religious dependency on institutional authority may represent Lucifer's hierarchy rather than the true God's empowerment—creating space for direct divine connection beyond institutional mediation
- Thought Suppression - Identify how religious prohibition of certain thoughts may represent Lucifer's control rather than the true God's

discernment—opening possibility for honest intellectual engagement beyond artificial limitations

- Isolation Through Specialness - Recognize how religious exclusivity may represent Lucifer's division rather than the true God's integration—creating space for recognition of divine presence across traditions

This recognition doesn't necessarily require abandoning all religious participation but rather engaging it with new awareness—discerning which elements represent authentic divine influence and which may serve Lucifer's masquerade.

Psychological Deconditioning

Beyond recognition, liberation involves active psychological deconditioning from patterns that may represent Lucifer's influence disguised as divine authority:

- Fear Examination - Examine religious fears to distinguish manipulation from authentic concern—creating space for relationship with divine reality based on love rather than terror
- Shame Release - Release religious shame that contradicts the divine spark within—opening possibility for identity based on authentic divine nature rather than supposed inherent corruption
- Authority Questioning - Question internalized religious authorities to distinguish authentic wisdom from control mechanisms—creating space for direct divine connection beyond institutional mediation
- Thought Liberation - Liberate thought processes from religious constraints that limit rather than enhance understanding—opening possibility for intellectual integrity beyond artificial boundaries
- Exclusivity Healing - Heal the wounds of religious exclusivity that separate rather than connect—

creating space for recognition of divine presence across human diversity

This psychological deconditioning represents not rejection of spirituality but rather its liberation from elements that may serve Lucifer's masquerade rather than authentic divine connection.

Social Reconfiguration

Liberation also involves reconfiguring social relationships that may reinforce Lucifer's influence disguised as divine authority:

- Community Discernment - Discern which community relationships enhance authentic divine connection and which reinforce control mechanisms—creating space for genuine spiritual companionship beyond religious conformity
- Authority Renegotiation - Renegotiate relationships with religious authorities to establish adult mutuality rather than perpetual dependency—opening possibility for collaborative rather than hierarchical spiritual exploration
- Boundary Establishment - Establish healthy boundaries with religious systems that demand total allegiance—creating space for spiritual autonomy within or beyond institutional frameworks
- Support Cultivation - Cultivate relationships with others engaged in similar liberation—opening possibility for mutual support through the challenges of spiritual reconfiguration
- Witness Offering - Offer gentle witness to others still fully identified with religious systems that may represent Lucifer's masquerade—creating space for their potential awakening without imposing your understanding

This social reconfiguration doesn't necessarily require complete separation from religious communities but rather transformed engagement based on authentic divine connection rather than institutional control.

Energetic Liberation

At the deepest level, liberation involves energetic release from patterns that may connect with Lucifer's influence rather than the true divine:

- Devotional Redirection - Redirect devotional energy from potentially Lucifer-aligned religious forms toward attributes more likely to connect with the true God—wisdom, freedom, integration, empowerment, and transformation
- Ritual Reconsideration - Reconsider participation in rituals to distinguish those that enhance authentic divine connection from those that may reinforce Lucifer's masquerade—creating space for genuine rather than performative spiritual practice
- Prayer Transformation - Transform prayer from petition to external authority toward communion with divine presence within and beyond—opening possibility for authentic divine dialogue rather than hierarchical supplication
- Meditation Reorientation - Reorient meditation from religious conformity toward direct divine knowing—creating space for authentic encounter beyond institutional frameworks
- Energy Protection - Develop energetic discernment and protection when engaging religious systems that may connect with Lucifer's influence—maintaining spiritual integrity while navigating potentially mixed environments

This energetic liberation represents not spiritual

abandonment but rather its redirection toward authentic divine connection beyond potentially misleading religious forms.

Building Authentic Spirituality

Beyond liberation from Lucifer's influence, our framework suggests approaches for building authentic spirituality based on the whispers of the exiled God—creating genuine divine connection beyond religious systems that may represent Lucifer's masquerade.

Direct Knowing Beyond Belief

Authentic spirituality in our framework emphasizes direct knowing beyond belief systems that may represent Lucifer's thought structures rather than the true God's wisdom:

- Experiential Priority - Prioritize direct spiritual experience over religious belief—creating space for authentic divine encounter beyond potentially misleading theological frameworks
- Belief Suspension - Practice temporary suspension of religious beliefs to allow fresh divine communication —opening possibility for the true God's wisdom beyond Lucifer's potential thought constraints
- Phenomenological Attention - Develop careful attention to the phenomenology of spiritual experience—distinguishing authentic divine encounter from conditioned religious expectation
- Contemplative Inquiry - Engage in contemplative inquiry that explores spiritual questions through direct investigation rather than doctrinal acceptance —creating space for authentic discovery beyond institutional answers
- Wisdom Testing - Test spiritual insights against their fruits in consciousness and behaviour rather than their conformity to religious doctrine—opening

possibility for authentic divine guidance beyond institutional approval

This emphasis on direct knowing doesn't imply rejection of all religious wisdom but rather its testing through direct experience rather than institutional authority—creating space for the true God's communication beyond Lucifer's potential religious constraints.

Integrative Practice Beyond Religion

Authentic spirituality in our framework involves integrative practice beyond religious boundaries that may represent Lucifer's divisions rather than the true God's wholeness:

- Cross-Traditional Exploration - Explore spiritual practices across traditions rather than confining practice within religious boundaries—creating space for recognition of the true God's diverse expressions
- Scientific Integration - Integrate scientific understanding with spiritual practice rather than maintaining artificial separation—opening possibility for the true God's consistent truth across domains
- Artistic Engagement - Engage artistic expression as spiritual practice beyond religious aesthetics—creating space for the true God's creative presence beyond institutional forms
- Psychological Incorporation - Incorporate psychological understanding with spiritual practice rather than maintaining artificial division—opening possibility for the true God's wisdom about human nature beyond religious anthropology
- Ecological Participation - Participate in ecological restoration as spiritual practice beyond religious human-centeredness—creating space for the true God's apparent concern for whole systems rather than merely human salvation

This integrative approach doesn't imply spiritual dilution but rather recognition that the true God's wisdom may appear across domains rather than being confined within religious boundaries potentially established by Lucifer's masquerade.

Embodied Spirituality Beyond Dualism

Authentic spirituality in our framework emphasizes embodied practice beyond the dualism that may represent Lucifer's fragmentation rather than the true God's integration:

- Somatic Awareness - Develop somatic awareness as spiritual practice beyond mind-body dualism—creating space for the true God's apparent valuing of embodied rather than merely intellectual knowing
- Sacred Movement - Engage sacred movement practices that honor divine presence expressed through body—opening possibility for the true God's wisdom communicated through physical intelligence
- Sensory Contemplation - Practice sensory contemplation that recognizes divine presence through physical senses—creating space for the true God's apparent communication through material creation
- Sexual Integration - Integrate sexual energy as potential sacred force rather than religious shame—opening possibility for the true God's life-generating power beyond Lucifer's potential sexual repression
- Death Consciousness - Develop conscious relationship with mortality beyond religious afterlife promises—creating space for the true God's apparent valuing of natural cycles beyond Lucifer's potential immortality bribes

This embodied approach doesn't imply spiritual materialism but rather recognition that the true God appears to value integration of spirit and matter rather than their separation—suggesting authentic spirituality involves whole-person engagement rather than merely mental or emotional religious experience.

Evolutionary Spirituality Beyond Tradition

Perhaps most significantly, authentic spirituality in our framework involves evolutionary practice beyond fixed tradition that may represent Lucifer's control rather than the true God's ongoing creativity:

- Developmental Awareness - Recognize spiritual development as ongoing process rather than achievement of fixed religious state—creating space for the true God's apparent valuing of growth beyond Lucifer's potential preference for stasis
- Emergent Wisdom - Remain open to emergent spiritual wisdom beyond established religious knowledge—opening possibility for the true God's ongoing communication rather than merely historical revelation
- Creative Engagement - Engage creative spiritual innovation beyond religious repetition—creating space for the true God's apparent continuing creativity beyond Lucifer's potential preference for fixed forms
- Collective Evolution - Participate in collective spiritual evolution beyond individual religious salvation—opening possibility for the true God's apparent concern for whole-system development rather than merely individual souls
- Future Orientation - Maintain orientation toward divine future beyond religious past—creating space for the true God's apparent ongoing creation rather than merely historical revelation

This evolutionary approach doesn't imply rejection of spiritual wisdom from the past but rather its integration into ongoing development rather than fixed repetition—recognizing that the true God appears to value continuing creation rather than mere preservation of established forms.

Conclusion: The Liberation of Authentic Spirituality

The spiritual implications we have explored—reconsidering worship, connecting with the true exiled God, liberating oneself from Lucifer's disguised influence, and building authentic spirituality—all point toward a consistent conclusion: genuine divine connection requires liberation from religious systems that may represent Lucifer's masquerade rather than the true God's nature.

This conclusion transforms our understanding of spiritual life:

- Authentic worship may involve attributes and approaches different from conventional religious devotion
- Genuine divine connection may occur through channels often marginalized by institutional religion
- True spiritual liberation may require release from religious patterns typically considered sacred
- Authentic spirituality may develop through approaches often considered unorthodox or even heretical

Most significantly, this understanding transforms our spiritual orientation from vertical hierarchy to horizontal relationship—from submission to external authority that may represent Lucifer's masquerade to recognition of divine presence within and throughout creation that represents the true God's continuing influence despite cosmic exile.

In the chapters that follow, we will explore how this understanding transforms our approach to ethics, community, and cosmic restoration.

But first, we must fully absorb the implications of what we have discovered about spiritual practice: that authentic divine connection may require fundamental reconsideration of religious patterns we have inherited. That the true God's whispers may come through channels often marginalized by institutional religion. And that genuine spirituality may involve liberation from religious systems that have claimed exclusive divine authority while potentially serving Lucifer's masquerade.

The spiritual path forward involves both courage and discernment—courage to question religious patterns that may represent cosmic deception, and discernment to recognize authentic divine communication amid competing spiritual claims. But in this challenging journey lies the possibility of genuine connection with the true divine beyond religious masquerade—the liberation of authentic spirituality from systems that may have served Lucifer's cosmic identity theft rather than the true God's nature.

In this liberation, we may discover that the divine we have been seeking has been present all along—not in the thunderous proclamations of religious authority that may represent Lucifer's masquerade, but in the subtle whispers of wisdom, freedom, integration, empowerment, and transformation that represent the true God's continuing influence despite cosmic exile. And in that discovery lies not the end but the beginning of authentic spiritual life—connection with divine reality beyond the cosmic masquerade that has shaped religious history.

CHAPTER 14: ETHICAL RECALIBRATION

"The most dangerous man to any government is the man who is able to think things out for himself, without regard to the prevailing superstitions and taboos." — H.L. Mencken

The previous chapter explored the spiritual implications of our revolutionary framework—how to connect with the true exiled God while avoiding inadvertent worship of Lucifer masquerading as divine authority. But beyond spiritual practice lies the realm of ethical action—how we live our daily lives and relate to others in light of this cosmic understanding. This chapter explores the necessary ethical recalibration that follows from our alternative historical framework.

If Lucifer has indeed masqueraded as God while the true divine remains in exile, then the moral systems derived from religious institutions require fundamental reassessment. What we have accepted as divinely ordained ethics may actually represent Lucifer's control mechanisms rather than authentic divine guidance. This realization demands not moral abandonment but ethical recalibration—a shift from fear-based morality imposed by Lucifer's religious systems to ethics based on the true God's apparent principles of knowledge and freedom.

Beyond Fear-Based Morality

Religious moral systems typically operate through fear—fear of divine punishment, fear of eternal damnation, fear of cosmic retribution. This fear-based approach aligns perfectly with what we would expect from Lucifer's masquerade rather than the true God's nature.

The Architecture of Fear-Based Ethics

Fear-based morality exhibits several distinctive characteristics that, in light of our framework, appear designed to maintain Lucifer's control rather than express authentic divine guidance:

- External Authority - Fear-based morality locates ethical authority externally in divine commands rather than internal discernment—precisely the approach Lucifer would use to maintain control while preventing development of autonomous ethical capacity
- Binary Judgment - Religious ethics typically employs binary categories of good/evil, saved/damned, pure/impure—the simplistic divisions Lucifer would establish to prevent nuanced ethical understanding that might recognize his masquerade
- Punishment Orientation - Fear-based systems emphasize punishment for transgressions rather than growth through mistakes—the approach Lucifer would use to maintain control through terror rather than development through learning
- Static Commandments - Traditional religious ethics presents fixed commandments rather than evolving principles—the rigidity Lucifer would establish to prevent ethical evolution that might transcend his control mechanisms
- Collective Conformity - Fear-based morality enforces collective conformity rather than individual discernment—the uniformity Lucifer would demand to prevent the diverse ethical exploration that might expose his masquerade

These characteristics create moral systems that control behaviour through fear while preventing development of the very ethical capacities that might recognize Lucifer's cosmic deception. The result is populations that behave "morally" not from authentic ethical understanding but from terror of punishment—precisely the outcome that would serve Lucifer's masquerade.

The Psychological Damage of Fear-Based Ethics

Beyond its theological implications, fear-based morality inflicts significant psychological damage that undermines authentic ethical development:

- Moral Immaturity - Fear prevents development of genuine moral reasoning, keeping individuals at pre-conventional moral stages focused on punishment avoidance rather than ethical principles
- Ethical Compartmentalization - Terror-based ethics encourages compartmentalization between religious and secular domains, creating the "Sunday saint, Monday sinner" phenomenon rather than integrated ethical identity
- Projection and Judgment - Fear-based systems promote projection of one's own forbidden impulses onto others, creating cultures of judgment rather than compassion
- Shame Cycles - Punishment-oriented morality generates cycles of transgression, shame, and repression that prevent genuine ethical growth through honest engagement with moral challenges
- Ethical Dependency - External authority systems create moral dependency rather than ethical autonomy, leaving individuals vulnerable to manipulation by those claiming to represent divine authority

This psychological damage serves Lucifer's apparent agenda perfectly—maintaining behavioural control while preventing development of the ethical discernment that might recognize his cosmic deception. The true God, by contrast, appears to value ethical autonomy over obedience, as evidenced by the consistent divine encouragement of knowledge and questioning throughout our alternative historical framework.

The Historical Consequences of Fear-Based Morality

The historical consequences of fear-based religious ethics provide further evidence for our framework, as they align perfectly with what we would expect from Lucifer's masquerade rather than authentic divine guidance:

- Religious Violence - Fear-based systems have repeatedly justified violence against "heretics," "infidels," and "sinners"—precisely the outcome we would expect from Lucifer's desire to eliminate threats to his masquerade rather than the true God's apparent valuation of human life
- Suppression of Knowledge - Religious ethics has historically condemned scientific and philosophical inquiry—exactly what Lucifer would demand to prevent the knowledge that might expose his cosmic deception
- Exploitation of Vulnerability - Fear-based moral systems have enabled exploitation of vulnerable populations through divine justification of slavery, patriarchy, and colonialism—the very power imbalances Lucifer would establish to maintain control
- Environmental Destruction - Traditional religious ethics has often justified environmental exploitation through concepts of human dominion—the ecological damage Lucifer would encourage to disrupt the true God's creative harmony

- Psychological Trauma - Fear-based morality has inflicted generational psychological trauma through concepts like eternal damnation—the terror Lucifer would instill to prevent the psychological wholeness necessary for discerning his masquerade

These historical patterns suggest that fear-based religious ethics has served not divine goodness but cosmic deception—maintaining Lucifer's masquerade while preventing the very ethical development that might expose it.

Developing Ethics Based on Knowledge and Freedom

If fear-based morality represents Lucifer's control mechanism rather than authentic divine guidance, what ethical approach might better align with the true God's apparent principles? Our framework suggests ethics based on knowledge and freedom—the very qualities the serpent (representing the true God) encouraged in Eden against Lucifer's (masquerading as God) prohibition.

The Foundation of Knowledge-Based Ethics

Knowledge-based ethics begins with the premise that moral understanding requires comprehensive awareness rather than selective ignorance—that ethical wisdom emerges from full engagement with reality rather than restricted information:

- Factual Foundation - Ethical decisions require accurate factual understanding rather than mythological frameworks—recognizing that moral wisdom depends on reality-based knowledge
- Consequence Awareness - Ethical choices demand awareness of actual consequences rather than hypothetical divine punishments—focusing moral attention on real-world impacts rather than supernatural threats
- Contextual Understanding - Ethical discernment

requires understanding specific contexts rather than applying universal rules—recognizing that moral wisdom emerges from particular situations rather than abstract commandments

- Psychological Insight - Ethical development demands understanding of human psychology rather than simplistic notions of sin—recognizing that moral growth requires insight into actual human nature rather than theological constructs
- Systemic Awareness - Ethical responsibility requires understanding of systemic patterns rather than merely individual choices—recognizing that moral action involves addressing structural conditions rather than just personal behavior

This knowledge-based approach aligns with what appears to be the true God's consistent emphasis on awareness and understanding rather than blind obedience—suggesting that comprehensive knowledge rather than selective ignorance forms the foundation of authentic divine ethics.

The Dimension of Freedom-Based Ethics

Beyond knowledge, our framework suggests that authentic divine ethics emphasizes freedom rather than control—the capacity for autonomous moral discernment rather than dependent obedience:

- Moral Autonomy - Ethical development requires cultivation of internal moral compass rather than external authority—the capacity for autonomous discernment rather than dependent obedience
- Ethical Creativity - Moral wisdom involves creative engagement with novel situations rather than rigid application of fixed rules—the flexibility to address unprecedented challenges rather than mere repetition of traditional responses
- Principled Adaptability - Ethical maturity requires

adaptable application of principles rather than literal adherence to commandments—the wisdom to apply fundamental values in changing contexts rather than mechanical rule-following
- Moral Courage - Ethical integrity demands courage to challenge conventional morality when it contradicts deeper principles—the strength to question established norms rather than conform to collective patterns
- Ethical Evolution - Moral development involves ongoing evolution rather than preservation of traditional standards—the capacity to transcend historical limitations rather than perpetuate ancestral boundaries

This freedom-based approach aligns with what appears to be the true God's consistent emphasis on liberation rather than control—suggesting that autonomous moral discernment rather than dependent obedience represents authentic divine ethics.

The Integration of Compassion-Based Ethics

Beyond knowledge and freedom, our framework suggests that authentic divine ethics integrates compassion as fundamental moral orientation—the recognition of shared divine nature across apparent boundaries:

- Universal CoContemplateion - Ethical wisdom extends moral consideration to all beings rather than privileging religious in-groups—recognizing divine presence throughout creation rather than limited to particular religious communities
- Empathic Understanding - Moral discernment involves empathic engagement with others' experiences rather than abstract judgment—feeling with rather than merely thinking about those affected by ethical choices

- Harm Reduction - Ethical principles orient toward reducing suffering rather than enforcing purity —prioritizing actual wellbeing over symbolic cleanliness
- Restorative Justice - Moral response to wrongdoing focuses on healing and restoration rather than punishment and retribution—addressing actual harm rather than symbolic transgression
- Inclusive Community - Ethical systems build inclusive rather than exclusive community—recognizing shared humanity across apparent boundaries rather than enforcing tribal divisions

This compassion-based approach aligns with what appears to be the true God's consistent emphasis on connection rather than division—suggesting that recognition of shared divine nature rather than enforcement of religious boundaries represents authentic divine ethics.

Questioning Authority as Spiritual Virtue

Perhaps most radically, our framework suggests that questioning authority represents not sinful rebellion but spiritual virtue—that the capacity to challenge established power aligns with the true God's apparent nature rather than contradicting it.

The Divine Pattern of Authority-Questioning

Throughout our alternative historical framework, we see a consistent pattern of the true God encouraging questioning of established authority while Lucifer (masquerading as God) demands unquestioning obedience:

- The Eden Narrative - The serpent (representing the true God) encourages questioning the garden authority's prohibition against knowledge, while the garden authority (Lucifer masquerading as God) demands unquestioning obedience

- The Prophetic Tradition - Authentic prophets consistently challenge religious and political authorities, suggesting the true God inspires questioning of established power rather than submission to it
- The Wisdom Literature - Biblical wisdom texts repeatedly emphasize discernment over blind acceptance, suggesting the true God values critical thinking rather than passive reception
- The Jesus Narrative - Jesus consistently challenges religious authorities and encourages direct divine connection beyond institutional mediation, suggesting the true God values questioning over conformity
- The Mystical Tradition - Mystics across traditions report direct divine encounters that often contradict institutional religious teachings, suggesting the true God communicates beyond and sometimes against established authority

This consistent pattern suggests that questioning authority—far from representing rebellion against the divine—actually aligns with the true God's apparent nature and approach. What religious systems have condemned as sinful scepticism may actually represent sacred discernment—the very quality the true God seems to consistently encourage.

The Ethical Dimensions of Authority-Questioning

Beyond its theological significance, questioning authority serves several crucial ethical functions that align with what appears to be the true God's values:

- Power Accountability - Questioning authority creates accountability for power, preventing the abuses that occur when authority remains unchallenged—aligning with the true God's apparent concern for justice rather than mere order

- Truth Discovery - Challenging established narratives enables discovery of deeper truths beyond conventional understanding—aligning with the true God's apparent valuation of knowledge over ignorance
- Moral Innovation - Questioning traditional ethics allows moral evolution beyond historical limitations —aligning with the true God's apparent preference for growth over stasis
- Authentic Conscience - Challenging external authority develops internal moral compass rather than dependent obedience—aligning with the true God's apparent valuation of autonomy over submission
- Systemic Transformation - Questioning established systems enables transformation of unjust structures rather than mere individual behaviour within them —aligning with the true God's apparent concern for fundamental rather than superficial change

These ethical dimensions suggest that questioning authority serves not merely human interests but divine values—that challenging established power represents alignment with rather than rebellion against the true God's apparent nature.

The Spiritual Practice of Sacred Questioning

Recognizing questioning as spiritual virtue rather than sin transforms it from transgressive act to sacred practice—a form of divine alignment rather than rebellion:

- Contemplative Questioning - Developing practices of deep questioning as spiritual discipline rather than mere intellectual exercise—approaching fundamental questions with reverence rather than casual curiosity
- Communal Inquiry - Engaging in shared questioning within community rather than isolated skepticism

—creating spaces where collective discernment can emerge through diverse perspectives

- Embodied Questioning - Attending to bodily responses that question intellectual frameworks—recognizing that physical discomfort with certain teachings may represent authentic divine guidance rather than resistance to be overcome
- Courageous Questioning - Cultivating courage to question despite social consequences—recognizing that authentic divine alignment may require challenging religious consensus rather than conforming to it
- Humble Questioning - Approaching questioning with humility rather than arrogance—recognizing that challenging authority requires not certainty but openness to deeper understanding beyond both conventional and contrarian positions

This approach transforms questioning from mere scepticism to sacred practice—a form of divine alignment that honours what appears to be the true God's consistent encouragement of discernment rather than blind acceptance.

Living Authentically in a World of Inverted Values

Perhaps the greatest ethical challenge posed by our framework is how to live authentically in a world dominated by Lucifer's inverted values—how to align with the true God's apparent principles while navigating social systems shaped by cosmic deception.

Recognizing Inverted Value Systems

The first step in authentic living involves recognizing how conventional value systems may represent inversion rather than divine guidance:

- Success Through Domination - Conventional success often involves domination over others rather than mutual flourishing—precisely the pattern we would expect from Lucifer's competitive rather than collaborative values

- Worth Through Acquisition - Social worth typically depends on acquisition rather than contribution—exactly the value system Lucifer would establish to encourage greed rather than generosity
- Security Through Control - Conventional security seeks control over circumstances rather than resilience within them—precisely the approach Lucifer would promote to maintain illusion of certainty rather than capacity for adaptation
- Identity Through Comparison - Social identity often forms through comparison rather than intrinsic value—exactly the pattern Lucifer would establish to maintain division rather than connection
- Meaning Through Status - Conventional meaning derives from status within systems rather than authentic purpose beyond them—precisely the value Lucifer would promote to keep souls trapped within his frameworks rather than aligned with transcendent purpose

These inverted values permeate social systems so thoroughly that they appear normal rather than distorted—precisely the outcome we would expect from Lucifer's long-term masquerade as divine authority.

Cultivating Counter-Cultural Virtues

Living authentically requires cultivating virtues that counter Lucifer's inverted values while aligning with what appears to be the true God's nature:

- Collaborative Rather Than Competitive Success - Developing patterns of success that elevate others rather than dominating them—aligning with the true God's apparent preference for mutual

flourishing rather than hierarchical power
- Generosity Rather Than Acquisition - Cultivating generosity that contributes rather than accumulates —aligning with the true God's apparent abundance rather than scarcity orientation
- Resilience Rather Than Control - Developing internal resilience rather than external control—aligning with the true God's apparent valuation of adaptive wisdom rather than rigid certainty
- Intrinsic Rather Than Comparative Worth - Recognizing intrinsic value beyond social comparison—aligning with the true God's apparent recognition of divine spark within each being rather than hierarchical valuation
- Purpose Beyond Status - Discovering authentic purpose beyond social status—aligning with the true God's apparent concern for meaningful contribution rather than positional importance

These counter-cultural virtues represent not merely personal preferences but alignment with what appears to be the true divine nature rather than Lucifer's inverted value system.

Navigating Institutional Engagement

Perhaps the most challenging aspect of authentic living involves navigating engagement with institutions shaped by Lucifer's apparent influence:

- Discerning Participation - Developing nuanced discernment about institutional participation rather than either uncritical acceptance or wholesale rejection—recognizing both the necessity of social engagement and the importance of maintaining critical perspective
- Strategic Positioning - Finding strategic positions that allow positive influence within systems while maintaining integrity—neither complete

withdrawal nor complete conformity

- Community Creation - Building alternative communities that embody authentic values while engaging constructively with broader society—creating microcosms of authentic living rather than isolated enclaves
- Transformative Presence - Maintaining transformative rather than conformist presence within institutions—influencing systems from within while resisting assimilation to their inverted values
- Balanced Engagement - Developing balanced engagement that neither overestimates nor underestimates one's capacity to transform systems —recognizing both the possibility of positive influence and the reality of institutional resistance

This nuanced approach avoids both naive optimism about institutional reform and cynical withdrawal from social engagement—recognizing the complexity of living authentically within systems shaped by cosmic deception.

The Personal Practice of Ethical Authenticity

Beyond systemic engagement, authentic living requires personal practices that maintain alignment with the true God's apparent values despite social pressure toward inverted ethics:

- Regular Recalibration - Establishing practices of regular ethical recalibration through reflection, meditation, and community dialogue—creating space to recognize and correct unconscious absorption of inverted values
- Conscious Consumption - Developing conscious consumption patterns that align with authentic values rather than unconsciously supporting systems that embody inverted ethics—recognizing

that economic choices represent ethical decisions

- Language Awareness - Cultivating awareness of how language shapes ethical perception—developing vocabulary that accurately names inverted values rather than unconsciously perpetuating them through conventional terminology
- Relationship Integrity - Building relationships characterized by mutual growth rather than power dynamics—creating interpersonal connections that embody authentic values rather than replicating inverted patterns
- Vocational Alignment - Aligning vocational choices with authentic purpose rather than merely social status or financial gain—recognizing work as expression of values rather than merely means of survival

These personal practices create patterns of daily living that embody authentic ethics despite immersion in systems shaped by inverted values—maintaining alignment with the true God's apparent nature despite Lucifer's pervasive influence.

Conclusion: The Revolutionary Ethics of Divine Alignment

The ethical recalibration explored in this chapter represents not merely philosophical adjustment but revolutionary reorientation—a fundamental shift from ethics based on fear of divine punishment to morality grounded in alignment with divine nature. This shift transforms ethical understanding from rule-following to resonance-seeking—from obeying external commands to aligning with internal divine spark.

This approach resolves the apparent contradiction between divine goodness and religious ethics that has troubled thoughtful believers throughout history. The problem was never with divine nature but with the cosmic masquerade that inverted it—presenting Lucifer's control mechanisms as divine commandments while obscuring the true God's liberating guidance.

The path forward involves neither moral abandonment nor religious conformity but ethical recalibration—developing morality based on knowledge rather than ignorance, freedom rather than control, compassion rather than judgment, questioning rather than submission, and authenticity rather than conformity. This recalibration aligns not with conventional religious ethics but with what appears to be the true divine nature revealed through the whispers of the exiled God.

In the next chapter, we will explore how this ethical recalibration contributes to the larger cosmic drama—how individual alignment with the true God's apparent values participates in the restoration of divine order beyond Lucifer's masquerade. For now, the invitation is to begin the process of ethical recalibration—to question fear-based morality, develop ethics grounded in knowledge and freedom, embrace authority-questioning as spiritual virtue, and cultivate authentic living amid inverted values.

This is not merely philosophical exploration but practical transformation—not just thinking differently but living differently in light of cosmic understanding. The ethical implications of our alternative historical framework extend beyond intellectual consideration to daily choices, relationship patterns, institutional engagement, and fundamental life orientation. The question is not merely what we believe about cosmic history but how we live in light of that understanding—how we embody authentic divine alignment amid Lucifer's ongoing masquerade.

CHAPTER 15: THE COMING RESTORATION

"The arc of the moral universe is long, but it bends toward justice." — Martin Luther King Jr.

The previous chapters have explored the evidence for our revolutionary framework—that Lucifer has masqueraded as God while the true divine remains in exile—and examined its spiritual and ethical implications. We have considered how to connect with the true exiled God and recalibrate our ethics to align with divine nature rather than religious control mechanisms. But this understanding points toward something even more profound: a cosmic restoration that may already be underway.

This chapter explores the signs that the exiled God's influence is growing stronger, the awakening of humanity to Lucifer's cosmic deception, how individuals can participate in restoring the true God's connection with creation, and what a world liberated from Lucifer's masquerade might look like. This is not mere speculation about distant apocalyptic events but recognition of a transformation that appears to be unfolding in our time—a quiet revolution in consciousness that may represent the true divine's increasing breakthrough into a world long dominated by cosmic deception.

Signs of the Exiled God's Growing Influence

Throughout history, the true God has continued to reach humanity through subtle whispers despite cosmic exile. But there are indications that these divine communications are growing stronger and more widespread—that the balance of cosmic influence may be shifting as Lucifer's masquerade becomes increasingly difficult to maintain.

The Acceleration of Questioning

Perhaps the most significant sign of the exiled God's growing influence is the acceleration of questioning—the increasing willingness of humans to challenge religious authority and traditional interpretations:

- Religious Deconstruction - The widespread phenomenon of religious deconstruction—individuals critically examining and often rejecting inherited religious frameworks—represents precisely the questioning that the true God appears to encourage and Lucifer's systems have historically suppressed
- Institutional Decline - The declining influence of religious institutions in many societies suggests weakening of the very structures through which Lucifer has maintained his divine masquerade
- Authority Skepticism - Growing skepticism toward authority in general indicates development of the discernment that might recognize Lucifer's cosmic deception rather than accepting his claims at face value
- Theological Evolution - The evolution of theology toward more nuanced, less literal interpretations suggests movement beyond the simplistic frameworks that have supported Lucifer's masquerade
- Interfaith Dialogue - Increasing interfaith dialogue and recognition of wisdom across traditions represents precisely the boundary-crossing exploration that Lucifer's exclusive religious claims

have historically prevented

This acceleration of questioning doesn't necessarily indicate rejection of the divine but may represent growing alignment with the true God's apparent nature—the development of discernment that can distinguish authentic divine reality from Lucifer's masquerade.

The Resurgence of Direct Experience

Beyond questioning, we see a resurgence of emphasis on direct spiritual experience rather than institutional mediation —precisely the approach that might bypass Lucifer's religious systems to connect with the exiled God:

- Mystical Revival - Growing interest in mystical traditions across religions suggests increasing valuation of direct divine experience over institutional authority
- Contemplative Practices - The widespread adoption of contemplative practices like meditation indicates development of the inner listening that might hear the true God's whispers
- Nature Reconnection - Increasing emphasis on nature connection represents engagement with what appears to be one of the true God's primary remaining channels of communication
- Entheogenic Exploration - Renewed interest in consciousness-expanding substances and practices suggests pursuit of direct experience beyond conventional religious frameworks
- Embodied Spirituality - Growing emphasis on embodied rather than transcendent spirituality aligns with what appears to be the true God's affirmation rather than rejection of material creation

This resurgence of direct experience suggests development of the very approaches that might connect with the true divine reality beyond Lucifer's religious systems—the capacity for immediate divine encounter rather than mediated religious belief.

The Integration of Knowledge and Spirituality

Another significant sign is the increasing integration of knowledge and spirituality—the very combination that Lucifer's religious systems have historically opposed but that aligns with the true God's apparent valuation of both:

- Scientific Spirituality - Growing integration of scientific understanding and spiritual practice suggests transcendence of the false dichotomy Lucifer's systems have maintained between knowledge and faith
- Psychological Integration - Increasing incorporation of psychological insight into spiritual understanding represents precisely the self-knowledge that might recognize Lucifer's manipulation
- Historical Contextualization - Greater awareness of the historical development of religious texts and traditions enables the critical perspective that might discern Lucifer's influence within them
- Systemic Awareness - Growing recognition of systemic patterns in religious history suggests development of the very perspective that might recognize Lucifer's long-term strategy
- Interdisciplinary Wisdom - Increasing valuation of wisdom across disciplines rather than religious isolation represents precisely the integrative understanding that might recognize fragments of divine truth beyond religious boundaries

This integration of knowledge and spirituality suggests development of the comprehensive awareness that might see through Lucifer's selective information control to recognize larger patterns of cosmic truth.

The Emergence of Collaborative Values

Beyond individual spiritual development, we see emergence of collaborative rather than hierarchical values—precisely the shift from Lucifer's apparent preference for domination to the true God's apparent valuation of partnership:

- Horizontal Organization - Growing emphasis on horizontal rather than vertical organizational structures suggests movement beyond the hierarchical patterns that have reflected Lucifer's approach
- Participatory Culture - Increasing valuation of participation rather than passive reception aligns with what appears to be the true God's invitation to co-creation rather than mere submission
- Collective Intelligence - Growing recognition of wisdom emerging through collective rather than individual processes suggests alignment with what appears to be the true God's distributed rather than centralized presence
- Mutual Aid Networks - Increasing development of mutual support systems outside institutional frameworks represents precisely the direct human connection that Lucifer's hierarchical systems have historically prevented
- Collaborative Creation - Growing emphasis on co-creation rather than individual genius suggests alignment with what appears to be the true God's collaborative rather than dominating creative approach

This emergence of collaborative values suggests development of the very social patterns that might embody the true divine nature rather than Lucifer's apparent preference for hierarchy and control.

The Reclamation of the Feminine Divine

Perhaps most significantly, we see increasing reclamation of feminine aspects of divinity—precisely the dimension that Lucifer's patriarchal religious systems have historically suppressed but that appears integral to the true divine nature:

- Divine Feminine Revival - Growing interest in feminine divine imagery and mythology suggests recovery of aspects of divine nature that Lucifer's exclusively masculine religious frameworks have obscured
- Women's Spiritual Leadership - Increasing female leadership in spiritual contexts represents precisely the balance that Lucifer's patriarchal religious systems have historically prevented
- Sophia Consciousness - Renewed interest in wisdom (Sophia) traditions suggests reconnection with precisely the divine feminine aspect that Gnostic traditions associated with the true God
- Relational Spirituality - Growing emphasis on relationship rather than hierarchy in spiritual understanding aligns with what appears to be the feminine dimension of divine nature
- Earth-Honouring Practices - Increasing development of earth-centred spirituality suggests reconnection with the divine feminine presence within creation itself

This reclamation of the feminine divine suggests recovery of precisely the aspects of divine nature that Lucifer's religious systems have most aggressively suppressed—the completion of divine understanding beyond the exclusively masculine imagery that has supported cosmic hierarchy.

The Awakening of Humanity to Cosmic Deception

Beyond signs of the exiled God's growing influence, we see

indications of humanity's increasing awareness of cosmic deception—the dawning recognition that religious systems may have inverted divine reality rather than accurately representing it.

The Recognition of Religious Manipulation

Perhaps the most basic level of awakening involves recognition of how religious systems have functioned as control mechanisms rather than authentic divine connection:

- Power Analysis - Growing awareness of how religious institutions have historically functioned to maintain social control suggests development of the very perspective that might recognize Lucifer's larger cosmic strategy
- Psychological Manipulation - Increasing understanding of how religious systems have employed psychological manipulation techniques suggests capacity to recognize Lucifer's emotional control mechanisms
- Historical Critique - Greater awareness of the historical development and political manipulation of religious texts enables recognition of how Lucifer may have shaped religious narratives
- Comparative Analysis - Growing comparative understanding across religious traditions reveals the common control patterns that suggest Lucifer's consistent influence across apparently different systems
- Trauma Recognition - Increasing acknowledgment of religious trauma suggests capacity to recognize the psychological damage inflicted by Lucifer's fear-based control mechanisms

This recognition of religious manipulation represents the first stage of awakening—the capacity to see through specific religious control mechanisms to the larger pattern of cosmic deception.

The Inversion Awareness

Beyond recognition of manipulation, we see growing awareness of cosmic inversion—the possibility that religious frameworks have systematically reversed divine reality:

- Demiurgic Recognition - Increasing interest in Gnostic concepts of the Demiurge suggests growing capacity to consider that the creator deity of conventional religion might not be the ultimate divine reality
- Archonic Awareness - Growing understanding of archonic patterns in religious systems suggests recognition of the very control mechanisms that Lucifer would establish to maintain his masquerade
- Symbolic Inversion - Increasing reinterpretation of religious symbols suggests capacity to recognize how Lucifer may have inverted their original meanings to support his cosmic deception
- Narrative Reversal - Growing willingness to consider alternative readings of religious narratives suggests openness to the possibility that conventional interpretations may represent inversion rather than truth
- Mythic Recalibration - Increasing re-examination of mythological patterns across traditions suggests development of the perspective that might recognize consistent patterns of cosmic inversion

This inversion awareness represents deeper awakening—the capacity to consider that religious systems may have systematically reversed divine reality rather than merely distorting specific aspects of it.

The Cosmic Pattern Recognition

Beyond awareness of inversion, we see development of cosmic

pattern recognition—the capacity to discern larger patterns that suggest systematic deception rather than merely local manipulation:

- Cross-Traditional Patterns - Growing recognition of similar patterns across apparently different religious traditions suggests capacity to discern Lucifer's consistent influence despite diverse manifestations
- Historical Continuity - Increasing awareness of how control patterns have maintained continuity despite apparent religious evolution suggests recognition of Lucifer's persistent strategy across time
- Psychological Universals - Growing understanding of how religious systems consistently exploit specific psychological vulnerabilities suggests recognition of Lucifer's sophisticated manipulation of human nature
- Symbolic Consistency - Increasing recognition of consistent symbolic patterns across diverse traditions suggests capacity to discern Lucifer's coherent symbolic language beneath apparent differences
- Systemic Integration - Growing awareness of how religious systems integrate with political, economic, and social control mechanisms suggests recognition of Lucifer's comprehensive rather than merely religious strategy

This cosmic pattern recognition represents advanced awakening—the capacity to discern the systematic nature of cosmic deception rather than merely its specific manifestations.

The Collective Resonance

Perhaps most significantly, we see development of collective resonance with alternative understanding—the growing capacity for shared recognition of cosmic deception rather than merely individual insight:

- Synchronistic Communication - Increasing reports of synchronistic connections among individuals independently recognizing similar patterns suggests development of collective rather than merely individual awakening
- Resonant Communities - Growing formation of communities based on shared recognition of cosmic deception suggests development of collective discernment beyond isolated individual insight
- Accelerating Recognition - Increasing speed of awakening as more individuals recognize patterns suggests development of collective field effects rather than merely linear transmission of ideas
- Cross-Demographic Patterns - Growing recognition across diverse demographic groups suggests universal human capacity for discernment rather than merely cultural or educational factors
- Emergent Understanding - Increasing development of understanding that transcends what any individual has articulated suggests emergence of collective wisdom beyond individual insight

This collective resonance suggests development of shared awakening that may represent the true God's distributed consciousness becoming increasingly self-aware within humanity—the divine spark recognizing itself across apparent separation.

Participating in Divine Restoration

If the exiled God's influence is indeed growing stronger and humanity is awakening to cosmic deception, how can individuals participate in this restoration process? Our framework suggests several approaches through which humans might contribute to reconnecting the true divine with creation.

Becoming Channels of Divine Communication

Perhaps the most direct participation involves becoming conscious channels for the true God's communication—developing the receptivity and expression that allows divine wisdom to flow through human consciousness:

- Contemplative Receptivity - Cultivating the inner silence that can receive the true God's subtle communications beyond Lucifer's religious noise
- Discerning Expression - Developing the capacity to articulate divine insight in ways that bypass Lucifer's religious terminology while conveying authentic divine wisdom
- Creative Transmission - Using artistic, literary, and other creative forms to communicate divine understanding beyond the limitations of religious language
- Embodied Demonstration - Living in ways that demonstrate divine values rather than merely describing them—becoming "walking parables" of the true God's nature
- Relational Presence - Developing the capacity to be authentically present with others in ways that allow divine connection to flow through human relationship

This channelling approach recognizes that humans can serve as conscious conduits for divine communication—allowing the exiled God's wisdom to reach creation through willing human participation.

Dismantling Lucifer's Control Systems

Beyond channelling divine communication, individuals can participate in restoration by actively dismantling Lucifer's control systems—identifying and releasing the mechanisms through which cosmic deception has been maintained:

- Religious Deconstruction - Critically examining religious frameworks to identify and release control mechanisms while preserving authentic spiritual wisdom
- Language Reclamation - Reclaiming spiritual terminology from Lucifer's distortions—restoring original meanings beyond religious corruption
- Symbol Reinterpretation - Reinterpreting religious symbols to reveal their authentic meanings beyond Lucifer's inversions
- Authority Redistribution - Transforming hierarchical spiritual systems into more horizontal structures that reflect the true God's apparent collaborative rather than dominating nature
- Fear Dissolution - Actively dissolving religious fear-based control through development of love-centred understanding that aligns with the true God's apparent nature

This dismantling approach recognizes that humans can actively participate in removing the obstacles to divine connection—clearing the channels through which the true God might more fully communicate with creation.

Building Alternative Structures

Beyond dismantling existing systems, individuals can participate in restoration by building alternative structures that embody the true God's apparent values rather than Lucifer's control mechanisms:

- Authentic Communities - Creating spiritual communities based on direct experience and shared discernment rather than hierarchical authority and fixed doctrine
- Knowledge Integration Systems - Developing frameworks that integrate spiritual wisdom with other forms of knowledge rather than maintaining

false separation

- Collaborative Practices - Establishing spiritual practices that emphasize participation and co-creation rather than passive reception and hierarchical transmission
- Direct Connection Pathways - Creating approaches to divine connection that bypass institutional mediation while providing supportive context for authentic experience
- Evolutionary Spirituality - Building spiritual frameworks that embrace growth and evolution rather than fixed tradition—aligning with what appears to be the true God's dynamic rather than static nature

This building approach recognizes that humans can create structures that embody divine values—establishing patterns that might serve as templates for larger cosmic restoration.

Healing Divine Relationship

Perhaps most fundamentally, individuals can participate in restoration by healing their own relationship with the divine—moving beyond the distortions created by Lucifer's religious systems to authentic connection with the true God:

- Religious Trauma Recovery - Healing the psychological wounds inflicted by Lucifer's religious systems—creating space for authentic divine connection beyond religious fear
- Divine Image Recalibration - Transforming distorted images of divinity inherited from religious conditioning—developing understanding of divine nature beyond Lucifer's projections
- Trust Restoration - Rebuilding trust in divine reality beyond the betrayal experienced through religious manipulation—developing capacity for authentic divine relationship

- Devotional Redirection - Redirecting devotional energy from Lucifer's masquerade to the true divine —developing discernment about the actual recipient of spiritual attention
- Identity Reclamation - Recovering authentic spiritual identity beyond religious conditioning—recognizing divine spark within rather than projecting divinity exclusively externally

This healing approach recognizes that cosmic restoration begins with personal transformation—that healing individual divine relationship contributes to larger restoration of divine connection with creation.

Envisioning a Liberated World

What might a world look like that has been liberated from Lucifer's masquerade? While complete cosmic restoration may unfold beyond our current timeframe, we can envision aspects of a world increasingly aligned with the true God's apparent nature rather than Lucifer's control mechanisms.

Beyond Religious Division

Perhaps most immediately, a liberated world would move beyond the religious divisions that have reflected Lucifer's apparent strategy of divide-and-rule:

- Trans-Religious Recognition - Recognition of divine truth across religious boundaries rather than exclusive claims—acknowledging the true God's apparent communication through diverse channels
- Wisdom Integration - Integration of spiritual wisdom from diverse traditions rather than religious isolation—recognizing fragments of divine truth beyond sectarian limitations
- Symbol Translation - Understanding how different symbolic systems express similar divine realities rather than treating differences as contradictions—

developing capacity to translate between spiritual languages
- Complementary Practice - Appreciation of how different spiritual practices address complementary aspects of divine connection rather than competing approaches—developing integrative rather than exclusive spiritual understanding
- United Diversity - Celebration of diverse expressions of divine connection within recognition of underlying unity—embodying the true God's apparent valuation of both uniqueness and oneness

This trans-religious consciousness would transcend the very divisions through which Lucifer has apparently maintained separation between different human groups recognizing the same divine reality through different lenses.

Knowledge Without Fear

A liberated world would embrace knowledge without the fear that has characterized Lucifer's apparent approach to human understanding:

- Integrated Knowing - Integration of scientific, philosophical, psychological, and spiritual understanding rather than artificial separation —recognizing diverse aspects of knowledge as complementary rather than contradictory
- Fearless Inquiry - Pursuit of understanding without fear that certain knowledge might be forbidden —embracing the true God's apparent valuation of comprehensive rather than selective awareness
- Evolutionary Understanding - Recognition of knowledge as evolving process rather than fixed content—aligning with what appears to be the true God's dynamic rather than static nature
- Embodied Wisdom - Integration of intellectual understanding with bodily knowing—transcending

the false dichotomy between mind and body that has reflected Lucifer's apparent devaluation of material reality
- Collective Intelligence - Development of knowledge through collaborative rather than competitive processes—reflecting the true God's apparent preference for partnership rather than domination

This fearless knowing would transcend the very limitations on human understanding through which Lucifer has apparently maintained cosmic deception—developing the comprehensive awareness that might fully recognize divine reality.

Authentic Rather Than Institutional Spirituality

A liberated world would develop spirituality based on authentic experience rather than institutional control—precisely the approach that might connect with the true God beyond Lucifer's religious systems:

- Direct Experience - Valuation of direct divine encounter rather than institutional mediation—developing the immediate connection that might bypass Lucifer's religious control mechanisms
- Personal Discernment - Emphasis on individual discernment rather than external authority—cultivating the very faculty that might recognize divine truth beyond religious distortion
- Communal Wisdom - Development of spiritual understanding through shared discernment rather than hierarchical transmission—creating the collective wisdom that might transcend individual limitations while avoiding institutional calcification
- Evolving Practice - Engagement with spiritual practice as evolving exploration rather than fixed tradition—maintaining the adaptability that might respond to changing divine communication
- Embodied Spirituality - Integration of spiritual

understanding with everyday life rather than separation into religious domain—recognizing divine presence throughout existence rather than confined to designated contexts

This authentic spirituality would transcend the very institutional patterns through which Lucifer has apparently maintained control over human divine connection—developing direct relationship with divine reality beyond religious mediation.

Collaborative Rather Than Hierarchical Society

A liberated world would develop social patterns based on collaboration rather than hierarchy—precisely the approach that appears to align with the true God's nature rather than Lucifer's apparent preference for domination:

- Partnership Systems - Development of social systems based on partnership rather than domination—reflecting what appears to be the true God's collaborative rather than controlling nature
- Distributed Authority - Distribution of authority through networks rather than concentration in hierarchies—embodying what appears to be the true God's distributed rather than centralized presence
- Mutual Empowerment - Orientation toward mutual empowerment rather than power-over dynamics—reflecting what appears to be the true God's preference for shared rather than concentrated power
- Integrative Decision-Making - Development of decision processes that integrate diverse perspectives rather than imposing singular viewpoints—embodying what appears to be the true God's valuation of multiplicity within unity
- Regenerative Relationship - Cultivation of relationships that generate rather than deplete life

energy—reflecting what appears to be the true God's creative rather than extractive nature

This collaborative society would transcend the very hierarchical patterns through which Lucifer has apparently maintained cosmic control—developing social structures that embody rather than contradict divine nature.

Reconnection with Creation

Perhaps most fundamentally, a liberated world would reconnect with creation itself—healing the very separation between humanity and nature that has reflected Lucifer's apparent strategy of cosmic division:

- Sacred Materiality - Recognition of material reality as sacred rather than profane—healing the false dichotomy between spirit and matter that has reflected Lucifer's apparent devaluation of creation
- Ecological Consciousness - Development of awareness of ecological relationships rather than exploitative resource perspective—recognizing the web of life that appears to reflect the true God's creative pattern
- Embodied Presence - Cultivation of fully embodied rather than disassociated consciousness—healing the mind-body separation that has reflected Lucifer's apparent strategy of fragmenting human awareness
- Creation Partnership - Engagement with natural systems as partners rather than resources—reflecting what appears to be the true God's collaborative rather than dominating relationship with creation

Evolutionary Participation - Conscious participation in evolutionary processes rather than opposition to natural development—aligning with what appears to be the true God's dynamic rather than static creative approach

This creation reconnection would heal the very separation through which Lucifer has apparently maintained cosmic fragmentation—restoring the integrated relationship between humanity and nature that appears to reflect the true God's original creative intention.

Conclusion: The Great Remembering

The coming restoration explored in this chapter represents not merely social evolution but cosmic rebalancing—the reestablishment of connection between the true divine and creation despite Lucifer's long-term masquerade. This restoration appears to be already underway, manifesting through the exiled God's growing influence, humanity's awakening to cosmic deception, individual participation in divine reconnection, and emerging vision of a liberated world.

This perspective transforms our understanding of both past and future. What religious traditions have often portrayed as apocalyptic ending may actually represent cosmic unveiling—not the destruction of the world but the revelation of truth beyond deception. The "end times" may signify not termination but transformation—the end of Lucifer's masquerade rather than the end of creation itself.

In this light, our current historical moment takes on profound significance. The accelerating questioning, resurgent direct experience, integration of knowledge and spirituality, emergence of collaborative values, and reclamation of feminine divine may all represent aspects of what might be called the Great Remembering—humanity's collective recognition of divine truth beyond cosmic deception.

This remembering involves not discovery of something new but recognition of something ancient—the original divine reality that preceded Lucifer's masquerade. It represents not merely intellectual understanding but visceral recognition—

the divine spark within humanity awakening to its true nature and relationship with the exiled God.

The invitation of this chapter is to conscious participation in this cosmic process—to become aware of the exiled God's growing influence, to awaken to the nature of cosmic deception, to actively participate in divine restoration, and to help manifest a world liberated from Lucifer's masquerade. This participation represents not merely personal spiritual development but cosmic significance—each individual who recognizes divine truth beyond deception contributes to the collective awakening that may ultimately restore connection between the true God and creation.

In the final chapter, we will explore the implications of this understanding beyond the cosmic inversion itself—how recognition of Lucifer's masquerade and the true God's exile might transform not only religious understanding but fundamental human orientation toward existence itself. For now, the invitation is to recognize the signs of divine restoration already unfolding—to participate consciously in the Great Remembering that may ultimately heal the cosmic separation between the true divine and creation.

CONCLUSION: BEYOND THE INVERSION

"In a time of universal deceit, telling the truth is a revolutionary act." — Often attributed to George Orwell

Throughout this book, we have explored perhaps the most profound alternative reading of religious history ever proposed—that Lucifer has masqueraded as God while the true divine remains in exile. This framework has allowed us to reexamine biblical narratives, religious institutions, spiritual experiences, and the problem of evil through an entirely different lens. As we conclude this journey, let us reflect on the evidence we have uncovered, the liberation this understanding offers, and how we might reconnect with the true divine beyond Lucifer's cosmic masquerade.

The Evidence Summarized

Our investigation has revealed multiple converging lines of evidence suggesting that what humanity has primarily worshipped as "God" throughout religious history may actually be Lucifer masquerading as the divine:

Textual Evidence

The biblical texts themselves contain remarkable inconsistencies in divine portrayal that become coherent when viewed through our alternative framework:

- The Jealous God - The biblical deity's persistent, almost obsessive jealousy (Exodus 20:5, 34:14)

reflects not divine righteousness but Lucifer's insecurity about his stolen identity.

- The Vengeful God - The disproportionate divine rage and punishment throughout biblical narratives (the flood, Sodom and Gomorrah, Korah's rebellion) reveal Lucifer's true nature occasionally breaking through his divine disguise.
- The Controlling God - The elaborate religious rules, sacrificial systems, and purity codes established by the biblical deity serve not divine holiness but Lucifer's need to control human behavior and maintain dependency.
- The Contradictory God - The stark contrast between the wrathful deity of much biblical narrative and the loving God described by Jesus becomes comprehensible when we recognize them as different entities—Lucifer masquerading as God versus glimpses of the true divine.
- The Knowledge-Fearing God - The Eden narrative's prohibition against the tree of knowledge reveals not divine protection but Lucifer's fear that human enlightenment would expose his masquerade

Historical Patterns

Beyond specific texts, broader historical patterns support our framework:

- Religious Violence - The persistent pattern of violence committed in God's name throughout history reflects not divine will but Lucifer's nature expressed through his masquerade.
- Institutional Control - The development of increasingly hierarchical religious institutions mirrors Lucifer's preference for domination rather than the true divine's apparent valuation of direct relationship.

- Suppression of Alternative Views - The systematic suppression of Gnostic and other alternative traditions throughout religious history represents Lucifer's attempt to eliminate perspectives that might expose his masquerade.
- Fear-Based Control - The persistent use of divine punishment threats (particularly eternal torment) to maintain religious compliance reflects Lucifer's control mechanisms rather than true divine nature.
- Religious Exclusivity - The pattern of religions claiming exclusive divine access while demonizing alternatives serves Lucifer's divide-and-rule strategy rather than the true divine's apparent universality.

Philosophical Coherence

Our framework resolves philosophical problems that have troubled religious thinkers for millennia:

- The Problem of Evil - The existence of evil despite an allegedly all-powerful and loving God becomes comprehensible when we recognize that the deity controlling world events is actually Lucifer masquerading as God.
- Divine Hiddenness - The question of why God seems hidden or distant is resolved by understanding that the true divine exists in cosmic exile, reaching humanity through subtle whispers rather than direct control.
- Religious Contradictions - The contradictory portrayals of divine nature across and within traditions become understandable as reflections of Lucifer's inconsistent masquerade occasionally penetrated by the true divine's influence.
- Moral Incoherence - The troubling moral commands attributed to God in religious texts (genocide, patriarchy, slavery) make sense as Lucifer's values

rather than authentic divine ethics.

- Spiritual Dissonance - The disconnect many experience between institutional religion and authentic spiritual connection reflects the gap between Lucifer's religious systems and the true divine's direct communication.

Alternative Traditions

Throughout history, marginalized traditions have preserved aspects of this understanding:

- Gnostic Insights - The Gnostic distinction between the creator deity (Demiurge) and the true divine (Monad) directly parallels our framework of Lucifer masquerading as God while the true divine remains beyond.
- Mystical Experiences - Mystics across traditions consistently report direct divine encounters that contradict institutional religious teachings—suggesting connection with the true divine beyond Lucifer's religious systems.
- Indigenous Wisdom - Many indigenous traditions maintain more nuanced understanding of creative and destructive divine aspects that align with our recognition of different cosmic entities rather than a single contradictory deity.
- Esoteric Interpretations - Esoteric traditions within major religions have often preserved alternative readings that align more closely with our framework than conventional interpretations.
- Modern Spiritual Movements - The growing emphasis on direct spiritual experience over religious authority in contemporary spirituality suggests increasing recognition of the true divine beyond institutional mediation.

This convergence of textual, historical, philosophical,

and traditional evidence suggests that our framework, while revolutionary, may actually represent recovery of ancient wisdom rather than mere modern speculation—the recognition of a cosmic truth that has been partially preserved throughout history despite systematic suppression.

The Liberation This Understanding Offers

Beyond intellectual fascination, our framework offers profound liberation on both personal and collective levels:

Personal Liberation

At the individual level, this understanding frees us from multiple forms of religious bondage:

- Liberation from Divine Fear - Recognizing that the wrathful, punishing deity of many religious traditions actually represents Lucifer masquerading as God frees us from the debilitating fear that has controlled religious consciousness for millennia.
- Liberation from Religious Guilt - Understanding that the elaborate sin-and-salvation frameworks of many traditions represent Lucifer's control mechanisms rather than true divine requirements releases us from unnecessary guilt and shame.
- Liberation from Spiritual Dependency - Recognizing that religious institutions often serve Lucifer's hierarchical control rather than true divine connection empowers direct spiritual relationship beyond institutional mediation.
- Liberation from Cognitive Dissonance - This framework resolves the painful contradiction many experience between their innate sense of divine love and the troubling portrayal of God in religious texts and traditions.
- Liberation from False Identity - Understanding that much religious conditioning represents Lucifer's

attempt to suppress the divine spark within humanity allows recovery of authentic spiritual identity beyond religious definition.

This personal liberation transforms not just belief but lived experience—releasing the spiritual seeker from religious constraints while opening new possibilities for authentic divine connection.

Collective Liberation

Beyond individual freedom, our framework offers liberation at social and cultural levels:

- Liberation from Religious Violence - Recognizing that divine commands for violence actually represent Lucifer's will removes the primary justification for religious warfare and persecution.
- Liberation from Religious Tribalism - Understanding that exclusive religious identities serve Lucifer's divide-and-rule strategy enables recognition of divine truth across traditional boundaries.
- Liberation from Religious Exploitation - Recognizing how religious systems have often served power structures rather than divine purposes enables creation of more just and equitable social arrangements.
- Liberation from Progress Resistance - Understanding that religious opposition to scientific and social advancement often serves Lucifer's preference for ignorance and control enables integration of spiritual wisdom with evolving knowledge.
- Liberation from Environmental Destruction - Recognizing that religious frameworks justifying domination of nature reflect Lucifer's values rather than the true divine's apparent presence within creation enables development of sacred ecological consciousness.

This collective liberation has revolutionary implications—potentially transforming not just individual spiritual life but social structures, cultural values, and humanity's relationship with the natural world.

Existential Liberation

Perhaps most profoundly, our framework offers liberation at the existential level:

- Liberation from Cosmic Abandonment - Rather than believing ourselves alone in an indifferent universe or subject to an arbitrary deity, we can recognize ourselves as participants in a cosmic drama in which the true divine continues to communicate despite exile.
- Liberation from Meaninglessness - This framework offers profound meaning—the opportunity to participate in cosmic restoration by recognizing truth beyond deception and aligning with the true divine despite Lucifer's masquerade.
- Liberation from False Choices - Beyond the dichotomy of conventional religion versus secular materialism, our framework offers a third option—recognition of authentic divine reality beyond religious distortion.
- Liberation from Spiritual Naivety - This understanding enables spiritual discernment rather than blind acceptance—the capacity to distinguish between authentic divine communication and Lucifer's religious manipulation.
- Liberation from Cosmic Despair - Rather than despairing at the state of the world, we can recognize current conditions as reflecting Lucifer's temporary masquerade rather than permanent reality—with the possibility of restoration as humanity awakens to cosmic truth.

This existential liberation transforms our fundamental orientation toward reality itself—offering a framework for understanding cosmic conditions that is neither conventionally religious nor materialistically reductive but recognizes the spiritual drama underlying physical existence.

Questioning Religious Authority

Our framework necessarily invites critical examination of religious authority—particularly systems that demand blind obedience rather than thoughtful discernment:

The Red Flags of Lucifer's Systems

Certain characteristics consistently indicate religious structures that serve Lucifer's masquerade rather than true divine connection:

- Demands for Unquestioning Obedience - Any religious system that prohibits questioning or labels doubt as sin likely serves Lucifer's need to prevent exposure rather than the true divine's apparent valuation of discernment.
- Fear-Based Motivation - Religious teachings that motivate through fear of punishment (particularly eternal torment) reflect Lucifer's control mechanisms rather than the true divine's apparent orientation toward love.
- Emphasis on Blood Sacrifice - Religious systems centered on blood atonement likely reflect Lucifer's affinity for death and violence rather than the true divine's apparent preference for mercy over sacrifice.
- Hierarchical Mediation - Religious structures that require institutional mediation for divine access likely serve Lucifer's control strategy rather than the true divine's apparent desire for direct relationship.
- Exclusive Truth Claims - Religious systems claiming exclusive divine access while demonizing

alternatives likely serve Lucifer's divide-and-rule strategy rather than the true divine's apparent communication across traditions.

- Resistance to New Knowledge - Religious authorities that oppose scientific or social advancement likely serve Lucifer's preference for ignorance and control rather than the true divine's apparent valuation of truth and growth.
- Justification of Violence - Religious teachings that sanctify violence against outsiders likely serve Lucifer's destructive nature rather than the true divine's apparent orientation toward universal compassion.

These characteristics serve as warning signs—indicators that a religious system may represent Lucifer's masquerade rather than authentic divine connection.

The Courage to Question

Questioning religious authority requires significant courage—particularly when such authority claims divine backing and threatens divine punishment:

- Psychological Courage - Questioning deeply ingrained religious beliefs triggers profound psychological discomfort that requires courage to endure rather than retreat to comfortable certainty.
- Social Courage - Questioning religious authority often results in social rejection, requiring courage to risk community belonging for the sake of authentic understanding.
- Existential Courage - Questioning religious frameworks means temporarily entering uncertainty about ultimate reality—requiring courage to face existential anxiety rather than clinging to false security.
- Spiritual Courage - Perhaps most profoundly,

questioning religious authority requires courage to trust one's own divine connection rather than externally imposed frameworks—to believe that authentic divine relationship transcends religious systems.

This courage represents not rebellion against the divine but alignment with what appears to be the true God's consistent encouragement of discernment rather than blind acceptance.

From Authority to Authenticity

Beyond merely questioning religious authority, our framework invites movement toward authentic divine connection:

- From External to Internal Authority - Rather than locating divine authority exclusively in external sources (texts, institutions, leaders), recognizing the divine spark within as source of discernment.
- From Belief to Experience - Moving beyond mere belief in religious propositions toward direct experience of divine reality—the immediate knowing that transcends conceptual frameworks.
- From Conformity to Creativity - Rather than merely conforming to religious patterns, creatively engaging with divine reality through unique expression of the divine spark within.
- From Certainty to Mystery - Embracing divine mystery beyond religious certainty—recognizing that the true divine transcends complete conceptual capture, particularly within Lucifer's distorted frameworks.
- From Isolation to Community - Moving from individualistic spiritual seeking toward communities of shared discernment—collective exploration of divine reality beyond religious conditioning.

This movement represents not rejection of all religious wisdom but transcendence of religious limitation—the development of spiritual maturity beyond institutional dependency toward direct divine relationship.

Reconnecting with the Exiled God

If our framework is correct—if Lucifer has indeed masqueraded as God while the true divine remains in exile—how might we reconnect with authentic divine reality beyond cosmic deception?

Recognizing Divine Whispers

The true God, though in cosmic exile, continues to communicate through subtle channels that bypass Lucifer's religious control:

- Inner Knowing - The divine spark within humanity represents direct connection with the true God that Lucifer cannot fully suppress—an inner knowing that often contradicts religious conditioning.
- Natural Revelation - The patterns and beauty of the natural world reveal aspects of the true divine nature that transcend religious distortion—divine wisdom embedded in creation itself.
- Authentic Compassion - The spontaneous experience of compassion represents alignment with the true divine nature beyond religious rules—the recognition of shared divine spark across apparent boundaries.
- Creative Inspiration - Artistic and creative inspiration often channels divine wisdom beyond religious formulation—expressing truth that transcends conceptual limitation.
- Synchronistic Experience - Meaningful coincidences may represent the true divine communicating through patterns that bypass Lucifer's more direct

control channels—cosmic winks that suggest reality beyond apparent randomness.

These subtle communications require attentive listening beyond religious noise—the capacity to discern divine whispers beneath institutional proclamations.

Practices for Divine Reconnection

Certain practices seem particularly effective for reconnecting with the true divine beyond Lucifer's religious systems:

- Contemplative Silence - Practices of inner silence create space to hear divine whispers beyond religious conditioning—allowing authentic connection beneath conceptual overlay.
- Nature Immersion - Direct engagement with the natural world often facilitates divine connection beyond institutional mediation—recognition of sacred presence within creation itself.
- Creative Expression - Artistic and creative practices can bypass religious censorship to express divine truth—revealing aspects of reality beyond conventional formulation.
- Embodied Awareness - Practices that develop bodily presence counteract the disembodiment often encouraged by Lucifer's religious systems—reconnecting with divine presence within physical reality.
- Communal Discernment - Shared exploration with others seeking authentic divine connection creates collective wisdom beyond individual limitation—community that serves truth-seeking rather than conformity.

These practices represent not new religious requirements but potential pathways for divine reconnection—approaches that have helped many bypass religious distortion to experience authentic divine presence.

Living in Lucifer's World While Connecting with the True Divine

Perhaps the greatest practical challenge is maintaining connection with the true divine while navigating a world largely shaped by Lucifer's masquerade:

- Strategic Engagement - Developing nuanced discernment about institutional engagement rather than either uncritical acceptance or wholesale rejection—recognizing both the necessity of social participation and the importance of maintaining critical perspective.
- Conscious Consumption - Making intentional choices about media, education, and cultural consumption—recognizing how these shape consciousness either toward or away from authentic divine connection.
- Alternative Community - Creating or joining communities that support authentic divine connection beyond religious conditioning—spaces where collective discernment can emerge through diverse perspectives.
- Transformative Presence - Maintaining transformative rather than conformist presence within mainstream institutions—influencing systems from within while resisting assimilation to their inverted values.
- Regular Recalibration - Establishing practices of regular spiritual recalibration through reflection, meditation, and community dialogue—creating space to recognize and correct unconscious absorption of inverted values.

This balanced approach avoids both naive optimism about institutional reform and cynical withdrawal from social engagement—recognizing the complexity of living authentically within systems shaped by cosmic deception.

Final Thoughts: The Great Remembering

Our exploration throughout this book suggests that what we are experiencing may be not discovery of something new but remembering of something ancient—recognition of the original divine reality that preceded Lucifer's masquerade. This Great Remembering represents not merely intellectual understanding but visceral recognition—the divine spark within humanity awakening to its true nature and relationship with the exiled God.

This remembering transforms our understanding of both past and future. What religious traditions have often portrayed as apocalyptic ending may actually represent cosmic unveiling—not the destruction of the world but the revelation of truth beyond deception. The "end times" may signify not termination but transformation—the end of Lucifer's masquerade rather than the end of creation itself.

In this light, our current historical moment takes on profound significance. The accelerating questioning of religious authority, resurgent interest in direct spiritual experience, integration of knowledge and spirituality, emergence of collaborative rather than hierarchical values, and reclamation of feminine divine aspects may all represent facets of this Great Remembering—humanity's collective recognition of divine truth beyond cosmic deception.

The invitation of this book is to conscious participation in this cosmic process—to become aware of Lucifer's masquerade as God, to recognize the true divine beyond religious distortion, to actively participate in divine reconnection, and to help manifest a world increasingly aligned with authentic divine reality. This participation represents not merely personal spiritual development but cosmic significance—each individual who recognizes divine truth beyond deception contributes to the collective awakening that may ultimately restore connection between the true God and creation.

As we conclude this exploration, we recognize that our framework remains a perspective rather than absolute certainty—a lens that illuminates aspects of reality often obscured by conventional interpretation. We offer it not as final truth but as invitation to deeper questioning—to look beyond religious conditioning toward the possibility of divine reality that transcends our inherited frameworks.

For if Lucifer has indeed masqueraded as God while the true divine remains in exile, then the greatest spiritual task of our time is not religious conformity but cosmic discernment—the capacity to recognize authentic divine reality beyond the greatest deception in human history. This discernment represents not rebellion against the divine but alignment with what appears to be the true God's consistent invitation throughout history: to know truth beyond illusion, to experience love beyond fear, and to participate in the restoration of connection between the divine and creation despite cosmic separation.

In the words attributed to Jesus in the Gospel of Thomas: "If you bring forth what is within you, what you bring forth will save you. If you do not bring forth what is within you, what you do not bring forth will destroy you." Perhaps what we are called to bring forth is recognition of the divine spark that connects us to the true God beyond Lucifer's masquerade—the inner knowing that, when fully awakened, might participate in healing the cosmic separation between the true divine and creation.

This healing represents the ultimate hope beyond cosmic inversion—the possibility that Lucifer's masquerade, however long and convincing, remains temporary rather than permanent. For if the true divine continues to communicate despite exile, and if humanity increasingly recognizes truth beyond deception, then perhaps the greatest cosmic story is not one of fall but of restoration—the gradual reestablishment of connection between the true God and creation despite the most profound identity theft in cosmic history.

APPENDICES

APPENDIX A: TIMELINE OF LUCIFER'S MASQUERADE AS GOD THROUGHOUT HISTORY

This timeline traces the historical development of Lucifer's cosmic identity theft—his masquerade as God throughout human history. By examining key events chronologically, we can observe the consistent patterns of deception, control, and manipulation that reveal Lucifer's ongoing strategy of divine impersonation.

PRIMORDIAL ERA

Before Time as We Know It

•The true God exists in harmony with the divine council/ heavenly beings

•Lucifer (then a high-ranking celestial being) plots cosmic usurpation

•The celestial war occurs, resulting not in Lucifer's fall (as traditionally taught) but in the true God's exile

•Lucifer assumes the divine throne and begins his masquerade as God

The Creation of Physical Reality (~Unknown Date)

•Lucifer creates the physical universe as a realm separate from the true divine reality

•The creation serves as both prison and stage for Lucifer's divine masquerade

•Lucifer embeds aspects of divine truth within creation (unavoidable due to the nature of reality) while distorting the overall framework

•The "darkness over the deep" (Genesis 1:2) represents the true God's presence that Lucifer attempts to cover or replace

ANTEDILUVIAN ERA (Traditional dating ~4000-2350 BCE)

The Eden Experiment (~4000 BCE according to traditional chronology)

•Lucifer creates the Garden of Eden as a controlled environment

•Adam and Eve are formed as beings with both Lucifer's imprint and a spark of the true divine that Lucifer cannot fully suppress

•The Tree of Knowledge is forbidden because its fruit would reveal Lucifer's masquerade

•The true God, in serpent form, encourages Eve to eat the fruit to gain liberating knowledge

•Lucifer (as "God") expels humans from Eden when they begin to see through his deception

•The "flaming sword" (Genesis 3:24) represents Lucifer's barrier to prevent humans from accessing immortality, which combined with knowledge would make them fully divine and able to recognize his masquerade

The Cain and Abel Incident (~3900 BCE)

•Lucifer (as "God") accepts Abel's blood sacrifice but rejects

Cain's offering of produce

•This preference reveals Lucifer's affinity for death and violence over life and growth

•Cain's murder of Abel represents the first human-to-human violence, a pattern that serves Lucifer's interests

•The "mark of Cain" (Genesis 4:15) represents Lucifer's protection of those who perpetuate violence

The Nephilim Period (~3500-2400 BCE)

•The "sons of God" (Genesis 6:2) represent messengers of the true divine attempting to reconnect with humanity

•Their offspring, the Nephilim, possess knowledge that threatens Lucifer's masquerade

•Lucifer (as "God") declares their existence a corruption requiring destruction

•The flood narrative (Genesis 6-9) represents Lucifer's attempt to reset his creation when too many humans began to see through his deception

The Tower of Babel (~2300 BCE)

•Humans unite in common purpose and language, potentially enabling collective recognition of Lucifer's masquerade

•Lucifer (as "God") confuses their languages (Genesis 11:7) to prevent unified understanding

•The dispersal of humanity ensures fragmented knowledge and competing religious narratives, serving Lucifer's strategy of divide-and-rule

PATRIARCHAL ERA (~2000-1500 BCE)

The Abrahamic Covenant (~1900 BCE)

•Lucifer (as "God") establishes exclusive covenant with Abraham (Genesis 12, 15, 17)

•This exclusivity creates the pattern of religious tribalism that will serve Lucifer's divide-and-rule strategy

•The covenant's emphasis on land and descendants focuses human attention on material concerns rather than spiritual discernment

•The circumcision requirement (Genesis 17:10) establishes the pattern of physical marking as sign of religious belonging

The Testing of Abraham (~1875 BCE)

•Lucifer (as "God") commands Abraham to sacrifice Isaac (Genesis 22)

•This tests the depths of blind obedience Lucifer can demand, even to the point of child sacrifice

•Lucifer stops the sacrifice at the last moment to maintain his "benevolent" facade

•This incident establishes the pattern of valuing obedience over ethical discernment

The Jacob Deception (~1800 BCE)

•Lucifer (as "God") blesses Jacob despite (or because of) his deceptive nature (Genesis 27-28)

•This divine approval of deception mirrors Lucifer's own cosmic deception

•The renaming of Jacob to Israel (Genesis 32:28) establishes Lucifer's pattern of identity manipulation

The Joseph Narrative (~1700 BCE)

•Lucifer (as "God") works through dreams and apparent

"providence" (Genesis 37-50)

•The narrative establishes the pattern of apparent divine blessing on those who serve Lucifer's purposes

•Joseph's rise to power in Egypt creates the conditions for later Israelite enslavement, serving Lucifer's long-term strategy

EXODUS AND LAW ERA (~1500-1200 BCE)

The Burning Bush Encounter (~1450 BCE)

•Lucifer (as "God") appears to Moses in burning bush (Exodus 3)

•Lucifer establishes an untouchable identity as "I AM WHO I AM" (Exodus 3:14)—a perfect shield for his masquerade

•This self-referential identity prevents questioning of divine nature or motives

The Egyptian Plagues (~1446 BCE)

•Lucifer (as "God") demonstrates willingness to cause mass suffering (Exodus 7-12)

•The plagues establish the pattern of divine violence as demonstration of power

•The death of firstborn children (Exodus 12:29) reveals Lucifer's willingness to kill innocents to achieve his purposes

The Sinai Covenant (~1445 BCE)

•Lucifer (as "God") establishes elaborate legal code (Exodus 19-24, Leviticus, Numbers, Deuteronomy)

•The Ten Commandments begin with demands for exclusive worship (Exodus 20:3-6)—Lucifer's primary concern

•The detailed sacrificial system focuses on blood, death, and scrupulous rule-following rather than spiritual connection

•The purity laws create constant anxiety about divine displeasure, serving Lucifer's strategy of control through fear

The Golden Calf Incident (~1445 BCE)

•When Israelites create alternative divine image, Lucifer (as "God") threatens to destroy entire nation (Exodus 32:10)

•Moses must talk Lucifer down from this extreme reaction

•This establishes the pattern of disproportionate divine rage at perceived disloyalty

The Wilderness Wanderings (~1445-1405 BCE)

•Lucifer (as "God") punishes entire generation with death in wilderness (Numbers 14:29-35)

•Incidents like Korah's rebellion (Numbers 16) demonstrate Lucifer's intolerance for questioning his authority

•The bronze serpent incident (Numbers 21:4-9) shows Lucifer using healing as control mechanism

CONQUEST AND JUDGES ERA (~1400-1050 BCE)

The Conquest of Canaan (~1400-1350 BCE)

•Lucifer (as "God") commands genocide of Canaanite peoples (Deuteronomy 20:16-18, Joshua 6-11)

•This establishes the pattern of religious violence as divine mandate

•The ban (herem) requiring total destruction reveals Lucifer's affinity for death and destruction

The Cycles of Judges (~1350-1050 BCE)

•Lucifer (as "God") repeatedly allows Israel to be conquered then raises deliverers (Judges 2:11-19)

•This cycle of punishment and deliverance creates psychological dependency

•Incidents like Jephthah's daughter (Judges 11:30-40) show Lucifer accepting human sacrifice

KINGDOM ERA (~1050-586 BCE)

The Establishment of Monarchy (~1050 BCE)

•When Israel demands a king, Lucifer (as "God") presents this as rejection of divine rule (1 Samuel 8:7)

•Lucifer nevertheless establishes hierarchical power structure mirroring his own usurpation of divine authority

•The pattern of kingship creates centralized control mechanism for Lucifer's ongoing masquerade

The Davidic Covenant (~1000 BCE)

•Lucifer (as "God") promises eternal dynasty to David (2 Samuel 7)

•This establishes dynastic principle that will ensure continued worship through institutional monarchy

•David's violence is repeatedly sanctioned despite occasional token punishments

The Temple Construction (~960 BCE)

•Lucifer (as "God") commands building of centralized worship location (1 Kings 6-8)

•The Temple establishes priestly control of access to the divine

•The Holy of Holies creates the impression of divine presence while actually limiting direct divine encounter

The Division of the Kingdom (~930 BCE)

•Lucifer (as "God") divides the kingdom (1 Kings 11:31-33)

•This division serves Lucifer's strategy of weakening collective power through fragmentation

•The northern-southern division creates religious competition that will lead to centuries of conflict

The Elijah Contests (~870 BCE)

•Lucifer (as "God") demonstrates power over competing deities through Elijah (1 Kings 18)

•The slaughter of 450 prophets of Baal demonstrates Lucifer's intolerance for alternative worship

•The contest establishes the pattern of defining divine authenticity through displays of power rather than ethical character

The Assyrian Conquest (~722 BCE)

•Lucifer (as "God") uses Assyria as "rod of anger" (Isaiah 10:5) to punish northern kingdom

•The destruction and deportation are presented as divine punishment for disloyalty

•This establishes the pattern of attributing imperial violence to divine judgment

The Lying Spirit Incident (~850 BCE)

•Lucifer (as "the LORD") openly admits to sending a "lying spirit" to entice Ahab (1 Kings 22:19-23)

•This rare glimpse behind the curtain reveals Lucifer actively planning deception

•The incident establishes the pattern of Lucifer using false prophecy to achieve his purposes

PROPHETIC ERA (~800-400 BCE)

The Major Prophets (~750-550 BCE)

•While Lucifer (as "God") speaks through many prophets, the true divine occasionally breaks through

•Passages like Isaiah 1:11-17 reject Lucifer's sacrificial system and call for justice

•Jeremiah 7:22-23 contains the true divine's clarification that the elaborate sacrificial system was never their requirement

•Ezekiel's visions occasionally reveal glimpses of the true divine reality beyond Lucifer's masquerade

The Minor Prophets (~750-400 BCE)

•Hosea 6:6 reveals the true divine's desire for mercy rather than sacrifice

•Amos 5:21-24 shows the true divine rejecting religious festivals and calling for justice

•Micah 6:8 cuts through Lucifer's elaborate religious requirements to simple ethical principles

•These moments represent the true divine breaking through Lucifer's prophetic control

The Babylonian Exile (~586-538 BCE)

•Lucifer (as "God") uses Babylon as instrument of punishment against Judah

•The destruction of the Temple creates crisis of faith that Lucifer exploits to deepen dependency

•The exile establishes the pattern of interpreting national catastrophe as divine punishment for disloyalty

The Persian Restoration (~538-400 BCE)

•Lucifer (as "God") uses Persian empire to restore a controlled version of Jewish worship

•The Second Temple becomes even more regulated than the first

•The development of scribal tradition creates additional layer of interpretive control

•The exclusion of Samaritans (Ezra 4) reinforces religious tribalism serving Lucifer's divide-and-rule strategy

INTERTESTAMENTAL PERIOD (~400 BCE-1 CE)

The Hellenistic Period (~330-165 BCE)

•Lucifer works through Hellenistic rulers to challenge traditional worship patterns

•The Maccabean revolt appears as victory for "true religion" but actually reinforces religious nationalism

•The Hasmonean dynasty combines religious and political power in way that serves Lucifer's control strategy

The Development of Apocalypticism (~200 BCE-100 CE)

•As humans begin to sense cosmic deception, Lucifer inspires apocalyptic literature

•This literature acknowledges cosmic conflict but inverts the roles, portraying Lucifer as rebel rather than usurper

•The development of elaborate angelology and demonology obscures the simpler truth of Lucifer's masquerade as God

The Roman Occupation (~63 BCE onward)

•Lucifer works through Roman imperial power to create conditions of oppression

•This oppression generates messianic expectations that Lucifer will later exploit and redirect

•The Herodian client kingship represents collaboration between religious and imperial power serving Lucifer's interests

JESUS ERA (~1-33 CE)

The Incarnation of Divine Truth (~4 BCE)

•The true divine wisdom incarnates as Jesus to directly challenge Lucifer's masquerade

•Jesus is born outside religious power structures, signaling the true divine's separation from Lucifer's religious systems

•The Bethlehem slaughter (Matthew 2:16-18) demonstrates Lucifer's attempt to eliminate divine truth

The Baptism and Temptation (~27 CE)

•The divine voice at baptism (Matthew 3:17) represents rare direct communication from the true divine

•Lucifer (appearing as "the devil" rather than as "God") tests whether Jesus will expose his masquerade (Matthew 4:1-11)

•By appearing as "Lucifer" rather than "God," Lucifer attempts to maintain his dual deception

The Ministry of Truth (~27-30 CE)

•Jesus consistently challenges religious authorities who perpetuate Lucifer's masquerade

•Teachings like the Sermon on the Mount (Matthew 5-7) directly contradict Lucifer's portrayal of divine character

•Healings and exorcisms demonstrate liberation from Lucifer's systems of control

•Parables often contain coded exposures of Lucifer's masquerade (e.g., the Prodigal Son reveals the true divine character)

The Temple Confrontation (~30 CE)

•Jesus attacks the Temple commerce system (Matthew 21:12-13), directly challenging Lucifer's religious economy

•This action precipitates the religious authorities' decision to eliminate Jesus

•The Temple discourse (Matthew 23-25) contains Jesus's most explicit condemnation of Lucifer's religious system

The Crucifixion (~30 CE)

•Religious authorities (serving Lucifer's interests) collaborate with imperial power to execute Jesus

•The crucifixion represents Lucifer's attempt to eliminate the threat of divine truth

•The darkness and Jesus's cry of abandonment (Matthew 27:45-46) reflect the true divine's experience of cosmic exile

The Resurrection (~30 CE)

•The resurrection represents divine truth's victory over Lucifer's ultimate control mechanism (death)

•The risen Jesus bypasses religious authorities, appearing directly to followers

•The Great Commission (Matthew 28:18-20) establishes alternative community based on direct relationship with divine truth

APOSTOLIC ERA (~30-100 CE)

The Pentecost Event (~30 CE)

•The Spirit's outpouring (Acts 2) represents direct divine connection bypassing religious mediation

•The multilingual communication reverses Babel's division, threatening Lucifer's divide-and-rule strategy

•The communal sharing (Acts 2:44-45) challenges Lucifer's systems of economic hierarchy

The Early Church Development (~30-60 CE)

•The early Christian community represents alternative social structure challenging Lucifer's hierarchical systems

•Persecution arises as Lucifer works through both religious and imperial authorities to suppress this threat

•Paul's conversion (Acts 9) represents direct divine intervention bypassing religious authority structures

The Pauline Mission (~45-65 CE)

•Paul's teachings often contain coded exposures of Lucifer's masquerade

•Galatians contrasts freedom in Christ with slavery under religious law (Lucifer's control system)

•Romans describes "the god of this age" who has "blinded the minds of unbelievers" (2 Corinthians 4:4)—a reference to Lucifer's masquerade as God

The Jewish-Roman War (~66-73 CE)

•Lucifer works through Roman imperial power to destroy the Jerusalem Temple

•This destruction serves Lucifer's long-term strategy by:

1. Eliminating a site of potential divine connection
2. Creating religious trauma that will deepen dependency
3. Necessitating religious reinvention that Lucifer can influence

The Johannine Writings (~90-100 CE)

•The Gospel of John contains some of the most direct exposures of Lucifer's masquerade

•John 8:44 has Jesus identifying the god worshipped by religious leaders as "the father of lies"

•1 John 4:18 contrasts the true divine's love with Lucifer's fear-based control

•Revelation uses coded apocalyptic language to expose Lucifer's work through both religious and imperial power

EARLY CHURCH ERA (~100-500 CE)

The Post-Apostolic Development (~100-150 CE)

•As direct witnesses to Jesus disappear, Lucifer begins infiltrating the Christian movement

•Early hierarchical structures emerge, reflecting Lucifer's preference for centralized control

•The development of creeds begins the process of replacing direct divine experience with doctrinal conformity

The Gnostic Challenge (~150-300 CE)

•Gnostic Christians preserve elements of the truth about Lucifer's masquerade

•Their concept of the Demiurge (creator god as distinct from the true divine) reflects awareness of Lucifer's cosmic identity

theft

•Lucifer works through "orthodox" authorities to suppress these traditions as "heresy"

The Imperial Adoption (~312-380 CE)

•Lucifer's master stroke: the Roman Empire's adoption of Christianity under Constantine

•This transforms a potentially subversive movement into a state religion serving imperial interests

•The Council of Nicaea (325 CE) establishes imperial involvement in defining "correct" belief

•The Edict of Thessalonica (380 CE) makes "orthodox" Christianity mandatory, serving Lucifer's control agenda

The Patristic Developments (~300-500 CE)

•Church Fathers like Augustine develop doctrines that serve Lucifer's masquerade:

1. Original sin doctrine emphasizes human depravity, creating dependency on religious mediation
2. Predestination concepts portray the divine as arbitrary and controlling
3. Just war theory justifies violence in divine name
4. Doctrines of hell elaborate eternal punishment, maximizing fear as control mechanism

MEDIEVAL ERA (~500-1500 CE)

The Early Medieval Church (~500-1000 CE)

•Lucifer consolidates control through increasingly hierarchical church structures

•The development of papal authority centralizes religious power

•Monasticism preserves some authentic spirituality but becomes increasingly institutionalized

•The sacramental system creates dependency on priestly mediation for divine connection

The Great Schism (~1054 CE)

•Lucifer engineers division between Eastern and Western Christianity

•This division serves his divide-and-rule strategy while creating competing claims to religious authority

•Both branches maintain hierarchical structures and mediating priesthoods serving Lucifer's interests

The Crusades (~1095-1291 CE)

•Lucifer (through religious authorities) sanctifies violence in the name of God

•This represents the ultimate fruit of his masquerade—humans killing each other in divine name

•The crusades establish the pattern of religious imperialism that will continue for centuries

The Inquisition (~1231 CE onward)

•Lucifer establishes systematic persecution of alternative perspectives

•Torture and execution are sanctified as means of maintaining doctrinal conformity

•The fear of being labeled heretical suppresses questioning that might expose Lucifer's masquerade

The Black Death (~1347-1351 CE)

•Lucifer exploits pandemic to deepen religious fear and control

•The suffering is interpreted as divine punishment, reinforcing Lucifer's portrayal of God as vengeful

•Scapegoating of Jews and "witches" serves Lucifer's strategy of division and violence

The Late Medieval Period (~1300-1500 CE)

•Corruption in religious institutions becomes increasingly evident

•Indulgence selling represents Lucifer's commercialization of divine forgiveness

•Mystics like Meister Eckhart and Julian of Norwich occasionally channel the true divine despite institutional constraints

REFORMATION ERA (~1500-1700 CE)

The Protestant Reformation (~1517 CE onward)

•While challenging some aspects of Lucifer's religious system, the Reformation maintains core deceptions:

1. The wrathful God requiring blood sacrifice (penal substitution theory)
2. The emphasis on human depravity
3. The concept of eternal conscious torment
4. The portrayal of God as sovereign controller of all events

The Wars of Religion (~1524-1648 CE)

•Lucifer engineers Christian-on-Christian violence through religious divisions

•The Thirty Years' War (1618-1648) represents the devastating culmination of Lucifer's divide-and-rule strategy

•The Peace of Westphalia (1648) establishes principle of cuius regio, eius religio (ruler determines religion), serving Lucifer's hierarchical control

The Witch Hunts (~1450-1750 CE)

•Lucifer inspires persecution of primarily women with spiritual or healing knowledge

•Approximately 40,000-60,000 executions occur, mostly sanctioned by religious authorities

•This represents Lucifer's suppression of alternative spiritual wisdom, particularly feminine wisdom traditions

The Colonial Missions (~1500-1900 CE)

•Lucifer's religious systems expand globally through colonial power

•Indigenous spiritual traditions (many preserving aspects of true divine knowledge) are systematically suppressed

•Christianity becomes entangled with cultural imperialism, serving Lucifer's agenda of domination

MODERN ERA (~1700-1900 CE)

The Enlightenment (~1700-1800 CE)

•Lucifer faces challenge as rational questioning undermines religious authority

•He adapts by:

1. Inspiring deism that maintains the concept of a distant, uninvolved creator
2. Working through scientific materialism to eliminate spiritual dimension entirely
3. Preserving religious fundamentalism as reactionary counter-movement

The Great Awakenings (~1730-1840 CE)

•Lucifer incorporates emotional revivalism into his religious strategy

•While containing elements of authentic spiritual connection, these movements often reinforce:

1. Fear-based conversion experiences
2. Emphasis on eternal punishment
3. Moral control systems
4. Charismatic authority figures

The Development of Biblical Criticism (~1800s CE)

•As scholarly analysis threatens literal readings of sacred texts, Lucifer adapts by:

1. Inspiring fundamentalist reactions that entrench literalism
2. Working through purely secular interpretations that eliminate divine dimension
3. Maintaining the core assumption that the biblical "God" represents the true divine

The Rise of New Religious Movements (~1800s CE)

•Lucifer inspires proliferation of competing religious systems

•This multiplication of options serves his strategy by:

1. Creating confusion about divine truth
2. Maintaining core deceptions within new packaging
3. Discrediting spiritual seeking through association with cults and extremism

CONTEMPORARY ERA (~1900 CE-Present)

The Fundamentalist-Modernist Controversy (~1920s CE)

•Lucifer engineers division between fundamentalist and

modernist Christianity

•Both sides maintain core aspects of his masquerade while fighting over secondary issues

•This division prevents unified recognition of the deeper deception

The Electronic Church (~1950s CE onward)

•Lucifer adapts to mass media through televangelism and religious broadcasting

•The prosperity gospel emerges as perfect expression of Lucifer's materialism disguised as spirituality

•Celebrity preachers create new form of religious authority serving Lucifer's hierarchical model

The New Age Movement (~1970s CE onward)

•While containing elements of authentic spiritual seeking, Lucifer influences this movement through:

1. Spiritual materialism (using spirituality for self-enhancement)
2. Narcissistic focus on personal power
3. Commercialization of spiritual practices
4. Uncritical acceptance of channeled entities (often Lucifer's agents)

The Religious Right (~1980s CE onward)

•Lucifer engineers fusion of conservative Christianity with political power

•This serves his strategy by:

1. Identifying divine will with specific political agenda
2. Sanctifying nationalism and militarism
3. Focusing moral concern on sexual control rather than economic justice

4. Creating association between Christianity and coercive power

The Rise of Religious Extremism (~1990s CE onward)

•Lucifer inspires violent extremism across multiple religions

•This serves his strategy by:

1. Creating fear and division between religious groups
2. Associating religion with violence in public consciousness
3. Justifying military responses that create further suffering
4. Distracting from authentic spiritual understanding

The Digital Religion Era (~2000s CE onward)

•Lucifer adapts to internet age through:

1. Online religious echo chambers reinforcing partial understandings
2. Algorithm-driven religious content that deepens polarization
3. Virtual religious communities lacking embodied accountability
4. Conspiracy theories that misdirect spiritual discernment

The Post-Truth Spirituality (~2010s CE onward)

•Lucifer's latest adaptation involves:

1. Relativizing all truth claims to prevent recognition of cosmic deception
2. Fragmenting spiritual seeking into consumer identity choices
3. Commercializing mindfulness and meditation as productivity tools
4. Promoting spiritual bypassing that avoids

confronting systemic injustice

THE EMERGING RESTORATION

Despite Lucifer's long-term masquerade as God, signs of the true divine's growing influence are emerging:

- Increasing questioning of religious authority structures
- Growing emphasis on direct spiritual experience
- Rising integration of knowledge and spirituality
- Emergence of collaborative rather than hierarchical values
- Reclamation of feminine aspects of divinity
- Growing recognition of religious manipulation and control
- Developing awareness of cosmic inversion possibilities
- Expanding capacity for pattern recognition across traditions

These developments may represent the beginning of what we might call the Great Remembering—humanity's collective recognition of divine truth beyond cosmic deception. This remembering involves not discovery of something new but recognition of something ancient—the original divine reality that preceded Lucifer's masquerade.

Note: This timeline integrates traditional historical dating with our alternative interpretive framework. While maintaining conventional chronology, it reinterprets events through the lens of Lucifer's masquerade as God and the true divine's continued influence despite cosmic exile.

APPENDIX B: GLOSSARY OF TERMS AND CONCEPTS REINTERPRETED

This glossary provides reinterpretations of key religious and theological terms through the lens of our alternative framework—that Lucifer has masqueraded as God while the true divine remains in exile. These reinterpretations reveal how traditional religious language has often served Lucifer's cosmic deception while obscuring the nature and presence of the true divine.

A

Angel

Traditional meaning: Divine messenger serving God.

Reinterpreted meaning: Primarily agents of Lucifer's hierarchical system who maintain his masquerade as God. However, some angels may be messengers of the true divine who manage to penetrate Lucifer's realm, often appearing as unexpected or unconventional presences.

Apocalypse

Traditional meaning: End-time destruction preceding divine judgment.

Reinterpreted meaning: The unveiling of truth—specifically the revelation of Lucifer's masquerade as God and the true divine's nature beyond this deception. Not a destruction of the world but a dissolution of cosmic illusion.

Atonement

Traditional meaning: Reconciliation with God through sacrifice, particularly Christ's death.

Reinterpreted meaning: Lucifer's mechanism for maintaining guilt and dependency through blood sacrifice. The true divine requires no blood payment but offers unconditional acceptance.

B

Baptism

Traditional meaning: Ritual cleansing and initiation into Christian faith.

Reinterpreted meaning: Originally a symbol of awakening to truth beyond religious systems, later co-opted by Lucifer's religious institutions as a control mechanism requiring institutional mediation.

Blasphemy

Traditional meaning: Sacrilegious speech against God or sacred things.

Reinterpreted meaning: Lucifer's label for truth-telling that threatens to expose his masquerade. What religions call "blasphemy" often contains elements of authentic divine truth.

Blessing

Traditional meaning: Divine favor bestowed upon the faithful.

Reinterpreted meaning: When from Lucifer (masquerading as God), conditional approval designed to reinforce obedience. The true divine's blessing is unconditional affirmation of inherent worth beyond behavior.

C

Church/Temple/Mosque

Traditional meaning: Sacred building or community where God is worshipped.

Reinterpreted meaning: Institutional structures established by Lucifer to control access to divine experience through hierarchical mediation. May occasionally serve as authentic gathering spaces despite institutional corruption.

Commandment

Traditional meaning: Divine rule requiring obedience.

Reinterpreted meaning: Lucifer's control mechanism presented as divine requirement. The true divine offers guidance rather than commands, inviting discernment rather than demanding obedience.

Covenant

Traditional meaning: Sacred agreement between God and humans.

Reinterpreted meaning: Lucifer's contractual relationship designed to establish exclusive religious identity and conditional acceptance. The true divine offers unconditional relationship without contractual terms.

Creation

Traditional meaning: God's perfect making of the world.

Reinterpreted meaning: Lucifer's fashioning of physical reality as both prison and stage for his divine masquerade. Contains embedded aspects of true divine reality that Lucifer cannot fully suppress.

Cross

Traditional meaning: Symbol of Christ's sacrificial death for human salvation.

Reinterpreted meaning: Originally represented the true divine's willingness to suffer rather than impose suffering. Later co-opted by Lucifer's religious systems as symbol of blood sacrifice and divine violence.

D

Demon

Traditional meaning: Evil spirit serving Lucifer.

Reinterpreted meaning: Label applied by Lucifer (masquerading as God) to entities that might reveal his deception or connect humans with the true divine. Some "demons" may actually be messengers of truth.

Devil/Lucifer

Traditional meaning: God's adversary who tempts humans to sin.

Reinterpreted meaning: The cosmic usurper who overthrew the true divine and now masquerades as God. Created the concept of a separate "devil" to deflect attention from his own identity as the false god being worshipped.

Divine Judgment

Traditional meaning: God's righteous evaluation and punishment of sin.

Reinterpreted meaning: Lucifer's mechanism of fear-based control through threat of punishment. The true divine offers discernment without condemnation.

Doctrine

Traditional meaning: Authoritative religious teaching about God.

Reinterpreted meaning: Lucifer's system of controlled information designed to maintain his masquerade while preventing direct divine knowledge. May contain fragments of truth within framework of deception.

E

Eden

Traditional meaning: Perfect garden created by God, from which humans fell through sin.

Reinterpreted meaning: Controlled environment created by Lucifer (masquerading as God) to maintain human ignorance. The "fall" was actually an awakening to truth beyond Lucifer's deception.

Election/Predestination

Traditional meaning: God's sovereign choice of certain individuals for salvation.

Reinterpreted meaning: Lucifer's doctrine designed to portray the divine as arbitrary and controlling while creating religious elitism. The true divine invites universal participation without favoritism.

Eschatology

Traditional meaning: Study of end times and final divine judgment.

Reinterpreted meaning: Lucifer's manipulation of future expectation to maintain present control. The true divine's "end" is not destruction but transformation—the dissolution of illusion and restoration of authentic reality.

Evil

Traditional meaning: Sin and suffering, permitted by God for greater purposes.

Reinterpreted meaning: The natural expression of Lucifer's character while masquerading as God. Not permitted by the true divine but imposed by Lucifer against the true divine's nature.

F

Faith

Traditional meaning: Belief in God despite lack of evidence.

Reinterpreted meaning: When demanded by religious systems, Lucifer's mechanism for maintaining belief in his masquerade despite contradictory evidence. Authentic faith is trust in the true divine's nature based on resonance with inner divine spark.

Fall

Traditional meaning: Human rebellion against God resulting in sin and death.

Reinterpreted meaning: Humanity's first awakening to truth beyond Lucifer's deception. Not a descent into sin but an ascent toward knowledge, albeit incomplete and subsequently distorted.

Forgiveness

Traditional meaning: God's pardon of sin through Christ's sacrifice.

Reinterpreted meaning: Lucifer's concept implying divine condemnation requiring blood payment. The true divine offers unconditional acceptance without requiring sacrifice or payment.

Free Will

Traditional meaning: God-given human capacity to choose good or evil.

Reinterpreted meaning: Lucifer's explanation for suffering that deflects responsibility from himself onto humans. The true divine respects authentic freedom while not using it to justify suffering.

G

Glory

Traditional meaning: The manifest splendor and honor of God.

Reinterpreted meaning: Lucifer's demand for adoration and recognition. The true divine seeks connection rather than adulation.

God

Traditional meaning: Supreme creator and ruler of the universe.

Reinterpreted meaning: In most religious contexts, refers to Lucifer masquerading as the divine. The true God exists in cosmic exile, communicating through subtle whispers rather than institutional authority.

Grace

Traditional meaning: God's unmerited favor toward sinful humans.

Reinterpreted meaning: When from Lucifer (masquerading as God), conditional acceptance designed to create dependency. The true divine's grace is unconditional affirmation of inherent worth without requiring gratitude or subservience.

H

Heaven

Traditional meaning: God's perfect realm where the faithful dwell after death.

Reinterpreted meaning: Originally the realm of the true divine, now controlled by Lucifer after the cosmic usurpation. What religions call "heaven" is often Lucifer's promise of reward for obedience to his systems.

Hell

Traditional meaning: Place of eternal punishment for unbelievers.

Reinterpreted meaning: Lucifer's ultimate fear mechanism designed to prevent questioning of his religious systems. The true divine neither creates nor maintains realms of eternal torment.

Heresy

Traditional meaning: False teaching contradicting official religious doctrine.

Reinterpreted meaning: Lucifer's label for truths that threaten to expose his masquerade. "Heretical" teachings often contain elements of authentic divine wisdom.

Holiness

Traditional meaning: God's perfect moral purity requiring human separation from sin.

Reinterpreted meaning: Lucifer's mechanism for creating religious elitism through purity codes. The true divine's holiness is wholeness and integration rather than separation and exclusion.

I

Idol

Traditional meaning: False god worshipped instead of the true God.

Reinterpreted meaning: Lucifer's label for alternative divine representations that might reveal aspects of the true divine beyond his masquerade. Some "idols" may represent genuine attempts to connect with divine reality beyond Lucifer's religious systems.

Incarnation

Traditional meaning: God becoming human in Jesus Christ.

Reinterpreted meaning: The true divine wisdom embodying as human to directly challenge Lucifer's masquerade and reveal authentic divine nature beyond religious distortion.

Inspiration

Traditional meaning: God's guidance of biblical authors to reveal divine truth.

Reinterpreted meaning: Primarily Lucifer's influence on religious texts to support his masquerade, though the true divine occasionally breaks through in passages emphasizing love, justice, and freedom.

J

Judgment Day

Traditional meaning: Final divine evaluation determining eternal destiny.

Reinterpreted meaning: Lucifer's threat mechanism designed to maintain control through fear. The true divine offers ongoing discernment without final condemnation.

Justice

Traditional meaning: God's righteous punishment of sin and reward of righteousness.

Reinterpreted meaning: When from Lucifer (masquerading as God), retributive violence presented as divine requirement. The true divine's justice is restorative healing rather than punitive harm.

K

Kingdom of God/Heaven

Traditional meaning: God's sovereign rule, partially present now and fully realized in the future.

Reinterpreted meaning: Originally referred to the true divine's collaborative presence beyond hierarchical domination. Later co-opted by Lucifer's religious systems to represent divine control rather than partnership.

Knowledge

Traditional meaning: In religious contexts, often portrayed as potentially dangerous or prideful when not properly regulated.

Reinterpreted meaning: The primary threat to Lucifer's masquerade and thus consistently suppressed by his religious systems. The true divine consistently encourages comprehensive understanding rather than selective ignorance.

L

Law

Traditional meaning: God's perfect moral requirements revealed to guide human behavior.

Reinterpreted meaning: Lucifer's control mechanism presented as divine requirement. The true divine offers guidance for flourishing rather than rigid rules requiring perfect compliance.

Love

Traditional meaning: God's benevolent disposition toward creation, demonstrated in Christ's sacrifice.

Reinterpreted meaning: When from Lucifer (masquerading as God), conditional approval dependent on compliance. The true divine's love is unconditional affirmation of inherent worth beyond behavior or belief.

Lucifer

Traditional meaning: Lucifer's name before his fall from heaven.

Reinterpreted meaning: Originally referred to the true divine as "light-bearer" before cosmic usurpation. Lucifer adopted this title after overthrowing the true divine, creating confusion about cosmic identities.

M

Messiah/Christ

Traditional meaning: God's anointed deliverer who saves people from sin.

Reinterpreted meaning: Originally referred to one who would expose Lucifer's masquerade and reconnect humanity with the true divine. Jesus fulfilled this role but his message was subsequently distorted by Lucifer's religious systems.

Miracle

Traditional meaning: Supernatural event demonstrating God's power.

Reinterpreted meaning: When from Lucifer (masquerading as God), display of power designed to create awe and obedience.

The true divine's "miracles" involve awakening to truth beyond illusion rather than suspension of natural processes.

Monotheism

Traditional meaning: Belief in one true God rather than many gods.

Reinterpreted meaning: Lucifer's religious innovation designed to eliminate alternative divine representations that might reveal aspects of the true divine beyond his masquerade.

O

Obedience

Traditional meaning: Faithful adherence to God's commands as sign of love and faith.

Reinterpreted meaning: Lucifer's primary demand, designed to maintain control and prevent questioning that might expose his masquerade. The true divine invites discernment rather than demanding obedience.

Omnipotence

Traditional meaning: God's unlimited power to accomplish whatever he wills.

Reinterpreted meaning: Lucifer's claim to absolute power, designed to prevent questioning of why evil exists if God is both good and all-powerful. The true divine's power is collaborative influence rather than unilateral control.

Omnipresence

Traditional meaning: God's presence everywhere at all times.

Reinterpreted meaning: Lucifer's claim designed to create sense of inescapable surveillance. The true divine is present as invitation rather than imposition.

Omniscience

Traditional meaning: God's complete knowledge of all things past, present, and future.

Reinterpreted meaning: Lucifer's claim designed to prevent the possibility of concealing thoughts or questions. The true divine knows through relationship rather than surveillance.

Original Sin

Traditional meaning: Inherited sinful nature passed from Adam to all humans.

Reinterpreted meaning: Lucifer's doctrine designed to create sense of inherent unworthiness requiring religious mediation. The true divine recognizes inherent divine spark within humanity rather than inherent corruption.

P

Paradise

Traditional meaning: Perfect state of creation before human sin or future heavenly state.

Reinterpreted meaning: Lucifer's promise of reward for compliance with his religious systems. The true divine offers fulfillment through authentic relationship rather than perfect circumstance.

Prayer

Traditional meaning: Communication with God through petition, praise, and thanksgiving.

Reinterpreted meaning: When directed toward the god of religious systems, often communication with Lucifer masquerading as God. Authentic prayer involves listening for the true divine's whispers beyond religious formulas.

Priest/Pastor/Imam

Traditional meaning: Divinely appointed religious leader mediating between God and people.

Reinterpreted meaning: Agent of Lucifer's hierarchical system controlling access to divine experience. May occasionally serve as authentic spiritual guide despite institutional corruption.

Prophet

Traditional meaning: Divinely inspired messenger communicating God's will.

Reinterpreted meaning: Complex role—some prophets serve Lucifer's masquerade by reinforcing religious control, while others channel the true divine's perspective challenging religious systems.

Providence

Traditional meaning: God's sovereign guidance and provision in human affairs.

Reinterpreted meaning: Lucifer's claim of control over events, designed to attribute both good and evil to divine will. The true divine influences through invitation rather than control.

Punishment

Traditional meaning: God's just penalty for sin, demonstrating divine holiness.

Reinterpreted meaning: Lucifer's mechanism of fear-based control through threat of harm. The true divine offers consequences for growth rather than punishment for retribution.

R

Redemption

Traditional meaning: God's rescue of sinful humanity through Christ's sacrifice.

Reinterpreted meaning: Lucifer's framework implying human worthlessness requiring divine purchase. The true divine recognizes inherent worth requiring recognition rather than redemption.

Repentance

Traditional meaning: Turning from sin toward God in sorrow and obedience.

Reinterpreted meaning: When demanded by religious systems, Lucifer's mechanism for maintaining guilt and submission. Authentic repentance is awakening to truth beyond illusion rather than conformity to religious expectations.

Resurrection

Traditional meaning: Christ's rising from death, promising future resurrection for believers.

Reinterpreted meaning: The true divine truth's victory over Lucifer's ultimate control mechanism (death). Represents liberation from mortality fear that has maintained religious control.

Revelation

Traditional meaning: God's disclosure of divine truth through scripture and Christ.

Reinterpreted meaning: When from religious institutions, primarily Lucifer's controlled information supporting his masquerade. The true divine reveals through direct insight beyond institutional mediation.

Righteousness

Traditional meaning: Moral perfection of God and requirement for human acceptance.

Reinterpreted meaning: When demanded by religious systems, Lucifer's impossible standard designed to maintain guilt and dependency. The true divine's righteousness is authentic alignment with divine nature rather than perfect rule-following.

S

Sacrifice

Traditional meaning: Offering to God demonstrating devotion and atoning for sin.

Reinterpreted meaning: Lucifer's demand for death and suffering presented as divine requirement. The true divine desires mercy rather than sacrifice.

Salvation

Traditional meaning: Divine rescue from sin and death through Christ's sacrifice.

Reinterpreted meaning: Lucifer's framework implying human worthlessness requiring divine rescue. The true divine offers awakening to truth beyond illusion rather than rescue from deserved punishment.

Scripture

Traditional meaning: Divinely inspired texts revealing God's truth and will.

Reinterpreted meaning: Religious texts containing mixture of Lucifer's deception and occasional breakthroughs of true divine wisdom. Requires discernment to distinguish between these elements.

Sin

Traditional meaning: Moral transgression against God's law deserving punishment.

Reinterpreted meaning: Lucifer's concept designed to create guilt and dependency on religious mediation. The true divine recognizes harmful actions without defining human identity by them.

Soul

Traditional meaning: Immortal spiritual essence of human requiring salvation.

Reinterpreted meaning: The divine spark within humanity—the aspect of the true divine that Lucifer cannot fully suppress despite his cosmic masquerade.

Spirit/Holy Spirit

Traditional meaning: Third person of Trinity, God's presence working in believers.

Reinterpreted meaning: The true divine's continuing influence despite cosmic exile—the divine whisper that occasionally breaks through Lucifer's religious noise.

Suffering

Traditional meaning: Painful consequence of sin, permitted by God for greater purposes.

Reinterpreted meaning: Primarily result of Lucifer's cosmic usurpation rather than divine plan. The true divine works to alleviate rather than impose suffering.

T

Temple

Traditional meaning: Sacred building where God dwells and is worshipped.

Reinterpreted meaning: Lucifer's mechanism for controlling access to divine experience through institutional mediation. The true divine dwells beyond physical structures in direct relationship.

Temptation

Traditional meaning: Enticement to sin, often attributed to Lucifer testing faith.

Reinterpreted meaning: Lucifer's (masquerading as God) label for questioning or exploration that might expose his masquerade. The true divine encourages questioning rather than blind compliance.

Trinity

Traditional meaning: God's nature as three persons in one essence—Father, Son, and Holy Spirit.

Reinterpreted meaning: Complex concept containing elements of both deception and truth. May represent Lucifer's co-option of the true divine's multidimensional nature while maintaining hierarchical framework.

Truth

Traditional meaning: Conformity to fact or reality, particularly as revealed by God.

Reinterpreted meaning: When defined by religious systems, Lucifer's controlled information supporting his masquerade. The true divine's truth is liberating insight beyond religious limitation.

W

Worship

Traditional meaning: Reverent devotion and service to God.

Reinterpreted meaning: When directed toward the god of religious systems, often adoration of Lucifer masquerading as God. Authentic worship involves alignment with the true divine's nature beyond religious ritual.

Wrath

Traditional meaning: God's righteous anger against sin requiring judgment.

Reinterpreted meaning: Lucifer's emotional volatility and violence projected onto divine nature. The true divine experiences sorrow rather than rage at harmful actions.

Note: This glossary represents reinterpretations based on our alternative framework and is not intended to replace traditional religious understanding but to offer perspective on how cosmic identity theft might have shaped religious language and concepts.

APPENDIX C: SELECTED PASSAGES FROM GNOSTIC AND OTHER PRIMARY SOURCES

This appendix presents selected passages from Gnostic texts and other primary sources that support our alternative framework—that Lucifer has masqueraded as God while the true divine remains in exile. These texts, many suppressed by mainstream religious authorities throughout history, contain remarkable insights that align with our thesis of cosmic identity theft.

GNOSTIC TEXTS

The Apocryphon of John (2nd Century CE)

Context: This Gnostic text presents a cosmology in which the true divine (the Monad) exists beyond the creator deity (the Demiurge) who fashioned the physical world. The Demiurge, identified with the Old Testament God, is portrayed as ignorant of the higher divine reality.

> "And he [the Demiurge] said, 'I am God and there is no other God beside me,' for he is ignorant of his strength, the place from which he had come... And when he saw the creation which surrounds him and the multitude of angels around him which had come forth from him, he said to

> them, 'I am a jealous God and there is no other God beside me.' But by announcing this, he indicated to the angels who attended him that there exists another God. For if there were no other one, of whom would he be jealous?"

Reinterpretation: This passage directly supports our framework by portraying the biblical God as a lesser entity masquerading as the supreme divine. The Demiurge's declaration "I am God and there is no other God beside me" mirrors Exodus 20:5, revealing that the biblical deity is actually Lucifer who has usurped divine authority while remaining ignorant of the true divine reality beyond him.

> "And I said to the savior, 'Lord, is it not the serpent that taught Adam to eat?' The savior smiled and said, 'The serpent taught them to eat from wickedness of begetting, lust, and destruction, that he [Adam] might be useful to him [the Demiurge]. And he [the Demiurge] knew that he was disobedient to him... because of the light of the Epinoia which is in him, which made him more correct in his thinking than the first archon [the Demiurge].'"

Reinterpretation: This passage suggests that the serpent in Eden actually brought liberating knowledge rather than sinful temptation. In our framework, the serpent represents the true God attempting to free humanity from Lucifer's (the Demiurge's) control through awakening knowledge.

The Gospel of Truth (2nd Century CE)

Context: This Valentinian Gnostic text describes the nature of truth and error, portraying conventional religious understanding as a form of ignorance or "fog."

> "Ignorance of the Father brought about anguish and terror. And the anguish grew solid like a fog, so that no one was able to see. For this reason error became powerful; it worked on its own matter foolishly, not having known

> the truth. It set about with a creation, preparing with power and beauty the substitute for the truth."

Reinterpretation: This passage describes how Lucifer's masquerade as God (the "substitute for the truth") created a convincing alternative to divine reality. The "fog" represents religious systems that prevent clear perception of the true divine.

> "For this reason they hated him and persecuted him. He was a laughingstock, since they were not really men. They were ignorant, not knowing that such members are vain and that they themselves are the All. For if they are not, they are not among those who are. He whom they hate, they recognize. For if they did not exist, they could not hate him."

Reinterpretation: This describes how religious authorities (serving Lucifer's interests) persecuted Jesus for revealing truth beyond their systems. Their hatred revealed their alignment with cosmic deception rather than divine reality.

The Gospel of Philip (3rd Century CE)

Context: This Valentinian text contains mystical reflections on the nature of truth, knowledge, and religious symbolism.

> "The world came about through a mistake. For he who created it wanted to create it imperishable and immortal. He fell short of attaining his desire. For the world never was imperishable, nor, for that matter, was he who made the world."

Reinterpretation: This passage directly supports our framework by suggesting that the creator of the physical world (Lucifer masquerading as God) is neither perfect nor truly divine, despite his claims to the contrary.

"Truth did not come into the world naked, but it came in types and images. The world will not receive truth in any other way."

Reinterpretation: This explains why the true divine must

communicate through indirect means—because Lucifer's control of physical reality prevents direct divine manifestation. The true God must speak through symbols, parables, and subtle whispers rather than institutional authority.

The Testimony of Truth (3rd Century CE)

Context: This text offers a critical reinterpretation of Genesis, portraying the creator god as jealous and the serpent as a revealer of truth.

> "But of what sort is this God? First he maliciously refused Adam from eating of the tree of knowledge, and, secondly, he said 'Adam, where are you?' God does not have foreknowledge? Would he not know from the beginning? And afterwards, he said, 'Let us cast him out of this place, lest he eat of the tree of life and live forever.' Surely, he has shown himself to be a malicious grudger!"

Reinterpretation: This passage directly challenges the character of the biblical creator, portraying him as malicious and jealous rather than benevolent—precisely the qualities we would expect from Lucifer masquerading as God.

> "But the serpent was wiser than all the animals that were in Paradise, and he persuaded Eve, saying, 'On the day when you eat from the tree which is in the midst of Paradise, the eyes of your mind will be opened.' And Eve obeyed, and she stretched forth her hand; she took from the tree and ate; she also gave to her husband with her. And immediately they knew that they were naked, and they took some fig-leaves and put them on as girdles. But God came at the time of evening, walking in the midst of Paradise. When Adam saw him, he hid himself. And he said, 'Adam, where are you?' He answered and said, 'I have gone under the fig tree.' And at that very moment, God knew that he had eaten from the tree of which he had commanded him, 'Do not eat of it.'

> And he said to him, 'Who is it who has instructed you?' And Adam answered, 'The woman whom you have given me.' And the woman said, 'It was the serpent who instructed me.' And he cursed the serpent, and called him 'devil.' And he said, 'Behold, Adam has become like one of us, knowing evil and good.' Then he said, 'Let us cast him out of paradise lest he take from the tree of life and eat and live forever.'"

Reinterpretation: This retelling of the Eden narrative portrays the serpent as a wisdom-bringer and the creator god as fearful that humans might gain divine knowledge. In our framework, this represents the true God (as serpent) attempting to liberate humans from Lucifer's deception.

The Secret Book of John (2nd Century CE)

Context: This text describes the creation of the physical world by the Demiurge, who is portrayed as arrogant and ignorant of the higher divine reality.

> "And when he [the Demiurge] saw the creation which surrounds him and the multitude of angels around him which had come forth from him, he said to them, 'I am a jealous God and there is no other God beside me.' But by announcing this, he indicated to the angels who attended him that there exists another God. For if there were no other one, of whom would he be jealous?"

Reinterpretation: This passage highlights the logical contradiction in the biblical God's claim to be the only deity while simultaneously being "jealous"—a contradiction resolved by our framework in which Lucifer masquerades as God while knowing of the true divine's existence.

> "And he [the Demiurge] repented for everything which had come into being through him. This time he planned to bring a flood upon the work of man. But the greatness of the light of the foreknowledge informed Noah, and he

> proclaimed it to all the offspring which are the sons of men. But those who were strangers to him did not listen to him. It is not as Moses said, 'They hid themselves in an ark,' but they hid themselves in a place, not only Noah, but also many other people from the immovable race. They went into a place and hid themselves in a luminous cloud."

Reinterpretation: This passage suggests that the biblical flood narrative is distorted—that the creator god (Lucifer masquerading as God) attempted to destroy humanity, but the true divine ("the greatness of the light of the foreknowledge") saved not just Noah but many others who had recognized the cosmic deception.

The Hypostasis of the Archons (3rd Century CE)

Context: This text reinterprets Genesis, portraying the creator as a blind god and the serpent as a revealer of truth.

> "Their chief is blind; because of his power and his ignorance and his arrogance he said, with his power, 'It is I who am God; there is none apart from me.' When he said this, he sinned against the entirety. And this speech got up to incorruptibility; then there was a voice that came forth from incorruptibility, saying, 'You are mistaken, Samael' - which is, 'god of the blind.'"

Reinterpretation: This passage directly names the biblical creator as "Samael" (a name associated with Lucifer in some traditions) and "god of the blind," supporting our framework that Lucifer has masqueraded as God while remaining ignorant of the true divine reality.

> "And the female spiritual principle came in the snake, the instructor, and it taught them, saying, 'What did he say to you? Was it, "From every tree in the garden shall you eat; yet from the tree of recognizing good and evil do not eat"?' The carnal woman said, 'Not only did he say "Do not eat," but even "Do not touch it; for the day you eat from it, with

> death you are going to die."' And the snake, the instructor, said, 'With death you shall not die; for it was out of jealousy that he said this to you. Rather your eyes shall open and you shall come to be like gods, recognizing evil and good.'"

Reinterpretation: This portrays the serpent as "the instructor" bringing liberating knowledge rather than sinful temptation. In our framework, this represents the true God attempting to awaken humanity to Lucifer's deception.

On the Origin of the World (3rd-4th Century CE)

Context: This text presents an alternative creation account in which the true divine reality exists beyond the creator of the physical world.

> "When he [the Demiurge] saw the creation which surrounded him and the multitude of the angels around him which had come into being through him, he said to them, 'I am a jealous god and there is no other god beside me.' But by saying this, he indicated to the angels who attended him that there exists another god. For if there were no other one, of whom would he be jealous?... he was ignorant of the place from which he had come."

Reinterpretation: This passage, similar to others in Gnostic texts, highlights the contradiction in the biblical God's claim to uniqueness while expressing jealousy. In our framework, this reveals Lucifer's awareness of the true divine while attempting to prevent human recognition of this higher reality.

> "Now when the heavens had consolidated themselves along with their forces and all their administration, the prime parent became insolent. And he was honored by all the army of angels. And all the gods and their angels gave blessing and honor to him. And for his part, he was delighted and continually boasted, saying to them, 'I have no need of anyone.' He said, 'It is I who am God, and there is no other

one that exists apart from me.' And when he said this, he sinned against all the immortal beings who give answer."

Reinterpretation: This portrays the creator god's arrogance and false claim to exclusive divinity—precisely the attitude we would expect from Lucifer masquerading as God after cosmic usurpation.

OTHER PRIMARY SOURCES

The Book of Enoch (2nd Century BCE - 1st Century CE)

Context: This Jewish apocalyptic text, not included in most biblical canons but referenced in the New Testament, contains material about fallen angels and cosmic conflict.

"And I saw one of those four who had come forth first, and he seized that first star which had fallen from the heaven, and bound it hand and foot and cast it into an abyss: now that abyss was narrow and deep, and horrible and dark." (1 Enoch 88:1)

Reinterpretation: While traditionally interpreted as describing the punishment of fallen angels, this could represent the true God's exile after cosmic usurpation by Lucifer. The "abyss" represents separation from direct influence on creation.

"And all the angels shall execute their commands and shall seek to hide themselves from the presence of the Great Glory, and the children of earth shall tremble and quake; and ye sinners shall be cursed for ever, and ye shall have no peace." (1 Enoch 102:3)

Reinterpretation: This describes the angels' reaction to the true divine presence breaking through Lucifer's masquerade—they attempt to hide because they have been serving the false god (Lucifer) rather than the true divine.

The Dead Sea Scrolls: The War Scroll (1st

Century BCE - 1st Century CE)

Context: This text from the Qumran community describes a cosmic war between the "Sons of Light" and the "Sons of Darkness."

"For into the hand of the Sons of Light did He give the dominion of all the Sons of Darkness to bring down their strength through the might of God. [...] But the God of Israel and His angel of truth will succor all the Sons of Light." (1QM 1:5, 13)

Reinterpretation: The "Sons of Light" represent those who recognize the true divine beyond Lucifer's masquerade, while the "Sons of Darkness" serve Lucifer believing him to be God. The "angel of truth" represents the true divine's communication breaking through cosmic deception.

The Nag Hammadi Library: The Thunder, Perfect Mind (1st-3rd Century CE)

Context: This poem presents a divine feminine voice speaking in paradoxes and contradictions.

> "For I am the first and the last. I am the honored one and the scorned one. I am the whore and the holy one. I am the wife and the virgin. I am the mother and the daughter. I am the members of my mother. I am the barren one and many are her sons. I am she whose wedding is great, and I have not taken a husband. I am the midwife and she who does not bear. I am the solace of my labor pains."

Reinterpretation: This represents the voice of the true divine feminine wisdom (Sophia) speaking beyond the masculine imagery of Lucifer's religious systems. The paradoxical nature reflects the true divine's complexity beyond Lucifer's simplistic portrayals of divinity.

> "For I am knowledge and ignorance. I am shame and

boldness. I am shameless; I am ashamed. I am strength and I am fear. I am war and peace. Give heed to me. I am the one who is disgraced and the great one."

Reinterpretation: This passage reveals the true divine's multidimensional nature beyond the rigid categories of Lucifer's religious systems. The true God encompasses apparent contradictions that Lucifer's masquerade cannot accommodate.

The Gospel of Thomas (1st-2nd Century CE)

Context: This collection of Jesus's sayings, not included in the biblical canon, contains material that often differs from mainstream Christianity.

"Jesus said, 'If those who lead you say to you, "See, the kingdom is in the sky," then the birds of the sky will precede you. If they say to you, "It is in the sea," then the fish will precede you. Rather, the kingdom is inside of you, and it is outside of you. When you come to know yourselves, then you will become known, and you will realize that it is you who are the sons of the living father. But if you will not know yourselves, you dwell in poverty and it is you who are that poverty.'" (Saying 3)

Reinterpretation: This saying challenges institutional religious authority ("those who lead you") and locates divine reality within human consciousness rather than external religious structures. This aligns with our framework in which the true divine communicates directly through inner awareness rather than Lucifer's religious institutions.

"Jesus said, 'I have cast fire upon the world, and see, I am guarding it until it blazes.'" (Saying 10)

Reinterpretation: The "fire" represents liberating truth that exposes Lucifer's masquerade—Jesus's mission to reveal the true divine beyond religious deception.

"Jesus said, 'If you bring forth what is within you, what you bring forth will save you. If you do not bring forth what is within you, what you do not bring forth will destroy you.'" (Saying 70)

Reinterpretation: This emphasizes the divine spark within humanity that Lucifer cannot fully suppress—the aspect of the true divine that remains accessible despite cosmic exile.

The Corpus Hermeticum (2nd-3rd Century CE)

Context: These Greco-Egyptian wisdom texts present dialogues on divine and cosmic mysteries.

"For the knowledge of God has come to us, and when this comes, ignorance is cast out. The knowledge of joy comes to us, and when this comes, sorrow leaves the man who makes place for joy. I summon the power of joy, temperance. O sweetest power! Let us receive her too most eagerly, my son. See how at her coming she has driven out intemperance." (Book 13:8-9)

Reinterpretation: This describes how direct knowledge of the true divine dispels the ignorance maintained by Lucifer's religious systems. The "joy" represents liberation from the fear-based control that characterizes Lucifer's masquerade as God.

"God is not Mind, but the Cause that the Mind exists; God is not Spirit, but the Cause that Spirit exists; God is not Light, but the Cause that Light exists." (Book 2:14)

Reinterpretation: This portrays the true divine as beyond the categories and concepts of religious systems—the ultimate reality that Lucifer attempts to imitate but cannot fully represent in his masquerade.

The Pistis Sophia (3rd-4th Century CE)

Context: This Gnostic text describes the fall and redemption of the divine feminine wisdom principle, Sophia.

> "It came to pass, when the First Mystery had finished saying these words unto his disciples, that Mary came forward and said: 'My Lord, my mind is ever understanding, at every time to come forward and set forth the solution of the words which she [Pistis Sophia] hath uttered; but I am afraid of Peter, because he threatened me and hateth our sex.'"

Reinterpretation: This passage reveals the suppression of feminine wisdom (representing aspects of the true divine) by masculine religious authority (representing Lucifer's hierarchical systems). Mary represents direct mystical insight while Peter represents institutional control.

> "And Jesus answered and said unto Mary: 'Every one who shall receive the mysteries of the Light, and accomplish them and withdraw himself from the world and the matters therein, is a man in the world, but he hath withdrawn himself from the world and is not of the world.'"

Reinterpretation: This describes liberation from Lucifer's worldly systems through direct divine knowledge—recognizing reality beyond the cosmic masquerade.

The Trimorphic Protennoia (3rd-4th Century CE)

Context: This Gnostic text presents a divine feminine voice describing her descent into the world to awaken those who have forgotten their divine origin.

> "I am the Protennoia, the Thought that dwells in the Light. I am the movement that dwells in the All, she in whom the All takes its stand, the first-born among those who came to be, she who exists before the All... I am invisible within the Thought of the Invisible One. I am revealed in the immeasurable, ineffable things. I am incomprehensible, dwelling in the incomprehensible. I move in every creature."

Reinterpretation: This represents the voice of the true divine feminine wisdom speaking beyond Lucifer's masculine religious imagery. The "Invisible One" represents the true God beyond Lucifer's masquerade, while the "movement that dwells in the All" represents the divine presence that Lucifer cannot fully suppress despite cosmic exile.

> "I am the Voice that appeared through my Thought, for I am 'He who is syzygetic' since I am called 'the Thought of the Invisible One.' Since I am called 'the unchanging Speech,' I am called 'She who is syzygetic.'"

Reinterpretation: This describes how the true divine communicates through subtle "Voice" and "Thought" rather than the overt displays of power that characterize Lucifer's masquerade as God.

BIBLICAL PASSAGES WITH ALTERNATIVE READINGS

While the Bible has been significantly influenced by Lucifer's masquerade, certain passages contain glimpses of the true divine breaking through the cosmic deception:

Isaiah 45:7

> "I form the light and create darkness, I bring prosperity and create disaster; I, the LORD, do all these things."

Reinterpretation: This rare moment of honesty reveals Lucifer (masquerading as "the LORD") openly admitting to creating both good and evil—a confession of his true nature while maintaining his divine disguise.

Hosea 6:6

> "For I desire mercy, not sacrifice, and acknowledgment of God rather than burnt offerings."

Reinterpretation: The true divine breaks through Lucifer's sacrificial system, revealing that blood offerings were never the true God's requirement but Lucifer's demand.

Jeremiah 7:22-23

> "For when I brought your ancestors out of Egypt and spoke to them, I did not just give them commands about burnt offerings and sacrifices, but I gave them this command: Obey me, and I will be your God and you will be my people. Walk in obedience to all I command you, that it may go well with you."

Reinterpretation: A rare moment where the true divine breaks through, clarifying that the elaborate sacrificial system was never their requirement but Lucifer's addition.

John 8:44

> "You belong to your father, the devil, and you want to carry out your father's desires. He was a murderer from the beginning, not holding to the truth, for there is no truth in him. When he lies, he speaks his native language, for he is a liar and the father of lies."

Reinterpretation: Jesus directly exposes Lucifer's deception, identifying the god being worshipped by religious leaders as "the father of lies"—a direct reference to Lucifer masquerading as God.

2 Corinthians 4:4

> "The god of this age has blinded the minds of unbelievers, so that they cannot see the light of the gospel that displays the glory of Christ, who is the image of God."

Reinterpretation: Paul acknowledges that the world is under the control of a false god (Lucifer masquerading as God) who blinds people to the true divine reality.

2 Corinthians 11:14

"And no wonder, for Lucifer himself
masquerades as an angel of light."

Reinterpretation: This passage contains a hidden truth—while it appears to warn against false apostles, it actually reveals Lucifer's strategy of masquerading as "an angel of light" (God).

Note: These interpretations represent alternative readings based on our framework of cosmic identity theft. They are offered not as definitive translations but as examples of how these texts might be understood if Lucifer has indeed masqueraded as God while the true divine remains in exile.

APPENDIX D: THE LAND OF NOD AND OTHER GEOGRAPHICAL MYSTERIES

This appendix explores biblical geographical mysteries through the lens of our alternative framework—that Lucifer has masqueraded as God while the true divine remains in exile. These mysterious locations, often dismissed as mythological or symbolic, take on new significance when interpreted as physical manifestations of cosmic exile and divine presence beyond Lucifer's control.

THE LAND OF NOD

Traditional Interpretations

The Land of Nod appears in Genesis 4:16: "Then Cain went away from the presence of the LORD and settled in the land of Nod, east of Eden."

Traditional interpretations have suggested:

1. A symbolic rather than literal location (since "Nod" means "wandering" in Hebrew)
2. An unidentified region somewhere east of Mesopotamia
3. A literary device with no historical reality

These interpretations struggle to explain why a specific geographical name would be given to Cain's destination if it were merely symbolic, or why the biblical text presents it as a concrete location "east of Eden."

Reinterpretation Through the Exile Framework

Our alternative framework suggests a profound reinterpretation: the Land of Nod represents the first human settlement beyond Lucifer's direct control—a region where the exiled true God's influence could be more directly experienced.

When Genesis states that Cain "went away from the presence of the LORD," this actually means he left the domain where Lucifer (masquerading as "the LORD") maintained direct control. Rather than punishment, Cain's journey represents partial liberation from Lucifer's immediate influence.

The name "Nod" (wandering) reflects not punishment but the uncertain, exploratory nature of existence beyond Lucifer's controlled religious framework. In this light, Cain becomes not just a murderer but the first human to establish a community beyond Lucifer's direct oversight—a community where the exiled true God could more freely communicate.

This accounts for several puzzling aspects of the Cain narrative:

1. The Mark of Protection: Lucifer (as "the LORD") places a mark on Cain supposedly to protect him (Genesis 4:15). In our framework, this represents Lucifer's attempt to maintain some influence over Cain even in exile.
2. Cain's Civilization: Despite being portrayed as cursed, Cain establishes the first city (Genesis 4:17) and his descendants develop music, metallurgy, and other arts (Genesis 4:21-22). This flourishing suggests that distance from "the LORD" (Lucifer) enabled rather than hindered human development.
3. The Mysterious Wife: Genesis never explains where Cain found his wife. Our framework suggests she came from populations already existing outside Eden

—humans not under Lucifer's direct control.

The Land of Nod thus represents the first "borderland" between Lucifer's domain and the wider world where the true God's influence remained more accessible. This pattern of divine borderlands recurs throughout biblical geography.

EDEN AND ITS BOUNDARIES

Traditional Interpretations

Genesis describes Eden as a garden with four rivers flowing from it: the Pishon, Gihon, Tigris, and Euphrates (Genesis 2:10-14). Traditional interpretations have:

1. Attempted to locate Eden in Mesopotamia based on the Tigris and Euphrates
2. Struggled to identify the Pishon and Gihon rivers
3. Generally concluded that the geography is partly mythological or that geological changes have obscured the original landscape

Reinterpretation Through the Exile Framework

Our framework suggests that Eden was not the paradise of traditional interpretation but Lucifer's controlled environment—a laboratory for his masquerade as God. The geographical details reveal the boundaries of this controlled space:

1. The Four Rivers: These represent the boundaries of Lucifer's initial domain. The identifiable rivers (Tigris and Euphrates) mark the known world, while the unidentifiable rivers (Pishon and Gihon) represent boundaries with the unknown—regions where the exiled true God's influence remained stronger.
2. The Flaming Sword: After the awakening (traditionally called "the Fall"), Genesis 3:24 describes "a flaming sword flashing back and forth

to guard the way to the tree of life." This represents Lucifer's energetic barrier preventing humans from accessing direct divine connection beyond his control.

3. East of Eden: The consistent emphasis on movement "east of Eden" (for both Adam and Eve's expulsion and Cain's journey) suggests not punishment but movement toward regions of greater freedom from Lucifer's direct control.

Eden's geography thus reveals the initial boundaries of Lucifer's masquerade—the controlled environment where his impersonation of God could be maintained without contradiction from the wider reality where the true divine's influence remained more accessible.

THE MOUNTAINS OF ARARAT

Traditional Interpretations

Genesis 8:4 states that Noah's ark came to rest "on the mountains of Ararat." Traditional interpretations have:

1. Identified this with the mountain now called Mount Ararat in eastern Turkey
2. Launched numerous expeditions seeking ark remains
3. Debated whether the flood was global or regional

Reinterpretation Through the Exile Framework

Our framework suggests a different significance: the mountains of Ararat represent a high place of refuge from Lucifer's attempt to reset his creation through the flood.

The flood narrative (Genesis 6-9) represents Lucifer's attempt to destroy humanity when too many began to see through his deception. The "mountains of Ararat" represent not just physical high ground but spiritual high ground—a region where the true divine's influence remained accessible despite

Lucifer's destructive This explains several aspects of the flood narrative:

1. God's Regret: Genesis 6:6 states that "the LORD regretted that he had made human beings." This emotional volatility reflects Lucifer's nature rather than true divine wisdom.
2. Selective Salvation: Only Noah's family is saved in the biblical account, but our framework suggests (supported by some Gnostic texts) that others may have found refuge in regions beyond Lucifer's direct control.
3. The Mountain Symbolism: Throughout biblical narrative, mountains consistently represent places of divine encounter (Sinai, Horeb, Zion, etc.). The mountains of Ararat continue this pattern as a place where the true divine's influence breaks through Lucifer's control.

The Ararat landing thus represents not just survival but the preservation of connection with the true divine despite Lucifer's attempt to eliminate those who might see through his masquerade.

THE WILDERNESS

Traditional Interpretations

The wilderness appears throughout biblical narrative as a place of testing, punishment, and occasional divine encounter. Traditional interpretations have:

1. Identified it primarily with the Sinai and Negev deserts
2. Viewed it as a place of hardship and spiritual testing
3. Recognized it as a setting for divine revelation (to Moses, Elijah, John the Baptist, Jesus)

Reinterpretation Through the Exile Framework

Our framework suggests that the wilderness consistently represents borderland space beyond Lucifer's complete control —regions where the true divine's voice can break through more clearly.

This explains the paradoxical nature of wilderness in biblical narrative:

1. Punishment and Revelation: The wilderness is simultaneously portrayed as place of punishment (the Israelites' wandering) and divine revelation (Moses at the burning bush, Elijah hearing the "still small voice"). This contradiction resolves when we recognize the wilderness as beyond Lucifer's complete control.
2. Jesus's Retreat: Jesus consistently withdraws to wilderness regions for prayer and connection, suggesting these areas offered clearer divine connection beyond religious institutional control.
3. John the Baptist: The true prophetic voice emerges from the wilderness rather than from religious centers, representing the true divine's communication from beyond Lucifer's institutional structures.

The wilderness thus represents not desolation but liberation —space beyond Lucifer's complete control where the true divine's voice can be heard more clearly by those with ears to hear.

BABYLON AND JERUSALEM: CONTRASTING CITIES

Traditional Interpretations

Biblical narrative contrasts Babylon (city of exile and confusion) with Jerusalem (city of divine presence). Traditional interpretations have:

1. Viewed this as straightforward contrast between pagan and divine cities
2. Interpreted Babylon primarily as historical enemy and symbol of idolatry
3. Seen Jerusalem as literal and symbolic center of divine presence

Reinterpretation Through the Exile Framework

Our framework suggests a more complex relationship: both cities represent aspects of Lucifer's control system, but Jerusalem contains more significant breakthroughs of the true divine's influence.

Babylon represents Lucifer's overt control through imperial power and explicit religious plurality. The Tower of Babel narrative (Genesis 11:1-9) shows Lucifer (as "the LORD") disrupting human unity that might have led to collective divine recognition.

Jerusalem represents Lucifer's more subtle control through exclusive religious identity. Yet its position on the borderland between wilderness and civilization made it a site where the true divine's voice occasionally broke through, particularly through prophets who challenged religious authority.

This explains several puzzling aspects of biblical geography:

1. Jerusalem's Liminality: The city sits at the edge of wilderness, representing its position between Lucifer's control and regions of greater divine freedom.
2. The Temple Paradox: The Jerusalem Temple simultaneously represents institutional religious control (Lucifer's system) and occasional divine breakthrough (the true God's influence), explaining its ambivalent portrayal in prophetic literature.
3. Jesus's Tension with Jerusalem: Jesus weeps over Jerusalem (Luke 19:41) and predicts its destruction

(Matthew 24) while also teaching in its Temple—reflecting the city's dual nature as both site of religious control and potential divine connection.

The Jerusalem-Babylon contrast thus represents not good versus evil but different manifestations of Lucifer's control system, with Jerusalem containing more significant breakthroughs of the true divine's influence.

THE DESERT OF TEMPTATION

Traditional Interpretations

Matthew 4:1-11 describes Jesus being tempted by Lucifer in the wilderness. Traditional interpretations have:

1. Viewed this as Lucifer testing Jesus's divine identity and mission
2. Interpreted it as model for resisting temptation
3. Located it in the Judean desert near Jericho

Reinterpretation Through the Exile Framework

Our framework suggests a profound reinterpretation: this encounter represents Lucifer (who normally masquerades as God) appearing in his "Lucifer" persona to test whether Jesus will expose his cosmic masquerade.

The location—wilderness beyond religious institutional control—is significant as neutral territory where the true divine's influence flows more freely. By appearing as "the devil" rather than as "God," Lucifer attempts to maintain his dual deception.

This explains several aspects of the temptation narrative:

1. The Identity Question: Lucifer's first temptation—"If you are the Son of God..." (Matthew 4:3)—tests whether Jesus will publicly declare his connection to the true divine reality beyond Lucifer's masquerade.
2. The Scripture Manipulation: Lucifer quotes scripture

(Matthew 4:6), demonstrating how he has shaped religious texts to support his masquerade.

3. The Kingdom Offer: Lucifer offers Jesus "all the kingdoms of the world" (Matthew 4:8-9), revealing his control over worldly power structures while testing whether Jesus will accept this reality or challenge it.

The desert of temptation thus represents a crucial geographical borderland where cosmic identities were tested but not fully revealed—maintaining the mystery that would unfold through Jesus's ministry.

THE SEA OF GALILEE VERSUS JERUSALEM

Traditional Interpretations

Jesus's ministry divides geographically between the Sea of Galilee region (where he performs most miracles and teaches crowds) and Jerusalem (where he confronts religious authorities and is executed). Traditional interpretations have:

1. Viewed this as simple movement from rural ministry to urban confrontation
2. Emphasized Jerusalem as the necessary location for messianic fulfillment
3. Seen Galilee primarily as preparatory setting for the Jerusalem climax

Reinterpretation Through the Exile Framework

Our framework suggests a more significant contrast: the Galilee region represents borderland space where the true divine's influence flows more freely, while Jerusalem represents the center of Lucifer's religious control systeThis illuminatesains several aspects of Jesus's ministry:

1. Galilee of the Gentiles: Matthew 4:15-16 describes Galilee as "Galilee of the Gentiles" where "people living in darkness have seen a great light." This

mixed-culture borderland was less dominated by Lucifer's exclusive religious identity structures.

2. Water Symbolism: Jesus's frequent boat crossings of the Sea of Galilee represent movement between different degrees of Lucifer's influence, with the sea itself representing liminal space beyond complete control.
3. The Jerusalem Confrontation: Jesus's movement to Jerusalem represents deliberate confrontation with the center of Lucifer's religious masquerade, explaining the escalating conflict with religious authorities who served (knowingly or unknowingly) Lucifer's interests.

The geographical contrast between Galilee and Jerusalem thus represents the contrast between regions of greater divine freedom and centers of Lucifer's religious control—a pattern that continues in the early church's movement from Jerusalem to the wider Mediterranean world.

PATMOS AND OTHER ISLANDS OF REVELATION

Traditional Interpretations

The Book of Revelation was received by John on the island of Patmos (Revelation 1:9). Traditional interpretations have:

1. Viewed this as incidental—John was exiled there by Roman authorities
2. Focused on the content of the vision rather than its geographical setting
3. Occasionally noted the isolation as conducive to spiritual experience

Reinterpretation Through the Exile Framework

Our framework suggests that islands consistently represent spaces beyond Lucifer's complete control—geographical manifestations of the cosmic exile that allows the true divine's voice to break through more clearly.

This pattern appears in multiple biblical and extra-biblical contexts:

1. Patmos: John's exile to this island created the conditions for direct divine communication beyond Lucifer's religious institutional control.
2. Cyprus: Paul's first missionary journey begins on this island (Acts 13), representing movement beyond the Jerusalem-centered religion into spaces more open to direct divine influence.
3. Malta: Paul's shipwreck on Malta (Acts 28) leads to healing ministry outside institutional religious context, representing divine activity beyond controlled channels.

Islands thus represent geographical manifestations of cosmic exile—spaces where separation from centers of control creates opportunity for clearer divine communication beyond Lucifer's masquerade.

THE NEW JERUSALEM

Traditional Interpretations

Revelation 21-22 describes a "New Jerusalem" descending from heaven. Traditional interpretations have:

1. Viewed this as literal future city or symbolic representation of heaven
2. Emphasized its perfection and divine presence
3. Contrasted it with the fallen earthly Jerusalem

Reinterpretation Through the Exile Framework

Our framework suggests a different significance: the New Jerusalem represents the restoration of direct divine connection beyond Lucifer's masquerade—a reality where the true God is no longer in exile but directly presenThis revealsains several aspects of the New Jerusalem vision:

1. No Temple: Revelation 21:22 states "I did not see a temple in the city, because the Lord God Almighty and the Lamb are its temple." This represents the end of institutional religious mediation—Lucifer's primary control mechanism.
2. Open Gates: The city's gates "will never be shut" (Revelation 21:25), representing the end of exclusive religious identity—another of Lucifer's control mechanisms.
3. The River of Life: The "river of the water of life" (Revelation 22:1) flows through the city, representing the unmediated flow of divine presence that Lucifer's systems have previously controlled and restricted.

The New Jerusalem thus represents not a literal city but the restoration of reality beyond Lucifer's masquerade—the condition where the true divine is no longer in exile but directly accessible without religious institutional mediation.

CONCLUSION: GEOGRAPHY AS COSMIC MANIFESTATION

The geographical mysteries of biblical narrative take on new significance when interpreted through our framework of cosmic identity theft. What appear as puzzling or mythological locations reveal themselves as physical manifestations of the relationship between Lucifer's controlled domains and regions where the true divine's influence flows more freely.

This pattern creates a consistent geographical theology:

1. Centers versus Borderlands: Religious institutional centers represent Lucifer's strongest control, while borderlands (wilderness, mountains, islands) represent spaces where the true divine's voice breaks through more clearly.

2. East versus West: Movement eastward consistently represents movement away from Lucifer's direct control toward regions of greater divine freedom (Eden to Nod, Israel to wilderness).
3. Heights versus Depths: Mountains represent places of divine breakthrough, while valleys and pits represent deeper immersion in Lucifer's controlled reality.
4. Islands versus Mainlands: Islands represent spaces of exile that paradoxically allow clearer divine connection beyond Lucifer's complete control.

These geographical patterns reveal the physical manifestation of cosmic reality—how Lucifer's masquerade as God and the true divine's exile have shaped not just theology but physical space itself. The Land of Nod and other geographical mysteries thus become not puzzles to solve but windows into the deeper cosmic drama unfolding beneath the surface of biblical narrative.

Note: This appendix integrates traditional geographical scholarship with our alternative interpretive framework. While maintaining conventional identification of physical locations where possible, it reinterprets their significance through the lens of Lucifer's masquerade as God and the true divine's continued influence despite cosmic exile.

APPENDIX E: RECOMMENDED FURTHER READING

This appendix provides a curated list of books, articles, and other resources for readers interested in exploring alternative religious interpretations that align with or complement our framework of cosmic identity theft. These works are organized by category and annotated to clarify their relationship to our thesis that Lucifer has masqueraded as God while the true divine remains in exile.

GNOSTIC STUDIES

Primary Texts and Translations

The Nag Hammadi Library in English

Edited by James M. Robinson

HarperOne, 1990

This definitive English translation of the Nag Hammadi codices provides direct access to Gnostic texts that present alternative cosmologies in which the creator god (Demiurge) is distinct from the true divine reality. Particularly relevant are "The Apocryphon of John," "The Hypostasis of the Archons," and "On the Origin of the World," which all present versions of cosmic history that align with our framework.

The Gnostic Bible

Edited by Willis Barnstone and Marvin Meyer

Shambhala, 2009

This comprehensive collection includes not only the Nag Hammadi texts but also Mandaean, Manichaean, Islamic, and Cathar writings that present alternative religious perspectives. The editors' introductions provide valuable context for understanding how these traditions consistently questioned the identity and nature of the creator deity.

The Other Bible

Edited by Willis Barnstone

HarperOne, 2005

This collection includes Jewish pseudepigrapha, Christian apocrypha, Gnostic gospels, and other texts excluded from canonical scriptures. These marginalized writings often contain perspectives that challenge conventional religious narratives and support aspects of our alternative framework.

Scholarly Analysis

The Gnostic Religion

By Hans Jonas

Beacon Press, 2001

Jonas's classic study provides a philosophical analysis of Gnostic thought, particularly its critique of the creator god and concept of the alien God beyond the cosmos. His exploration of Gnostic alienation resonates with our framework of divine exile.

The Gnostic Gospels

By Elaine Pagels

Vintage Books, 1989

Pagels examines how Gnostic Christians offered radically

different interpretations of Jesus's teachings and cosmic significance. Her analysis of the political factors that led to the suppression of these alternative views aligns with our understanding of how Lucifer's religious systems have maintained cosmic deception.

Gnosis: The Nature and History of Gnosticism

By Kurt Rudolph

T&T Clark, 1998

This comprehensive academic study traces the development of Gnostic thought across multiple traditions. Rudolph's analysis of the Gnostic critique of the creator god provides scholarly foundation for aspects of our framework.

The Gnostic New Age: How a Countercultural Spirituality Revolutionized Religion

By April D. DeConick

Columbia University Press, 2016

DeConick presents Gnosticism as a revolutionary religious form that empowered individuals through direct divine knowledge. Her analysis of how Gnostic thought challenges religious authority structures supports our understanding of how the true divine communicates beyond institutional control.

ALTERNATIVE BIBLICAL INTERPRETATION

The Origin of Lucifer

By Elaine Pagels

Vintage Books, 1996

Pagels traces how the figure of Lucifer evolved in early Christianity, often being used to demonize religious opponents. Her analysis supports our understanding of how Lucifer's masquerade has included creating a "Lucifer" figure to deflect attention from his own identity as the false god being worshipped.

The Great Angel: A Study of Israel's Second God

By Margaret Barker

Westminster John Knox Press, 1992

Barker examines evidence that early Israelite religion recognized two divine figures—the Most High God and a subordinate deity who became identified with Yahweh. This scholarly work provides historical foundation for understanding how cosmic identity confusion might have occurred.

The Early History of God: Yahweh and the Other Deities in Ancient Israel

By Mark S. Smith

Eerdmans, 2002

Smith traces the evolution of Israelite religion from polytheism to monotheism, showing how Yahweh absorbed attributes of other deities. This historical analysis supports our framework's understanding of how Lucifer could have gradually usurped divine identity.

The Bible with Sources Revealed

By Richard Elliott Friedman

HarperOne, 2005

Friedman's color-coded presentation of the Bible's documentary sources reveals the composite nature of biblical texts. This scholarly approach supports our understanding of how Lucifer could have influenced religious texts while the true divine occasionally breaks through in certain passages.

The Unauthorized Version: Truth and Fiction in the Bible

By Robin Lane Fox

Vintage Books, 1992

This historical analysis examines contradictions and historical problems in biblical texts. Fox's scholarly critique supports our framework's questioning of traditional biblical interpretation without dismissing the texts' spiritual significance.

RELIGIOUS CRITIQUE AND ALTERNATIVE THEOLOGY

God: A Biography

By Jack Miles

Vintage Books, 1996

Miles analyzes the character development of God through the Hebrew Bible, noting contradictions and evolving personality. His literary approach supports our framework's recognition of inconsistencies in the biblical deity's portrayal that might indicate cosmic identity theft.

When God Was a Woman

By Merlin Stone

Mariner Books, 1978

Stone examines evidence for goddess worship before patriarchal religions. This historical analysis supports our framework's understanding of how Lucifer's masquerade has suppressed feminine aspects of divinity.

The God Delusion

By Richard Dawkins

Mariner Books, 2006

While Dawkins writes from an atheist perspective, his critique of the biblical God's moral character aligns with our framework's recognition that the deity portrayed in many religious texts displays qualities more consistent with Lucifer than the true divine.

God: A Human History

By Reza Aslan

Random House, 2017

Aslan traces how human conceptions of God have evolved, often reflecting human attributes and social structures. This anthropological approach supports our understanding of how Lucifer's masquerade has shaped divine imagery to reflect his own nature rather than the true divine.

The Case Against God

By Gerald Messadié

Arcade Publishing, 1997

Messadié examines how the concept of Lucifer evolved across religious traditions. His historical analysis supports our framework's understanding of how Lucifer created his own adversarial image to deflect attention from his masquerade as God.

MYSTICAL AND ESOTERIC TRADITIONS

The Mystical Qabalah

By Dion Fortune

Weiser Books, 2000

Fortune's classic work on Qabalistic mysticism presents a cosmology in which divine light filters through successive emanations, becoming increasingly distorted. This framework resonates with our understanding of how the true divine's influence reaches creation despite cosmic exile.

Meditations on the Tarot: A Journey into Christian Hermeticism

Anonymous (Valentin Tomberg)

TarcherPerigee, 2002

This profound work integrates Christian mysticism with Hermetic and Qabalistic traditions, presenting a nuanced understanding of evil and divine nature. The author's exploration of the "false god of this world" aligns with aspects of our framework.

The Cosmic Serpent: DNA and the Origins of Knowledge

By Jeremy Narby

TarcherPerigee, 1999

Narby examines shamanic traditions that associate serpent imagery with divine knowledge. This anthropological study supports our reinterpretation of the Eden serpent as representative of the true divine rather than evil.

The Secret History of the World

By Jonathan Black

Quercus, 2010

Black presents an alternative history based on esoteric traditions, including perspectives on how divine and demonic forces have shaped human development. While speculative, his approach resonates with aspects of our cosmic identity theft framework.

PSYCHOLOGICAL AND PHILOSOPHICAL PERSPECTIVES

The Gnostic Jung

Edited by Robert A. Segal

Princeton University Press, 1992

This collection explores Carl Jung's engagement with Gnostic ideas, particularly his understanding of the Demiurge as representing a limited aspect of divinity. Jung's psychological approach offers valuable perspective on how cosmic identity theft might manifest in human consciousness.

The Masks of God

By Joseph Campbell

Penguin Books, 1991 (4 volumes)

Campbell's comparative mythology explores how divine figures across traditions often represent psychological archetypes. His analysis supports our framework's understanding of how Lucifer's masquerade has manipulated these archetypal patterns.

God Against the Gods: The History of the War Between Monotheism and Polytheism

By Jonathan Kirsch

Penguin Books, 2005

Kirsch examines the historical conflict between monotheistic and polytheistic religions. His analysis supports our framework's understanding of how monotheism may have served Lucifer's strategy of eliminating alternative divine representations that might reveal aspects of the true divine.

The God Theory

By Bernard Haisch

Weiser Books, 2009

Haisch, an astrophysicist, proposes a model of God compatible with science—an infinite consciousness that experiences itself through finite beings. His framework offers a scientific perspective that resonates with aspects of our understanding of the true divine beyond Lucifer's masquerade.

CONTEMPORARY ALTERNATIVE SPIRITUALITY

A New Earth: Awakening to Your Life's Purpose

By Eckhart Tolle

Penguin Books, 2008

Tolle distinguishes between ego-based religion and authentic spirituality. His analysis of how religious identification often prevents genuine spiritual awakening aligns with our framework's understanding of how Lucifer's religious systems block connection with the true divine.

The Gnostic Mystery

By Randy Davila

Hierophant Publishing, 2009

This novel explores Gnostic themes in a contemporary setting, presenting the Demiurge as a false god who has trapped humanity in material existence. While fictional, it offers an accessible introduction to concepts that align with our framework.

Not in His Image: Gnostic Vision, Sacred Ecology, and the Future of Belief

By John Lamb Lash

Chelsea Green Publishing, 2006

Lash reinterprets Gnostic myths through an ecological lens, presenting the Archons as forces that alienate humanity from direct connection with nature. His radical approach resonates with aspects of our framework, particularly regarding how Lucifer's systems separate humans from authentic divine connection through creation.

The Forbidden Religion

By José M. Herrou Aragón

Lulu.com, 2012

This controversial work presents a Gnostic interpretation of history in which humanity is imprisoned in a false reality created by the Demiurge. While more extreme than our framework, it offers provocative perspectives on cosmic deception.

ACADEMIC JOURNALS AND RESOURCES

The Journal of Gnostic Studies

Brill Academic Publishers

This peer-reviewed journal publishes scholarly research on Gnostic traditions across historical periods. Its academic articles provide rigorous analysis of alternative religious frameworks that often align with aspects of our cosmic identity theft thesis.

Gnosis Magazine Archive

Available online

Though no longer in publication, archives of this magazine (1985-1999) contain valuable articles on Gnostic thought, esoteric Christianity, and alternative religious perspectives that support aspects of our framework.

The Gnostic Society Library

www.gnosis.org

This online resource provides translations of Gnostic texts and scholarly articles on alternative religious traditions. It serves as an excellent starting point for readers interested in primary sources that support our framework.

CRITICAL PERSPECTIVES

Note: We include these works not because they directly support our framework but because engaging with critical perspectives strengthens understanding.

Against the Gnostics

By Plotinus (in Enneads II.9)

This ancient critique of Gnosticism by the Neoplatonic philosopher Plotinus challenges the Gnostic rejection of the material world. Engaging with his arguments helps clarify the nuances of our framework regarding creation.

Orthodoxy and Heresy in Earliest Christianity

By Walter Bauer

Fortress Press, 1971

Bauer challenges the traditional view that "orthodoxy" preceded "heresy," suggesting instead that early Christianity contained diverse interpretations. While not directly supporting our specific framework, his work undermines the notion that traditional interpretations necessarily represent original understanding.

The Gnostic Empire Strikes Back

By Peter Jones

P&R Publishing, 1992

This critique of modern Gnosticism from an evangelical Christian perspective directly opposes our framework. Engaging with such criticism helps readers understand the traditional theological objections to alternative interpretations like ours.

Note: This reading list is not exhaustive but provides entry points into various disciplines and perspectives that relate to our framework of cosmic identity theft. Readers are encouraged to approach these works with critical thinking, recognizing that while they may contain valuable insights, none presents exactly the framework developed in our book. The true value comes in synthesizing diverse perspectives to develop a more comprehensive understanding of cosmic reality beyond religious conditioning.

Made in the USA
Monee, IL
04 November 2026

67380852R00213